MASTERIN

THE IRREGULAR VERBS

Thunder Bay

AND MODALS

EDITORIAL STANLEY

Written by / Escrito por:
Edward R. Rosset
Member of the Bachelor of Arts Association of Euskadi.
Miembro del Colegio de Licenciados de Filosofía y Letras de Euskadi

Published by / Editado por:
Editorial Stanley

Layout / Diseño y Maquetación:
Angela Gómez Martín

Front page design / Diseño portada:
DISEÑO IRUNÉS

Apdo. 207 - 20302 IRUN - SPAIN
Telf. (943) 64 04 12 - Fax. (943) 64 38 63

ISBN: 84-7873-343-4
Dep. Leg. BI-2.267/99

First edition / Primera edición 1999

Printers / Imprime:
Imprenta Berekintza

Introducción

Los verbos ingleses tienen fama de ser fáciles y sencillos, tan sencillos que ninguna otra editorial se ha preocupado nunca de publicar un libro de verbos conjugados tal como los conocemos en español o francés, por ejemplo.
Sin embargo, no por ser fáciles dejan de tener sus dificultades. A muchos estudiantes les gustaría tener un libro de referencia, sobre todo de verbos irregulares y defectivos.
La Editorial Stanley, después de publicar **ENGLISH VERBS ONE BY ONE**, lanza al mercado **ENGLISH IRREGULAR and modal VERBS conjugated**.
Pongamos por caso que queremos traducir:

- **Si yo hubiese podido, habría venido más temprano.**

Puede ocurrir que los verbos no se nos dan muy bien, ni siquiera en castellano. Abrimos el libro de **IRREGULAR VERBS** en el verbo PODER y buscamos **hubiese podido**, lo encontramos en el pluscuamperfecto de Subjuntivo, y a su lado la traducción:

- ***I had been able.***

A continuación miramos, **habría venido** en el verbo VENIR, y lo encontramos en el condicional compuesto:

- ***I would have come.***

Así pues:

- ***If I had been able, I would have come earlier.***

Veamos otra frase:

- **Si hubiera habido menos tráfico, habrían ido en coche.**

En el verbo HABER (impersonal) encontraremos, **hubiera habido** en el pluscuamperfecto de subjuntivo y su traducción ***there had been***. Y si miramos, **habrían ido** en el verbo IR, veremos que es el Condicional compuesto, **they would have gone.**
Así pues:

- ***If there had been less traffic, they would have gone by car.***

Introduction

English verbs are reputed to be simple. Having relatively few inflected forms, they are indeed easier to master than the verbs of many other languages. For that reason, perhaps, no book of English verb conjugations like those we are accustomed to in Spanish and French, has, until now been published.
However, the fact that English verbs are relatively easy does not mean that they are entirely without difficulty. Quite the contrary. They have their own peculiarities, complexities and traps for the unwary. Consequently, we feel that many students can benefit from a reference work devoted wholly to the irregular and modal verbs, presenting each form methodically, completely and with the utmost clarity.
Suppose, for example, that your English is somewhat rusty and that you wish to translate a comparatively complex verbal pattern like:

- **Si yo hubiera podido, habría venido.**

Simply open the book at PODER and look for, **hubiese podido.** You will find it in the Past Perfect Subjunctive and next to it, the translation:

- ***I had been able.***

In the same way find, **habría venido,** the Conditional Perfect of VENIR:

- ***I would have come.***

All that remains is to put the two clauses together:

- **If I had been able, I would have come.**

This book is addressed not only to those who are beginning to study English, but also to those who, for whatever reason, are still uncertain about how to form verb tenses correctly. In both cases, ENGLISH IRREGULAR & MODAL VERBS will prove an invaluable tool.

INDEX

INDEX

MASTERING THE IRREGULAR VERBS AND MODALS

EDITORIAL STANLEY

ABIDE · ABODE/ABIDED · ABIDED

TOLERAR, SOPORTAR, ACATAR, CUMPLIR.

Indicative

Present

tolero
I abide
you abide
he/she/it abides
we abide
you abide
they abide

Present perfect

he tolerado
I have abided
you have abided
he/she/it has abided
we have abided
you have abided
they have abided

Past

toleraba/toleré
I abode/abided
you abode/abided
he/she/it abode/abided
we abode/abided
you abode/abided
they abode/abided

Past perfect

había/hube tolerado
I had abided
you had abided
he/she/it has abided
we had abided
you had abided
they had abided

Future

toleraré
I shall/will abide
you will abide
he/she/it will abide
we shall/will abide
you will abide
they will abide

Future perfect

habré tolerado
I shall/will have abided
you will have abided
he/she/it will have abided
we shall/will have abided
you will have abided
they will have abided

Conditional

Present

toleraría
I should/would abide
you would abide
he/she/it would abide
we should/would abide
you would abide
they would abide

Perfect

habría tolerado
I should/would have abided
you would have abided
he/she/it would have abided
we should/would have abided
you would have abided
they would have abided

Subjunctive

Present

tolere
I abide
you abide
he/she/it abides
we abide
you abide
they abide

Present perfect

haya tolerado
I have abided
you have abided
he/she/it has abided
we have abided
you have abided
they have abided

Past

tolerara o tolerase
I abode/abided
you abode/abided
he/she/it abode/abided
we abode/abided
you abode/abided
they abode/abided

Past perfect

hubiera o hubiese tolerado
I had abided
you had abided
he/she/it has abided
we had abided
you had abided
they had abided

Imperative

let me abide	***no existe (déjame tolerar)***
abide	***tolera tú***
let him/her/it abide	***tolere él/ella/ello***
let us (let's) abide	***toleremos nosotros***
abide	***tolerad vosotros***
let them abide	***toleren ellos***

Impersonal forms

Infinitive

tolerar
to abide

Perfect Infinitive

haber tolerado
to have abided

Gerund

tolerando
abiding

Perfect Gerund

habiendo tolerado
having abided

Participle

tolerado
abided

Perfect Participle

habiendo tolerado
having abided

ARISE · AROSE · ARISEN

SURGIR, LEVANTAR

Indicative

Present

surjo
I arise
you arise
he/she/it arises
we arise
you arise
they arise

Present perfect

he surgido
I have arisen
you have arisen
he/she/it has arisen
we have arisen
you have arisen
they have arisen

Past

surgía/surgí
I arose
you arose
he/she/it arose
we arose
you arose
they arose

Past perfect

había/hube surgido
I had arisen
you had arisen
he/she/it had arisen
we had arisen
you had arisen
they had arisen

Future

surgiré
I shall/will arise
you will arise
he/she/it will arise
we shall/will arise
you will arise
they will arise

Future perfect

habré surgido
I shall/will have arisen
you will have arisen
he/she/it will have arisen
we shall/will have arisen
you will have arisen
they will have arisen

Conditional

Present

surgiría
I should/would arise
you would arise
he/she/it would arise
we should/would arise
you would arise
they would arise

Perfect

habría surgido
I should/would have arisen
you would have arisen
he/she/it would have arisen
we should/would have arisen
you would have arisen
they would have arisen

Subjunctive

Present

surja
I arise
you arise
he/she/it arises
we arise
you arise
they arise

Present perfect

haya surgido
I have arisen
you have arisen
he/she/it has arisen
we have arisen
you have arisen
they have arisen

Past

surgiera o surgiese
I arose
you arose
he/she/it arose
we arose
you arose
they arose

Past perfect

hubiera o hubiese surgido
I had arisen
you had arisen
he/she/it had arisen
we had arisen
you had arisen
they had arisen

Imperative

let me arise	***no existe (déjame surgir)***
arise	***surge tú***
let him/her/it arise	***surja él/ella/ello***
let us arise	***surjamos nosotros***
arise	***surgid vosotros***
let them arise	***surjan ellos***

Impersonal forms

Infinitive

surgir
arise

Perfect Infinitive

haber surgido
to have arisen

Gerund

surgiendo
arising

Perfect Gerund

habiendo surgido
having arisen

Participle

surgido
arisen

Perfect Participle

habiendo surgido
having arisen

AWAKE · AWOKE · AWOKEN

DESPERTAR (SE)

Indicative

Present

(me) despierto
I awake
you awake
he/she/it awakes
we awake
you awake
they awake

Present perfect

(me) he despertado
I have awoken
you have awoken
he/she/it has awoken
we have awoken
you have awoken
they have awoken

Past

(me) despertaba/ desperté
I awoke
you awoke
he/she/it awoke
we awoke
you awoke
they awoke

Past perfect

(me) había/hube despertado
I had awoken
you had awoken
he/she/it had awoken
we had awoken
you had awoken
they had awoken

Future

(me) despertaré
I shall/will awake
you will awake
he/she/it will awake
we shall/will awake
you will awake
they will awake

Future perfect

(me) habré despertado
I shall/will have awoken
you will have awoken
he/she/it will have awoken
we shall/will have awoken
you will have awoken
they will have awoken

Conditional

Present

(me) despertaría
I should/would awake
you would awake
he/she/it would awake
we should/would awake
you would awake
they would awake

Perfect

(me) habría despertado
I should/would have awoken
you would have awoken
he/she/it would have awoken
we should/would have awoken
you would have awoken
they would have awoken

Subjunctive

Present

(me) despierte
I awake
you awake
he/she/it awakes
we awake
you awake
they awake

Present perfect

(me) haya despertado
I have awoken
you have awoken
he/she/it has awoken
we have awoken
you have awoken
they have awoken

Past

(me) despertara o despertase
I awoke
you awoke
he/she/it awoke
we awoke
you awoke
they awoke

Past perfect

(me) hubiera o hubiese despertado
I had awoken
you had awoken
he/she/it had awoken
we had awoken
you had awoken
they had awoken

Imperative

let me awake	***no existe (déjame despertar(me))***
awake	***despierta tú***
let him/her/it awake	***despierte él/ella/ello***
let us awake	***despertemos***
awake	***despertad***
let them awake	***despierten ellos***

Impersonal forms

Infinitive

despertar
to awake

Perfect Infinitive

haber despertado
to have awoken

Gerund

despertando
awaking

Perfect Gerund

habiendo despertado
having awoken

Participle

despertado
awoken

Perfect Participle

habiendo despertado
having awoken

BEAR · BORE · BORNE

AGUANTAR, RESISTIR, SOPORTAR

Indicative

Present

aguanto
I bear
you bear
he/she/it bears
we bear
you bear
they bear.

Present perfect

he aguantado
I have borne
you have borne
he/she/it has borne
we have borne
you have borne
they have borne

Past

aguantaba/aguanté
I bore
you bore
he/she/it bore
we bore
you bore
they bore

Past perfect

había /hube aguantado
I had borne
you had borne
he/she/it had borne
we had borne
you had borne
they had borne

Future

aguantaré
I shall/will bear
you will bear
he/she/it will bear
we shall/will bear
you will bear
they will bear.

Future perfect

habré aguantado
I shall/will have borne
you will have borne
he/she/it will have borne
we shall/will have borne
you will have borne
they will have borne

Conditional

Present

aguantaría
I should/would bear
you would bear
he/she/it would bear
we should/would bear
you would bear
they would bear

Perfect

habría aguantado
I should/would have borne
you would have borne
he/she/it would have borne
we should have borne
you would have borne
they would have borne

Subjunctive

Present

aguante
I bear
you bear
he/she/it bears
we bear
you bear
they bear

Present perfect

haya aguantado
I have borne
you have borne
he/she/it has borne
we have borne
you have borne
they have borne

Past

aguantara o aguantase
I bore
you bore
he/she/it bore
we bore
you bore
they bore

Past perfect

hubiera o hubiese aguantado
I had borne
you had borne
he/she/it had borne
we had borne
you had borne
they had borne

Imperative

let me bear	***no existe (déjame aguantar)***
bear	***aguanta tú***
let him/her/it bear	***aguante él/ella/ello***
let us (let's) bear	***aguantemos nosotros***
bear	***aguantad vosotros***
let them bear	***aguanten ellos/ellas***

Impersonal forms

Infinitive

aguantar
to bear

Perfect Infinitive

haber aguantado
to have borne

Gerund

aguantando
bearing

Perfect Gerund

habiendo aguantado
having borne

Participle

aguantado
borne

Perfect Participle

habiendo aguantado
having borne

BEAT · BEAT · BEATEN

DERROTAR, VENCER, GOLPEAR, BATIR, SACUDIR.

Indicative

Present

derroto
I beat
you beat
he/she/it beats
we beat
you beat
they beat

Present perfect

he derrotado
I have beaten
you have beaten
he/she/it has beaten
we have beaten
you have beaten
they have beaten

Past

derrotaba/derroté
I beat
you beat
he/she/it beat
we beat
you beat
they beat

Past perfect

había /hube derrotado
I had beaten
you had beaten
he/she/it had beaten
we had beaten
you had beaten
they had beaten

Future

derrotaré
I shall/will beat
you will beat
he/she/it will beat
we shall/will beat
you will beat
they will beat

Future perfect

habré derrotado
I shall/will have beaten
you will have beaten
he/she/it will have beaten
we shall/will have beaten
you will have beaten
they will have beaten

Conditional

Present

derrotaría
I should/would beat
you would beat
he/she/it would beat
we should/would beat
you would beat
they would beat

Perfect

habría derrotado
I should/would have beaten
you would have beaten
he/she/it would have beaten
we should/would have beaten
you would have beaten
they would have beaten

Subjunctive

Present

derrote
I beat
you beat
he/she/it beats
we beat
you beat
they beat

Present perfect

haya derrotado
I have beaten
you have beaten
he/she/it has beaten
we have beaten
you have beaten
they have beaten

Past

derrotara o derrotase
I beat
you beat
he/she/it beat
we beat
you beat
they beat

Past perfect

hubiera o hubiese derrotado
I had beaten
you had beaten
he/she/it had beaten
we had beaten
you had beaten
they had beaten

Imperative

let me beat	***no existe (déjame derrotar)***
beat	***derrota tú***
let him/her/it beat	***derrote él/ella/ello***
let us beat	***derrotemos nosotros***
beat	***derrotad vosotros***
let them beat	***derroten ellos***

Impersonal forms

Infinitive

derrotar
to beat

Perfect Infinitive

haber derrotado
to have beaten

Gerund

derrotando
beating

Perfect Gerund

habiendo derrotado
having beaten

Participle

derrotado
beaten

Perfect Participle

habiendo derrotado
having beaten

BECOME · BECAME · BECOME

LLEGAR A SER, HACERSE

Indicative

Present

llego a ser
I become
you become
he/she/it becomes
we become
you become
they become

Present perfect

he llegado a ser
I have become
you have become
he/she/it has become
we have become
you have become
they have become

Past

llegaba/llegué a ser
I became
you became
he/she/it became
we became
you became
they became

Past perfect

había/hube llegado a ser
I had become
you had become
he/she/it had become
we had become
you had become
they had become

Future

llegaré a ser
I shall/will become
you will become
he/she/it will become
we shall/will become
you will become
they will become

Future perfect

habré llegado a ser
I shall/will have become
you will have become
he/she/it will have become
we shall/will have become
you will have become
they will have become

Conditional

Present

llegaría a ser
I should/would become
you would become
he/she/it would become
we should/would become
you would become
they would become

Perfect

habría llegado a ser
I should/would have become
you would have become
he/she/it would have become
we should/would have become
you would have become
they would have become

Subjunctive

Present

llegue a ser
I become
you become
he/she/it becomes
we become
you become
they become

Present perfect

haya llegado a ser
I have become
you have become
he/she/it has become
we have become
you have become
they have become

Past

llegara o llegase a ser
I became
you became
he/she/it became
we became
you became
they became

Past perfect

hubiera o hubiese llegado a ser
I had become
you had become
he/she/it had become
we had become
you had become
they had become

Imperative

let me become	***no existe (déjame llegar a ser)***
become	***llega a ser tú***
let him/her/it become	***llegue a ser él/ella/ello***
let us (let's) become	***lleguemos a ser nosotros***
become	***llegad a ser vosotros***
let them become	***lleguen a ser ellos***

Impersonal forms

Infinitive

llegar a ser
to become

Perfect Infinitive

haber llegado a ser
to have become

Gerund

llegando a ser
becoming

Perfect Gerund

habiendo llegado a ser
having become

Participle

llegado a ser
become

Perfect Participle

habiendo llegado a ser
having become

BEGIN · BEGAN · BEGUN

EMPEZAR, COMENZAR

Indicative

Present

empiezo
I begin
you begin
he/she/it begins
we begin
you begin
they begin

Present perfect

he empezado
I have begun
you have begun
he/she/it has begun
we have begun
you have begun
they have begun

Past

empezaba/empecé
I began
you began
he/she/it began
we began
you began
they began

Past perfect

había/hube empezado
I had begun
you had begun
he/she/it had begun
we had begun
you had begun
they had begun

Future

empezaré
I shall/will begin
you will begin
he/she/it will begin
we shall/will begin
you will begin
they will begin

Future perfect

habré empezado
I shall/will have begun
you will have begun
he/she/it will have begun
we shall/will have begun
you will have begun
they will have begun

Conditional

Present

empezaría
I should/would begin
you would begin
he/she/it would begin
we should/would begin
you would begin
they would begin

Perfect

habría empezado
I should/would have begun
you would have begun
he/she/it would have begun
we should/would have begun
you would have begun
they would have begun

Subjunctive

Present

empiece
I begin
you begin
he/she/it begins
we begin
you begin
they begin

Present perfect

haya empezado
I have begun
you have begun
he/she/it has begun
we have begun
you have begun
they have begun

Past

empezara/empezase
I began
you began
he/she/it began
we began
you began
they began

Past perfect

hubiera/hubiese empezado
I had begun
you had begun
he/she/it had begun
we had begun
you had begun
they had begun

Imperative

let me begin	***no existe (déjame empezar)***
begin	***empieza tú***
let him/her/it begin	***empiece él/ella/ello***
let us (let's) begin	***empecemos nosotros***
begin	***empezad vosotros***
let them begin	***empiecen ellos***

Impersonal forms

Infinitive

empezar
to begin

Perfect Infinitive

haber empezado
to have begun

Gerund

empezando
beginning

Perfect Gerund

habiendo empezado
having begun

Participle

empezado
begun

Perfect Participle

habiendo empezado
having begun

BEND · BENT · BENT

DOBLAR, TORCER, CURVAR

Indicative

Present

doblo
I bend
you bend
he/she/it bends
we bend
you bend
they bend

Present perfect

he doblado
I have bent
you have bent
he/she/it has bent
we have bent
you have bent
they have bent

Past

doblaba/doblé
I bent
you bent
he/she/it bent
we bent
you bent
they bent

Past perfect

había/hube doblado
I had bent
you had bent
he/she/it had bent
we had bent
you had bent
they had bent

Future

doblaré
I shall/will bend
you will bend
he/she/it will bend
we shall/will bend
you will bend
they will bend

Future perfect

habré doblado
I shall/will have bent
you will have bent
he/she/it will have bent
we shall/will have bent
you will have bent
they will have bent

Conditional

Present

doblaría
I should/would bend
you would bend
he/she/it would bend
we should/would bend
you would bend
they would bend

Perfect

habría doblado
I should/would have bent
you would have bent
he/she/it would have bent
we should/would have bent
you would have bent
they would have bent

Subjunctive

Present

doble
I bend
you bend
he/she/it bends
we bend
you bend
they bend

Present perfect

haya doblado
I have bent
you have bent
he/she/it has bent
we have bent
you have bent
they have bent

Past

doblara/doblase
I bent
you bent
he/she/it bent
we bent
you bent
they bent

Past perfect

hubiera/hubiese doblado
I had bent
you had bent
he/she/it had bent
we had bent
you had bent
they had bent

Imperative

let me bend	***no existe (déjame doblar)***
bend	***dobla tú***
let him/her/it bend	***doble él/ella/ello***
let us (let's) bend	***doblemos nosotros***
bend	***doblad vosotros***
let them bend	***doblen ellos***

Impersonal forms

Infinitive

doblar
to bend

Perfect Infinitive

haber doblado
to have bent

Gerund

doblando
bending

Perfect Gerund

habiendo doblado
having bent

Participle

doblado
bent

Perfect Participle

habiendo doblado
having bent

BESEECH · BESOUGHT · BESOUGHT

SUPLICAR, IMPLORAR.

Indicative

Present

suplico
I beseech
you beseech
he/she/it beseeches
we beseech
you beseech
they beseech

Present perfect

he suplicado
I have besought
you have besought
he/she/it has besought
we have besought
you have besought
they have besought

Past

suplicaba/supliqué
I besought
you besought
he/she/it besought
we besought
you besought
they besought

Past perfect

había/ hube suplicado
I had besought
you had besought
he/she/it had besought
we had besought
you had besought
they had besought

Future

suplicaré
I shall/will beseech
you will beseech
he/she/it will beseech
we shall/will beseech
you will beseech
they will beseech

Future perfect

habré suplicado
I shall/will have besought
you will have besought
he/she/it will have besought
we shall/will have besought
you will have besought
they will have besought

Conditional

Present

suplicaría
I should/would beseech
you would beseech
he/she/it would beseech
we should/would beseech
you would beseech
they would beseech

Perfect

habría suplicado
I should/would have besought
you would have besought
he/she/it would have besought
we should/would have besought
you would have besought
they would have besought

Subjunctive

Present

suplique
I beseech
you beseech
he/she/it beseeches
we beseech
you beseech
they beseech

Present perfect

haya suplicado
I have besought
you have besought
he/she/it has besought
we have besought
you have besought
they have besought

Past

suplicara o suplicase
I besought
you besought
he/she/it besought
we besought
you besought
they besought

Past perfect

hubiera o hubiese suplicado
I had besought
you had besought
he/she/it had besought
we had besought
you had besought
they had besought

Imperative

let me beseech	***no existe (déjame suplicar)***
beseech	***suplica***
let him/her/it beseech	***suplique él/ella/ello***
let us (let's) beseech	***supliquemos***
beseech	***suplicad***
let them beseech	***supliquen***

Impersonal forms

Infinitive

suplicar
to beseech

Perfect Infinitive

haber suplicado
to have besought

Gerund

suplicando
beseeching

Perfect Gerund

habiendo suplicado
having besought

Participle

suplicado
besought

Perfect Participle

habiendo suplicado
having besought

BET · BET · BET

APOSTAR

Indicative

Present

apuesto
I bet
you bet
he/she/it bets
we bet
you bet
they bet

Present perfect

he apostado
I have bet
you have bet
he/she/it has bet
we have bet
you have bet
they have bet

Past

apostaba/aposté
I bet
you bet
he/she/it bet
we bet
you bet
they bet

Past perfect

había/hube apostado
I had bet
you had bet
he/she/it had bet
we had bet
you had bet
they had bet

Future

apostaré
I shall/will bet
you will bet
he/she/it will bet
we shall/will bet
you will bet
they will bet

Future perfect

habré apostado
I shall/will have bet
you will have bet
he/she/it will have bet
we shall/will have bet
you will have bet
they will have bet

Conditional

Present

apostaría
I should/would bet
you would bet
he/she/it would bet
we should/would bet
you would bet
they would bet

Perfect

habría apostado
I should/would have bet
you would have bet
he/she/it would have bet
we should/would have bet
you would have bet
they would have bet

Subjunctive

Present

apueste
I bet
you bet
he/she/it bets
we bet
you bet
they bet

Present perfect

haya apostado
I have bet
you have bet
he/she/it has bet
we have bet
you have bet
they have bet

Past

apostara/apostase
I bet
you bet
he/she/it bet
we bet
you bet
they bet

Past perfect

hubiera/hubiese apostado
I had bet
you had bet
he/she/it had bet
we had bet
you had bet
they had bet

Imperative

let me bet	***no existe (déjame apostar)***
bet	***apuesta tú***
let him/her/it bet	***apueste él/ella/ello***
let us (let's) bet	***apostemos nosotros***
bet	***apostad vosotros***
let them bet	***apuesten ellos***

Impersonal forms

Infinitive

apostar
to bet

Perfect Infinitive

haber apostado
to have bet

Gerund

apostando
betting

Perfect Gerund

habiendo apostado
having bet

Participle

apostado
bet

Perfect Participle

habiendo apostado
having bet

BID · BADE · BIDDEN

MANDAR, ORDENAR, INVITAR, DAR.

Indicative

Present	Present perfect
ordeno	***he ordenado***
I bid	I have bidden
you bid	you have bidden
he/she/it bids	he/she/it has bidden
we bid	we have bidden
you bid	you have bidden
they bid	they have bidden

Past	Past perfect
ordenaba/ordené	***había/hube ordenado***
I bade	I had bidden
you bade	you had bidden
he/she/it bade	he/she/it had bidden
we bade	we had bidden
you bade	you had bidden
they bade	they had bidden

Future	Future perfect
ordenaré	***habré ordenado***
I shall/will bid	I shall/will have bidden
you will bid	you will have bidden
he/she/it will bid	he/she/it will have bidden
we shall/will bid	we shall/will have bidden
you will bid	
they will bid	they will have bidden

Conditional

Present	Perfect
ordenaría	***habría ordenado***
I should/would bid	I should/would have bidden
you would bid	you would have bidden
he/she/it would bid	he/she/it would have bidden
we should/would bid	we should/would have bidden
you would bid	you would have bidden
they would bid	they would have bidden

Subjunctive

Present	Present perfect
ordene	***haya ordenado***
I bid	I have bidden
you bid	you have bidden
he/she/it bids	he/she/it has bidden
we bid	we have bidden
you bid	you have bidden
they bid	they have bidden

Past	Past perfect
ordenara/ordenase	***hubiera/hubiese ordenado***
I bade	I had bidden
you bade	you had bidden
he/she/it bade	he/she/it had bidden
we bade	we had bidden
you bade	you had bidden
they bade	they had bidden

Imperative

let me bid	***no existe (déjame ordenar)***
bid	***ordena tú***
let him/her/it bid	***ordene él/ella/ello***
let us (let's) bid	***ordenemos nosotros***
bid	***ordenad vosotros***
let them bid	***ordenen ellos***

Impersonal forms

Infinitive	Perfect Infinitive
ordenar	***haber ordenado***
to bid	to have bidden

Gerund	Perfect Gerund
ordenando	***habiendo ordenado***
bidding	having bidden

Participle	Perfect Participle
ordenado	***habiendo ordenado***
bidden	having bidden

BIND · BOUND · BOUND

ATAR, AMARRAR, ENVOLVER, UNIR, VENDAR

Indicative

Present

ato
I bind
you bind
he/she/it binds
we bind
you bind
they bind

Present perfect

he atado
I have bound
you have bound
he/she/it has bound
we have bound
you have bound
they have bound

Past

ataba/até
I bound
you bound
he/she/it bound
we bound
you bound
they bound

Past perfect

había/hube atado
I had bound
you had bound
he/she/it had bound
we had bound
you had bound
they had bound

Future

ataré
I shall/will bind
you will bind
he/she/it will bind
we shall/will bind
you will bind
they will bind

Future perfect

habré atado
I shall/will have bound
you will have bound
he/she/it will have bound
we shall/will have bound
you will have bound
they will have bound

Conditional

Present

ataría
I should/would bind
you would bind
he/she/it would bind
we should/would bind
you would bind
they would bind

Perfect

habría atado
I should/would have bound
you would have bound
he/she/it would have bound
we should/would have bound
you would have bound
they would have bound

Subjunctive

Present

ate
I bind
you bind
he/she/it binds
we bind
you bind
they bind

Present perfect

haya atado
I have bound
you have bound
he/she/it has bound
we have bound
you have bound
they have bound

Past

atara o atase
I bound
you bound
he/she/it bound
we bound
you bound
they bound

Past perfect

hubiera o hubiese atado
I had bound
you had bound
he/she/it had bound
we had bound
you had bound
they had bound

Imperative

let me bind	***no existe (déjame atar)***
bind	***ata tú***
let him/her/it bind	***ate él/ella/ello***
let us bind	***atemos nosotros***
bind	***atad vosotros***
they them bind	***aten ellos***

Impersonal forms

Infinitive

atar
to bind

Perfect Infinitive

haber atado
to have bound

Gerund

atando
binding

Perfect Gerund

habiendo atado
having bound

Participle

atado
bound

Perfect Participle

habiendo atado
having bound

BITE · BIT · BITTEN

MORDER, PICAR

Indicative

Present

muerdo
I bite
you bite
he/she/it bites
we bite
you bite
they bite

Present perfect

he mordido
I have bitten
you have bitten
he/she/it has bitten
we have bitten
you have bitten
they have bitten

Past

mordía/mordí
I bit
you bit
he/she/it bit
we bit
you bit
they bit

Past perfect

había/hube mordido
I had bitten
you had bitten
he/she/she/it had bitten
we had bitten
you had bitten
they had bitten

Future

morderé
I shall/will bite
you will bite
he/she/it will bite
we shall/will bite
you will bite
they will bite

Future perfect

habré mordido
I shall/will have bitten
you will have bitten
he/she/it will have bitten
we shall/will have bitten
you will have bitten
they will have bitten

Conditional

Present

mordería
I should/would bite
you would bite
he/she/it would bite
we should/would bite
you would bite
they would bite

Perfect

habría mordido
I should/would have bitten
you would have bitten
he/she/it would have bitten
we should/would have bitten
you would have bitten
they would have bitten

Subjunctive

Present

muerda
I bite
you bite
he/she/it bites
we bite
you bite
they bite

Present perfect

haya mordido
I have bitten
you have bitten
he/she/it has bitten
we have bitten
you have bitten
they have bitten

Past

mordiera o mordiese
I bit
you bit
he/she/it bit
we bit
you bit
they bit

Past perfect

hubiera o hubiese mordido
I had bitten
you had bitten
he/she/it had bitten
we had bitten
you had bitten
they had bitten

Imperative

let me bite	***no existe (déjame morder)***
bite	***muerde tú***
let him/her/it bite	***muerda él/ella/ello***
let us (let's) bite	***mordamos nosotros***
bite	***morded vosotros***
let them bite	***muerdan ellos***

Impersonal forms

Infinitive

morder
to bite

Perfect Infinitive

haber mordido
to have bitten

Gerund

mordiendo
biting

Perfect Gerund

habiendo mordido
having bitten

Participle

mordido
bitten

Perfect Participle

habiendo mordido
having bitten

BLEED · BLED · BLED

SANGRAR, DESANGRAR.

Indicative

Present

sangro
I bleed
you bleed
he/she/it bleeds
we bleed
you bleed
they bleed

Present perfect

he sangrado
I have bled
you have bled
he/she/it has bled
we have bled
you have bled
they have bled

Past

sangraba/sangré
I bled
you bled
he/she/it bled
we bled
you bled
they bled

Past perfect

había/hube sangrado
I had bled
you had bled
he/she/it had bled
we had bled
you had bled
they had bled

Future

sangraré
I shall/will bleed
you will bleed
he/she/it will bleed
we shall/will bleed
you will bleed
they will bleed

Future perfect

habré sangrado
I shall/will have bled
you will have bled
he/she/it will have bled
we shall/will have bled
you will have bled
they will have bled

Conditional

Present

sangraría
I should/would bleed
you would bleed
he/she/it would bleed
we should/would bleed
you would bleed
they would bleed

Perfect

habría sangrado
I should/would have bled
you would have bled
he/she/it would have bled
we should/would have bled
you would have bled
they would have bled

Subjunctive

Present

sangre
I bleed
you bleed
he/she/it bleeds
we bleed
you bleed
they bleed

Present perfect

hube sangrado
I have bled
you have bled
he/she/it has bled
we have bled
you have bled
they have bled

Past

sangrara/sangrase
I bled
you bled
he/she/it bled
we bled
you bled
they bled

Past perfect

hubiera/hubiese sangrado
I had bled
you had bled
he/she/it had bled
we had bled
you had bled
they had bled

Imperative

let me bleed	***no existe (déjame sangrar)***
bleed	***sangra tú***
let him/her/it bleed	***sangre él/ella/ello***
let us (let's) bleed	***sangremos nosotros***
bleed	***sangrad vosotros***
let them bleed	***sangren ellos***

Impersonal forms

Infinitive

sangrar
to bleed

Perfect Infinitive

haber sangrado
to have bled

Gerund

sangrando
bleeding

Perfect Gerund

habiendo sangrado
having bled

Participle

sangrado
bled

Perfect Participle

habiendo sangrado
having bled

BLOW · BLEW · BLOWN

SOPLAR

Indicative

Present	Present perfect
soplo	***he soplado***
I blow	I have blown
you blow	you have blown
he/she/it blows	he/she/it has blown
we blow	we have blown
you blow	you have blown
they blow	they have blown

Past	Past perfect
soplaba/soplé	***había/hube soplado***
I blew	I had blown
you blew	you had blown
he/she/it blew	he/she/it had blown
we blew	we had blown
you blew	you had blown
they blew	they had blown

Future	Future perfect
soplaré	***habré soplado***
I shall/will blow	I shall/will have blown
you will blow	you will have blown
he/she/it will blow	he/she/it will have blown
we shall/will blow	we shall/will have blown
you will blow	you will have blown
they will blow	they will have blown

Conditional

Present	Perfect
soplaría	***habría soplado***
I should/would blow	I should/would have blown
you would blow	you would have blown
he/she/it would blow	he/she/it would have blown
we should/would blow	we should/would have blown
you would blow	you would have blown
they would blow	they would have blown

Subjunctive

Present	Present perfect
sople	***haya soplado***
I blow	I have blown
you blow	you have blown
he/she/it blows	he/she/it has blown
we blow	we have blown
you blow	you have blown
they blow	they have blown

Past	Past perfect
soplara/soplase	***hubiera/hubiese soplado***
I blew	I had blown
you blew	you had blown
he/she/it blew	he/she/it had blown
we blew	we had blown
you blew	you had blown
they blew	they had blown

Imperative

let me blow	***no existe (déjame soplar)***
blow	***sopla tú***
let him/her/it blow	***sople él/ella/ello***
let us (let's) blow	***soplemos nosotros***
blow	***soplad vosotros***
let them blow	***soplen ellos***

Impersonal forms

Infinitive	Perfect Infinitive
soplar	***haber soplado***
to blow	to have blown

Gerund	Perfect Gerund
soplando	***habiendo soplado***
blowing	having blown

Participle	Perfect Participle
soplado	***habiendo soplado***
blown	having blown

BREAK · BROKE · BROKEN

ROMPER

Indicative

Present

rompo
I break
you break
he/she/it breaks
we break
you break
they break

Present perfect

he roto
I have broken
you have broken
he/she/it has broken
we have broken
you have broken
they have broken

Past

rompía/rompí
I broke
you broke
he/she/it broke
we broke
you broke
they broke

Past perfect

había/hube roto
I had broken
you had broken
he/she/it had broken
we had broken
you had broken
they had broken

Future

romperé
I shall/will break
you will break
he/she/it will break
we shall/will break
you will break
they will break

Future perfect

habré roto
I shall/will have broken
you will have broken
he/she/it will have broken
we shall/will have broken
you will have broken
they will have broken

Conditional

Present

rompería
I should/would break
you would break
he/she/it would break
we should/would break
you would break
they would break

Perfect

habría roto
I should/would have broken
you would have broken
he/she/it would have broken
we should/would have broken
you would have broken
they would have broken

Subjunctive

Present

rompa
I break
you break
he/she/it breaks
we break
you break
they break

Present perfect

haya roto
I have broken
you have broken
he/she/it has broken
we have broken
you have broken
they have broken

Past

rompiera/rompiese
I broke
you broke
he/she/it broke
we broke
you broke
they broke

Past perfect

hubiera/hubiese roto
I had broken
you had broken
he/she/it had broken
we had broken
you had broken
they had broken

Imperative

let me break	***no existe (déjame romper)***
break	***rompe tú***
let him/her/it break	***rompa él/ella/ello***
let us (let's) break	***rompamos nosotros***
break	***romped vosotros***
let them break	***rompan ellos***

Impersonal forms

Infinitive

romper
to break

Perfect Infinitive

haber roto
to have broken

Gerund

rompiendo
breaking

Perfect Gerund

habiendo roto
having broken

Participle

roto
broken

Perfect Participle

habiendo roto
having broken

BREED · BRED · BRED

CRIAR, GENERAR, ENGENDRAR

Indicative

Present

crío
I breed
you breed
he/she/it breeds
we breed
you breed
they breed

Present perfect

he criado
I have bred
you have bred
he/she/it has bred
we have bred
you have bred
they have bred

Past

criaba/crié
I bred
you bred
he/she/it bred
we bred
you bred
they bred

Past perfect

había/hube criado
I had bred
you had bred
he/she/it had bred
we had bred
you had bred
they had bred

Future

criaré
I shall/will breed
you will breed
he/she/it will breed
we shall/will breed
you will breed
they will breed

Future perfect

habré criado
I shall/will have bred
you will have bred
he/she/it will have bred
we shall/will have bred
you will have bred
they will have bred

Conditional

Present

criaría
I should/would breed
you would breed
he/she/it would breed
we should/would breed
you would breed
they would breed

Perfect

habría criado
I should/would have bred
you would have bred
he/she/it would have bred
we should/would have bred
you would have bred
they would have bred

Subjunctive

Present

críe
I breed
you breed
he/she/it breeds
we breed
you breed
they breed

Present perfect

haya criado
I have bred
you have bred
he/she/it has bred
we have bred
you have bred
they have bred

Past

criara o criase
I bred
you bred
he/she/it bred
we bred
you bred
they bred

Past perfect

hubiera o hubiese criado
I had bred
you had bred
he/she/it had bred
we had bred
you had bred
they had bred

Imperative

let me breed	***no existe (déjame criar)***
breed	***cría tú***
let him/her/it breed	***críe él/ella/ello***
let us (let's) breed	***criemos nosotros***
breed	***criad vosotros***
let them breed	***críen ellos***

Impersonal forms

Infinitive

criar
to breed

Perfect Infinitive

haber criado
to have bred

Gerund

criando
breeding

Perfect Gerund

habiendo criado
having bred

Participle

criado
bred

Perfect Participle

habiendo criado
having bred

BRING · BROUGHT · BROUGHT

TRAER

Indicative

Present

traigo
I bring
you bring
he/she/it brings
we bring
you bring
they bring

Present perfect

he traído
I have brought
you have brought
he/she/it has brought
we have brought
you have brought
they have brought

Past

traía/traje
I brought
you brought
he/she/it brought
we brought
you brought
they brought

Past perfect

había/hube traído
I had brought
you had brought
he/she/it had brought
we had brought
you had brought
they had brought

Future

traeré
I shall/will bring
you will bring
he/she/it will bring
we shall/will bring
you will bring
they will bring

Future perfect

habré traído
I shall/will have brought
you will have brought
he/she/it will have brought
we shall/will have brought
you will have brought
they will have brought

Conditional

Present

traería
I should/would bring
you would bring
he/she/it would bring
we should/would bring
you would bring
they would bring

Perfect

habría traído
I should/would have brought
you would have brought
he/she/it would have brought
we should/would have brought
you would have brought
they would have brought

Subjunctive

Present

traiga
I bring
you bring
he/she/it brings
we bring
you bring
they bring

Present perfect

haya traído
I have brought
you have brought
he/she/it has brought
we have brought
you have brought
they have brought

Past

trajera/trajese
I brought
you brought
he/she/it brought
we brought
you brought
they brought

Past perfect

hubiera/hubiese traído
I had brought
you had brought
he/she/it had brought
we had brought
you had brought
they had brought

Imperative

let me bring	***no existe (déjame traer)***
bring	***trae tú***
let him/her/it bring	***traiga él/ella/ello***
let us (let's) bring	***traigamos nosotros***
bring	***traed vosotros***
let them bring	***traigan ellos***

Impersonal forms

Infinitive

traer
to bring

Perfect Infinitive

haber traído
to have brought

Gerund

trayendo
bringing

Perfect Gerund

habiendo traído
having brought

Participle

traído
brought

Perfect Participle

habiendo traído
having brought

BUILD · BUILT · BUILT

CONSTRUIR, EDIFICAR

Indicative

Present

construyo
I build
you build
he/she/it builds
we build
you build
they build

Present perfect

he construido
I have built
you have built
he/she/it has built
we have built
you have built
they have built

Past

construía/construí
I built
you built
he/she/it built
we built
you built
they built

Past perfect

había/hube construido
I had built
you had built
he/she/it had built
we had built
you had built
they had built

Future

construiré
I shall/will build
you will build
he/she/it will build
we shall/will build
you will build
they will build

Future perfect

habré construido
I shall/will have built
you will have built
he/she/it will have built
we shall/will have built
you will have built
they will have built

Conditional

Present

construiría
I should/would build
you would build
he/she/it would build
we should/would build
you would build
they would build

Perfect

habría construido
I should/would have built
you would have built
he/she/it would have built
we should/would have built
you would have built
they would have built

Subjunctive

Present

construya
I build
you build
he/she/it builds
we build
you build
they build

Present perfect

haya construido
I have built
you have built
he/she/it has built
we have built
you have built
they have built

Past

construyera/construyese
I built
you built
he/she/it built
we built
you built
they built

Past perfect

hubiera/hubiese construido
I had built
you had built
he/she/it had built
we had built
you had built
they had built

Imperative

let me build	***no existe (déjame construir)***
build	***construye tú***
let him/her/it build	***construya él/ella/ello***
let us (let's) build	***construyamos nosotros***
build	***construid vosotros***
let them build	***construyan ellos***

Impersonal forms

Infinitive

construir
to build

Perfect Infinitive

haber construido
to have built

Gerund

construyendo
building

Perfect Gerund

habiendo construido
having built

Participle

construido
built

Perfect Participle

habiendo construido
having built

BURN · BURNT/BURNED · BURNT/BURNED

QUEMAR, ARDER

Indicative

Present

ardo
I burn
you burn
he/she/it burns
we burn
you burn
they burn

Present perfect

he ardido
I have burnt/burned
you have burnt/burned
he/she/it has burnt/burned
we have burnt/burned
you have burnt/burned
they have burnt/burned

Past

ardía/ardí
I burnt/burned
you burnt/burned
he/she/it burnt/burned
we burnt/burned
you burnt/burned
they burnt/burned

Past perfect

había/hube ardido
I had burnt/burned
you had burnt/burned
he/she/it had burnt/burned
we had burnt/burned
you had burnt/burned
they had burnt/burned

Future

arderé
I shall/will burn
you will burn
he/she/it will burn
we shall/will burn
you will burn
they will burn

Future perfect

habré ardido
I shall/will have burnt/burned
you will have burnt/burned
he/she/it will have burnt/burned
we shall/will have burnt/burned
you will have burnt/burned
they will have burnt/burned

Conditional

Present

ardería
I should/would burn
you would burn
he/she/it would burn
we should/would burn
you would burn
they would burn

Perfect

habría ardido
I should/would have burnt/burned
you would have burnt/burned
he/she/it would have burnt/burned
we should/would have burnt/burned
you would have burnt/burned
they would have burnt/burned

Subjunctive

Present

arda
I burn
you burn
he/she/it burns
we burn
you burn
they burn

Present perfect

haya ardido
I have burnt/burned
you have burnt/burned
he/she/it has burnt/burned
we have burnt/burned
you have burnt/burned
they have burnt/burned

Past

ardiera o ardiese
I burnt/burned
you burnt/burned
he/she/it burnt/burned
we burnt/burned
you burnt/burned
they burnt/burned

Past perfect

hubiera o hubiese ardido
I had burnt/burned
you had burnt/burned
he/she/it had burnt/burned
we had burnt/burned
you had burnt/burned
they had burnt/burned

Imperative

let me burn	***no existe (déjame arder)***
burn	***arde tú***
let him/her/it burn	***arda él/ella/ello***
let us (let's burn)	***ardamos nosotros***
burn	***arded vosotros***
let them burn	***ardan ellos***

Impersonal forms

Infinitive

arder
to burn

Perfect Infinitive

haber ardido
to have burnt/burned

Gerund

ardiendo
burning

Perfect Gerund

habiendo ardido
having burnt

Participle

ardido
burnt

Perfect Participle

habiendo ardido
having burnt

BURST · BURST · BURST

REVENTAR, DESBORDAR, ABRIRSE DE GOLPE

Indicative

Present

reviento
I burst
you burst
he/she/it bursts
we burst
you burst
they burst

Present perfect

he reventado
I have burst
you have burst
he/she/it has burst
we have burst
you have burst
they have burst

Past

reventaba/reventé
I burst
you burst
he/she/it burst
we burst
you burst
they burst

Past perfect

había/hube reventado
I had burst
you had burst
he/she/it had burst
we had burst
you had burst
they had burst

Future

reventaré
I shall/will burst
you will burst
he/she/it will burst
we shall/will burst
you will burst
they will burst

Future perfect

habré reventado
I shall/will have burst
you will have burst
he/she/it will have burst
we shall/will have burst
you will have burst
they will have burst

Conditional

Present

reventaría
I should/would burst
you would burst
he/she/it would burst
we should/would burst
you would burst
they would burst

Perfect

habría reventado
I should/would have burst
you would have burst
he/she/it would have burst
we should/would have burst
you would have burst
they would have burst

Subjunctive

Present

reviente
I burst
you burst
he/she/it bursts
we burst
you burst
they burst

Present perfect

haya reventado
I have burst
you have burst
he/she/it has burst
we have burst
you have burst
they have burst

Past

reventara o reventase
I burst
you burst
he/she/it burst
we burst
you burst
they burst

Past perfect

hubiera o hubiese reventado
I had burst
you had burst
he/she/it had burst
we had burst
you had burst
they had burst

Imperative

let me burst	***no existe (déjame reventar)***
burst	***revienta tú***
let him/her/it burst	***reviente él/ella/ello***
let us (let's) burst	***reventemos nosotros***
burst	***reventad vosotros***
let them burst	***revienten ellos***

Impersonal forms

Infinitive

reventar
to burst

Perfect Infinitive

haber reventado
to have burst

Gerund

reventando
bursting

Perfect Gerund

habiendo reventado
having burst

Participle

reventado
burst

Perfect Participle

habiendo reventado
having burst

BUY · BOUGHT · BOUGHT

COMPRAR, ADQUIRIR

Indicative

Present

compro
I buy
you buy
he/she/it buys
we buy
you buy
they buy

Present perfect

he comprado
I have bought
you have bought
he/she/it has bought
we have bought
you have bought
they have bought

Past

compraba/compré
I bought
you bought
he/she/it bought
we bought
you bought
they bought

Past perfect

había/hube comprado
I had bought
you had bought
he/she/it had bought
we had bought
you had bought
they had bought

Future

compraré
I shall/will buy
you will buy
he/she/it will buy
we shall/will buy
you will buy
they will buy

Future perfect

habré comprado
I shall/will have bought
you will have bought
he/she/it will have bought
we shall/will have bought
you will have bought
they will have bought

Conditional

Present

compraría
I should/would buy
you would buy
he/she/it would buy
we should/would buy
you would buy
they would buy

Perfect

habría comprado
I should/would have bought
you would have bought
he/she/it would have bought
we should/would have bought
you would have bought
they would have bought

Subjunctive

Present

compre
I buy
you buy
he/she/it buys
we buy
you buy
they buy

Present perfect

haya comprado
I have bought
you have bought
he/she/it has bought
we have bought
you have bought
they have bought

Past

comprara o comprase
I bought
you bought
he/she/it bought
we bought
you bought
they bought

Past perfect

hubiera o hubiese comprado
I had bought
you had bought
he/she/it had bought
we had bought
you had bought
they had bought

Imperative

let me buy	***no existe (déjame comprar)***
buy	***compra tú***
let him/her/it buy	***compre él/ella/ello***
let us (let's) buy	***compremos nosotros***
buy	***comprad vosotros***
let them buy	***compren ellos***

Impersonal forms

Infinitive

comprar
to buy

Perfect Infinitive

haber comprado
to have bought

Gerund

comprando
buying

Perfect Gerund

habiendo comprado
having bought

Participle

comprado
bought

Perfect Participle

habiendo comprado
having bought

CAST · CAST · CAST

ARROJAR, PROYECTAR, ECHAR

Indicative

Present

arrojo
I cast
you cast
he/she/it casts
we cast
you cast
they cast

Present perfect

haya arrojado
I have cast
you have cast
he/she/it has cast
we have cast
you have cast
they have cast

Past

arrojaba/arrojé
I cast
you cast
he/she/it cast
we cast
you cast
they cast

Past perfect

había/hube arrojado
I had cast
you had cast
he/she/it had cast
we had cast
you had cast
they had cast

Future

arrojaré
I shall/will cast
you will cast
he/she/it will cast
we shall/will cast
you will cast
they will cast

Future perfect

habré arrojado
I shall/will have cast
you will have cast
he/she/it will have cast
we shall/will have cast
you will have cast
they will have cast

Conditional

Present

arrojaría
I should/would cast
you would cast
he/she/it would cast
we should/would cast
you would cast
they would cast

Perfect

habría arrojado
I should/would have cast
you would have cast
he/she/it would have cast
we should/would have cast
you would have cast
they would have cast

Subjunctive

Present

arroje
I cast
you cast
he/she/it casts
we cast
you cast
they cast

Present perfect

haya arrojado
I have cast
you have cast
he/she/it has cast
we have cast
you have cast
they have cast

Past

arrojara/arrojase
I cast
you cast
he/she/it cast
we cast
you cast
they cast

Past perfect

hubiera/hubiese arrojado
I had cast
you had cast
he/she/it had cast
we had cast
you had cast
they had cast

Imperative

let me cast	***no existe (déjame arrojar)***
cast	***arroja tú***
let him/her/it cast	***arroje él/ella/ello***
let us (let's) cast	***arrojemos nosotros***
cast	***arrojad vosotros***
let them cast	***arrojen ellos***

Impersonal forms

Infinitive

arrojar
to cast

Perfect Infinitive

haber arrojado
to have cast

Gerund

arrojando
casting

Perfect Gerund

habiendo arrojado
having cast

Participle

arrojado
cast

Perfect Participle

habiendo arrojado
having cast

CATCH · CAUGHT · CAUGHT

AGARRAR, COGER, ATRAPAR, ASIR

Indicative

Present

agarro
I catch
you catch
he/she/it catches
we catch
you catch
they catch

Present perfect

he agarrado
I have caught
you have caught
he/she/it has caught
we have caught
you have caught
they have caught

Past

agarraba/agarré
I caught
you caught
he/she/it caught
we caught
you caught
they caught

Past perfect

había/hube agarrado
I had caught
you had caught
he/she/it had caught
we had caught
you had caught
they had caught

Future

agarraré
I shall/will catch
you will catch
he/she/it will catch
we shall/will catch
you will catch
they will catch

Future perfect

habré agarrado
I shall/will have caught
you will have caught
he/she/it will have caught
we shall/will have caught
you will have caught
they will have caught

Conditional

Present

agarraría
I should/would catch
you would catch
he/whe/it would catch
we should/would catch
you would catch
they would catch

Perfect

habría agarrado
I should/would have caught
you would have caught
he/she/it would have caught
we should/would have caught
you would have caught
they would have caught

Subjunctive

Present

agarre
I catch
you catch
he/she/it catches
we catch
you catch
they catch

Present perfect

haya agarrado
I have caught
you have caught
he/she/it has caught
we have caught
you have caught
they have caught

Past

agarrara o agarrase
I caught
you caught
he/she/it caught
we caught
you caught
they caught

Past perfect

hubiera o hubiese agarrado
I had caught
you had caught
he/she/it had caught
we had caught
you had caught
they had caught

Imperative

let me catch	***no existe (déjame agarrar)***
catch	***agarra tú***
let him/her/it catch	***agarre él/ella/ello***
let us (let's) catch	***agarremos nosotros***
catch	***agarrad vosotros***
let them catch	***agarren ellos***

Impersonal forms

Infinitive

agarrar
to catch

Perfect Infinitive

haber agarrado
to have caught

Gerund

agarrando
catching

Perfect Gerund

habiendo agarrado
having caught

Participle

agarrado
caught

Perfect Participle

habiendo agarrado
having caught

CHOOSE · CHOSE · CHOSEN

ELEGIR

Indicative

Present

elijo
I choose
you choose
he/she/it chooses
we choose
you choose
they choose

Present perfect

he elegido
I have chosen
you have chosen
he/she/it has chosen
we have chosen
you have chosen
they have chosen

Past

elegía/elegí
I chose
you chose
he/she/it chose
we chose
you chose
they chose

Past perfect

había/hube elegido
I had chosen
you had chosen
he/she/it had chosen
we had chosen
you had chosen
they had chosen

Future

elegiré
I shall/will choose
you will choose
he/she/it will choose
we shall/will choose
you will choose
they will choose

Future perfect

habré elegido
I shall/will have chosen
you will have chosen
he/she/it will have chosen
we shall/will have chosen
you will have chosen
they will have chosen

Conditional

Present

elegiría
I should/would choose
you would choose
he/she/it would choose
we should/would choose
you would choose
they would choose

Perfect

habría elegido
I should/would have chosen
you would have chosen
he/she/it would have chosen
we should/would have chosen
you would have chosen
they would have chosen

Subjunctive

Present

elija
I choose
you choose
he/she/it chooses
we choose
you choose
they choose

Present perfect

haya elegido
I have chosen
you have chosen
he/she/it has chosen
we have chosen
you have chosen
they have chosen

Past

eligiera/eligiese
I chose
you chose
he/she/it chose
we chose
you chose
they chose

Past perfect

hubiera/hubiese elegido
I had chosen
you had chosen
he/she/it had chosen
we had chosen
you had chosen
they had chosen

Imperative

let me choose	***no existe (déjame elegir)***
choose	***elige tú***
let him/her/it choose	***elija él/ella/ello***
let us (let's) choose	***elijamos nosotros***
choose	***elegid vosotros***
let them choose	***elijan ellos***

Impersonal forms

Infinitive

elegir
to choose

Perfect Infinitive

haber elegido
to have chosen

Gerund

eligiendo
choosing

Perfect Gerund

habiendo elegido
having chosen

Participle

elegido
chosen

Perfect Participle

habiendo elegido
having chosen

CLING · CLUNG · CLUNG

AFERRARSE, ADHERIRSE, PEGARSE

Indicative

Present

aferro
I cling
you cling
he/she/it clings
we cling
you cling
they cling

Present perfect

he aferrado
I have clung
you have clung
he/she/it has clung
we have clung
you have clung
they have clung

Past

aferraba/aferré
I clung
you clung
he/she/it clung
we clung
you clung
they clung

Past perfect

había/hube aferrado
I had clung
you had clung
he/she/it had clung
we had clung
you had clung
they had clung

Future

aferraré
I shall/will cling
you will cling
he/she/it will cling
we shall/will cling
you will cling
they will cling

Future perfect

habré aferrado
I shall/will have clung
you will have clung
he/she/it will have clung
we shall/will have clung
you will have clung
they will have clung

Conditional

Present

aferraría
I should/would cling
you would cling
he/she/it would cling
we should/would cling
you would cling
they would cling

Perfect

habría aferrado
I should/would have clung
you would have clung
he/she/it would have clung
we should/would have clung
you would have clung
they would have clung

Subjunctive

Present

aferre
I cling
you cling
he/she/it clings
we cling
you cling
they cling

Present perfect

haya aferrado
I have clung
you have clung
he/she/it has clung
we have clung
you have clung
they have clung

Past

aferrara o aferrase
I clung
you clung
he/she/it clung
we clung
you clung
they clung

Past perfect

hubiera o hubiese aferrado
I had clung
you had clung
he/she/it had clung
we had clung
you had clung
they had clung

Imperative

let me cling	***no existe (déjame aferrar)***
cling	***aferra tú***
let him/her/it cling	***aferre él/ella/ello***
let us (let's) cling	***aferremos nosotros***
cling	***aferrad vosotros***
let them cling	***aferren ellos***

Impersonal forms

Infinitive

aferrar
to cling

Perfect Infinitive

haber aferrado
to have clung

Gerund

aferrando
clinging

Perfect Gerund

habiendo aferrado
having clung

Participle

aferrado
clung

Perfect Participle

habiendo aferrado
having clung

COME · CAME · COME

VENIR

Indicative

Present

vengo
I come
you come
he/she/it comes
we come
you come
they come

Present perfect

he venido
I have come
you have come
he/she/it has come
we have come
you have come
they have come

Past

venía/vine
I came
you came
he/she/it came
we came
you came
they came

Past perfect

había/hube venido
I had come
you had come
he/she/it had come
we had come
you had come
they had come

Future

vendré
I shall/will come
you will come
he/she/it will come
we shall/will come
you will come
they will come

Future perfect

habré venido
I shall/will have come
you will have come
he/she/it will have come
we shall/will have come
you will have come
they will have come

Conditional

Present

vendría
I should/would come
you would come
he/she/it would come
we should/would come
you would come
they would come

Perfect

habría venido
I should/would have come
you would have come
he/she/it would have come
we should/would have come
you would have come
they would have come

Subjunctive

Present

venga
I come
you come
he/she/it comes
we come
you come
they come

Present perfect

haya venido
I have come
you have come
he/she/it has come
we have come
you have come
they have come

Past

viniera/viniese
I came
you came
he/she/it came
we came
you came
they came

Past perfect

hubiera/hubiese venido
I had come
you had come
he/she/it had come
we had come
you had come
they had come

Imperative

let me come	***no existe (déjame venir)***
come	***ven tú***
let him/her/it come	***venga él/ella/ello***
let us (let's) come	***vengamos nosotros***
come	***venid vosotros***
let them come	***vengan ellos***

Impersonal forms

Infinitive

venir
to come

Perfect Infinitive

haber venido
to have come

Gerund

viniendo
coming

Perfect Gerund

habiendo venido
having come

Participle

venido
come

Perfect Participle

habiendo venido
having come

COST · COST · COST

COSTAR

Indicative

Present

cuesto
I cost
you cost
he/she/it costs
we cost
you cost
they cost

Present perfect

he costado
I have cost
you have cost
he/she/it has cost
we have cost
you have cost
they have cost

Past

costaba/costé
I cost
you cost
he/she/it cost
we cost
you cost
they cost

Past perfect

había/hube costado
I had cost
you had cost
he/she/it had cost
we had cost
you had cost
they had cost

Future

costaré
I shall/will cost
you will cost
he/she/it will cost
we shall/will cost
you will cost
they will cost

Future perfect

habré costado
I shall/will have cost
you will have cost
he/she/it will have cost
we shall/will have cost
you will have cost
they will have cost

Conditional

Present

costaría
I should/would cost
you would cost
he/she/it would cost
we should/would cost
you would cost
they would cost

Perfect

habría costado
I should/would have cost
you would have cost
he/she/it would have cost
we should/would have cost
you would have cost
they would have cost

Subjunctive

Present

cueste
I cost
you cost
he/she/it costs
we cost
you cost
they cost

Present perfect

haya costado
I have cost
you have cost
he/she/it has cost
we have cost
you have cost
they have cost

Past

costara o costase
I cost
you cost
he/she/it cost
we cost
you cost
they cost

Past perfect

hubiera o hubiese costado
I had cost
you had cost
he/she/it had cost
we had cost
you had cost
they had cost

Imperative

let me cost	***no existe (déjame costar)***
cost	***cuesta tú***
let him/her/it cost	***cueste él/ella/ello***
let us (let's) cost	***costemos nosotros***
cost	***costad vosotros***
let them cost	***cuesten ellos***

Impersonal forms

Infinitive

costar
to cost

Perfect Infinitive

haber costado
to have cost

Gerund

costando
costing

Perfect Gerund

habiendo costado
having cost

Participle

costado
cost

Perfect Participle

habiendo costado
having cost

CREEP · CREPT · CREPT

ARRASTRARSE, DESLIZARSE

Indicative

Present	Present perfect
me deslizo	***me he deslizado***
I creep	I have crept
you creep	you have crept
he/she/it creeps	he/she/it has crept
we creep	we have crept
you creep	you have crept
they creep	they have crept

Past	Past perfect
me deslizaba/deslicé	***me había/hube deslizado***
I crept	I had crept
you crept	you had crept
he/she/it crept	he/she/it had crept
we crept	we had crept
you crept	you had crept
they crept	they had crept

Future	Future perfect
me deslizaré	***habré deslizado***
I shall/will creep	I shall/will have crept
you will creep	you will have crept
he/she/it will creep	he/she/it will have crept
we shall/will creep	we shall/will have crept
you will creep	you will have crept
they will creep	they will have crept

Conditional

Present	Perfect
me deslizaría	***me habría deslizado***
I should/would creep	I should/would have crept
you would creep	you would have crept
he/she/it would creep	he/she/it would have crept
we should/would creep	we should/would have crept
you would creep	you would have crept
they would creep	they would have crept

Subjunctive

Present	Present perfect
me deslice	***me haya deslizado***
I creep	I have crept
you creep	you have crept
he/she/it creeps	he/she/it has crept
we creep	we have crept
you creep	you have crept
they creep	they have crept

Past	Past perfect
me deslizara/deslizase	***me hubiera/hubiese deslizado***
I crept	I had crept
you crept	you had crept
he/she/it crept	he/she/it had crept
we crept	we had crept
you crept	you had crept
they crept	they had crept

Imperative

let me creep	***no existe (déjame***
creep	***deslizar(me)***
let him/her/it creep	***deslíza tú***
let us (let's) creep	***deslice él/ella/ello***
creep	***deslicemos nosotros***
let them creep	***deslizad vosotros***

Impersonal forms

Infinitive	Perfect Infinitive
deslizar	***haber deslizado***
to creep	to have crept
Gerund	**Perfect Gerund**
deslizando	***habiendo deslizado***
creeping	having crept
Participle	**Perfect Participle**
deslizado	***habiendo deslizado***
crept	having crept

CUT · CUT · CUT

CORTAR

Indicative

Present

corto
I cut
you cut
he/she/it cuts
we cut
you cut
they cut

Present perfect

he cortado
I have cut
you have cut
he/she/it has cut
we have cut
you have cut
they have cut

Past

cortaba/corté
I cut
you cut
he/she/it cut
we cut
you cut
they cut

Past perfect

había/hube cortado
I had cut
you had cut
he/she/it had cut
we had cut
you had cut
they had cut

Future

cortaré
I shall/will cut
you will cut
he/she/it will cut
we shall/will cut
you will cut
they will cut

Future perfect

habré cortado
I shall/will have cut
you will have cut
he/she/it will have cut
we shall/will have cut
you will have cut
they will have cut

Conditional

Present

cortaría
I should/would cut
you would cut
he/she/it would cut
we should/would cut
you would cut
they would cut

Perfect

habría cortado
I should/would have cut
you would have cut
he/she/it would have cut
we should/would have cut
you would have cut
they would have cut

Subjunctive

Present

corte
I cut
you cut
he/she/it cuts
we cut
you cut
they cut

Present perfect

haya cortado
I have cut
you have cut
he/she/it has cut
we have cut
you have cut
they have cut

Past

cortara o cortase
I cut
you cut
he/she/it cut
we cut
you cut
they cut

Past perfect

hubiera o hubiese costado
I had cut
you had cut
he/she/it had cut
we had cut
you had cut
they had cut

Imperative

let me cut	***no existe (déjame cortar)***
cut	***corta tú***
let him/her/it cut	***corte él/ella/ello***
let us (let's) cut	***cortemos nosotros***
cut	***cortad vosotros***
let them cut	***corten ellos***

Impersonal forms

Infinitive

cortar
to cut

Perfect Infinitive

haber cortado
to have cut

Gerund

cortando
cutting

Perfect Gerund

habiendo cortado
having cut

Participle

cortado
cut

Perfect Participle

habiendo cortado
having cut

DEAL · DEALT · DEALT

TRATAR CON, REPARTIR, DISTRIBUIR, DAR (NAIPES)

Indicative

Present

trato
I deal
you deal
he/she/it deals
we deal
you deal
they deal

Present perfect

he tratado
I have dealt
you have dealt
he/she/it has dealt
we have dealt
you have dealt
they have dealt

Past

trataba/traté
I dealt
you dealt
he/she/it dealt
we dealt
you dealt
they dealt

Past perfect

había/hube tratado
I had dealt
you had dealt
he/she/it had dealt
we had dealt
you had dealt
they had dealt

Future

trataré
I shall/will deal
you will deal
he/she/it will deal
we shall/will deal
you will deal
they will deal

Future perfect

habré tratado
I shall/will have dealt
you will have dealt
he/she/it will have dealt
we shall/will have dealt
you will have dealt
they will have dealt

Conditional

Present

trataría
I should/would deal
you would deal
he/she/it would deal
we should/would deal
you would deal
they would deal

Perfect

habría tratado
I should/would have dealt
you would have dealt
he/she/it would have dealt
we should/would have dealt
you would have dealt
they would have dealt

Subjunctive

Present

trate
I deal
you deal
he/she/it deals
we deal
you deal
they deal

Present perfect

haya tratado
I have dealt
you have dealt
he/she/it has dealt
we have dealt
you have dealt
they have dealt

Past

tratara/tratase
I dealt
you dealt
he/she/it dealt
we dealt
you dealt
they dealt

Past perfect

hubiera/hubiese tratado
I had dealt
you had dealt
he/she/it had dealt
we had dealt
you had dealt
they had dealt

Imperative

let me deal	***no existe (déjame tratar)***
deal	***trata tú***
let him/her/it deal	***trate él/ella/ello***
let us (let's) deal	***tratemos nosotros***
deal	***tratad vosotros***
let them deal	***traten ellos***

Impersonal forms

Infinitive

tratar
to deal

Perfect Infinitive

haber tratado
to have dealt

Gerund

tratando
dealing

Perfect Gerund

habiendo tratado
having dealt

Participle

tratado
dealt

Perfect Participle

habiendo tratado
having dealt

DIG · DUG · DUG

CAVAR, EXCAVAR

Indicative

Present	Present perfect
cavo	***he cavado***
I dig	I have dug
you dig	you have dug
he/she/it digs	he/she/it has dug
we dig	we have dug
you dig	you have dug
they dig	they have dug

Past	Past perfect
cavaba/cavé	***había/hube cavado***
I dug	I had dug
you dug	you had dug
he/she/it dug	he/she/it had dug
we dug	we had dug
you dug	you had dug
they dug	they had dug

Future	Future perfect
cavaré	***habré cavado***
I shall/will dig	I shall/will have dug
you will dig	you will have dug
he/she/it will dig	he/she/it will have dug
we shall/will dig	we shall/will have dug
you will dig	you will have dug
they will dig	they will have dug

Conditional

Present	Perfect
cavaría	***habría cavado***
I should/would dig	I should/would have dug
you would dig	you would have dug
he/she/it would dig	he/she/it would have dug
we should/would dig	we should/would have dug
you would dig	you would have dug
they would dig	they would have dug

Subjunctive

Present	Present perfect
cave	***haya cavado***
I dig	I have dug
you dig	you have dug
he/she/it digs	he/she/it has dug
we dig	we have dug
you dig	you have dug
they dig	they have dug

Past	Past perfect
cavara/cavase	***hubiera/hubiese cavado***
I dug	I had dug
you dug	you had dug
he/she/it dug	he/she/it had dug
we dug	we had dug
you dug	you had dug
they dug	they had dug

Imperative

let me dig	***no existe (déjame cavar)***
dig	***cava tú***
let him/her/it dig	***cave él/ella/ello***
let us (let's) dig	***cavemos nosotros***
dig	***cavad vosotros***
let them dig	***caven ellos***

Impersonal forms

Infinitive	Perfect Infinitive
cavar	***haber cavado***
to dig	to have dug
Gerund	**Perfect Gerund**
cavando	***habiendo cavado***
digging	having dug
Participle	**Perfect Participle**
cavado	***habiendo cavado***
dug	having dug

DO · DID · DONE

HACER

Indicative

Present

hago
I do
you do
he/she/it does
we do
you do
they do

Present perfect

he hecho
I have done
you have done
he/she/it has done
we have done
you have done
they have done

Past

hacía/hice
I did
you did
he/she/it did
we did
you did
they did

Past perfect

había/hube hecho
I had done
you had done
he/she/it had done
we had done
you had done
they had done

Future

haré
I shall/will do
you will do
he/she/it will do
we shall/will do
you will do
they will do

Future perfect

habré hecho
I shall/will have done
you will have done
he/she/it will have done
we shall/will have done
you will have done
they will have done

Conditional

Present

haría
I should/would do
you would do
he/she/it would do
we should/would do
you would do
they would do

Perfect

habría hecho
I should/would have done
you would have done
he/she/it would have done
we should/would have done
you would have done
they would have done

Subjunctive

Present

haga
I do
you do
he/she/it does
we do
you do
they do

Present perfect

haya hecho
I have done
you have done
he/she/it has done
we have done
you have done
they have done

Past

hiciera/hiciese
I did
you did
he/she/it did
we did
you did
they did

Past perfect

hubiera/hubiese hecho
I had done
you had done
he/she/it had done
we had done
you had done
they had done

Imperative

let me do	***no existe (déjame hacer)***
do	***haz tú***
let him/her/it do	***haga él/ella/ello***
let us (let's) do	***hagamos nosotros***
do	***haced vosotros***
let them do	***hagan ellos***

Impersonal forms

Infinitive

hacer
to do

Perfect Infinitive

haber hecho
to have done

Gerund

haciendo
doing

Perfect Gerund

habiendo hecho
having done

Participle

hecho
done

Perfect Participle

habiendo hecho
having done

DRAW · DREW · DRAWN

DIBUJAR, TRAZAR, TIRAR DE, SACAR, GIRAR (LETRAS)

Indicative

Present	Present perfect
dibujo	***he dibujado***
I draw	I have drawn
you draw	you have drawn
he/she/it draws	he/she/it has drawn
we draw	we have drawn
you draw	you have drawn
they draw	they have drawn

Past	Past perfect
dibujaba/dibujé	***había/hube dibujado***
I drew	I had drawn
you drew	you had drawn
he/she/it drew	he/she/it had drawn
we drew	we had drawn
you drew	you had drawn
they drew	they had drawn

Future	Future perfect
dibujaré	***habré dibujado***
I shall/will draw	I shall/will have drawn
you will draw	you will have drawn
he/she/it will draw	he/she/it will have drawn
we shall/will draw	we shall/will have drawn
you will draw	you will have drawn
they will draw	they will have drawn

Conditional

Present	Perfect
dibujaría	***habría dibujado***
I should/would draw	I should/would have drawn
you would draw	you would have drawn
he/she/it would draw	he/she/it would have drawn
we should/would draw	we should/would have drawn
you would draw	you would have drawn
they would draw	they would have drawn

Subjunctive

Present	Present perfect
dibuje	***haya dibujado***
I draw	I have drawn
you draw	you have drawn
he/she/it draws	he/she/it has drawn
we draw	we have drawn
you draw	you have drawn
they draw	they have drawn

Past	Past perfect
dibujara/dibujase	***hubiera/hubiese dibujado***
I drew	I had drawn
you drew	you had drawn
he/she/it drew	he/she/it had drawn
we drew	we had drawn
you drew	you had drawn
they drew	they had drawn

Imperative

let me draw	***no existe (déjame dibujar)***
draw	***dibuja tú***
let him/her/it draw	***dibuje él/ella/ello***
let us (let's) draw	***dibujemos nosotros***
draw	***dibujad vosotros***
let them draw	***dibujen ellos***

Impersonal forms

Infinitive	Perfect Infinitive
dibujar	***haber dibujado***
to draw	to have drawn

Gerund	Perfect Gerund
dibujando	***habiendo dibujado***
drawing	having drawn

Participle	Perfect Participle
dibujado	***habiendo dibujado***
drawn	having drawn

DREAM · DREAMT/DREAMED · DREAMT/DREAMED

SOÑAR

Indicative

Present

sueño
I dream
you dream
he/she/it dreams
we dream
you dream
they dream

Present perfect

he soñado
I have dreamt/dreamed
you have dreamt/dreamed
he/she/it has dreamt/dreamed
we have dreamt/dreamed
you have dreamt/dreamed
they have dreamt/dreamed

Past

soñaba/soñé
I dreamt/dreamed
you dreamt/dreamed
he/she/it dreamt/dreamed
we dreamt/dreamed
you dreamt/dreamed
they dreamt/dreamed

Past perfect

había/hube soñado
I had dreamt/dreamed
you had dreamt/dreamed
he/she/it had dreamt/dreamed
we had dreamt/dreamed
you had dreamet/dreamed
they had dreamt/dreamt

Future

soñaré
I shall/will dream
you will dream
he/she/it will dream
we shall/will dream
you will dream
they will dream

Future perfect

habré soñado
I shall/will have dreamt/dreamed
you will have dreamt/dreamed
he/she/it will have dreamt/dreamed
we shall/will have dreamt/dreamed
you will have dreamt/dreamed
they will have dreamt/dreamed

Conditional

Present

soñaría
I should/would dream
you would dream
he/she/it would dream
we should/would dream
you would dream
they would dream

Perfect

habría soñado
I should/would have dreamt/dreamed
you would have dreamt/dreamed
he/she/it would have dreamt/dreamed
we should/would have dreamt/dreamed
you would have dreamt/dreamed
they would have dreamt/dreamed

Subjunctive

Present

sueñe
I dream
you dream
he/she/it dreams
we dream
you dream
they dream

Present perfect

haya soñado
I have dreamt/dreamed
you have dreamt/dreamed
he/she/it has dreamt/dreamed
we have dreamt/dreamed
you have dreamt/dreamed
they have dreamt/dreamed

Past

soñara o soñase
I dreamt/dreamed
you dreamt/dreamed
he/she/it dreamt/dreamed
we dreamt/dreamed
you dreamt/dreamed
they dreamt/dreamed

Past perfect

hubiera o hubiese soñado
I had dreamt/dreamed
you had dreamt/dreamed
he/she/it had dreamt/dreamed
we had dreamt/dreamed
you had dreamt/dreamed
they had dreamt/dreamed

Imperative

let me dream	***no existe (déjame soñar)***
dream	***sueña tú***
let him/her/it dream	***sueñe él/ella/ello***
let us (let's) dream	***soñemos nosotros***
dream	***soñad vosotros***
let them dream	***sueñen ellos***

Impersonal forms

Infinitive

soñar
to dream

Perfect Infinitive

haber soñado
to have dreamt/dreamed

Gerund

soñando
dreaming

Perfect Gerund

habiendo soñado
having dreamt/dreamed

Participle

soñado
dreamt/dreamed

Perfect Participle

habiendo soñado
having dreamt/dreamed

DRINK · DRANK · DRUNK

BEBER

Indicative

Present

bebo
I drink
you drink
he/she/it drinks
we drink
you drink
they drink

Present perfect

he bebido
I have drunk
you have drunk
he/she/it has drunk
we have drunk
you have drunk
they have drunk

Past

bebía/bebí
I drank
you drank
he/she/it drank
we drank
you drank
they drank

Past perfect

había/hube bebido
I had drunk
you had drunk
he/she/it had drunk
we had drunk
you had drunk
they had drunk

Future

beberé
I shall/will drink
you will drink
he/she/it will drink
we shall/will drink
you will drink
they will drink

Future perfect

habré bebido
I shall/will have drunk
you will have drunk
he/she/it will have drunk
we shall/will have drunk
you will have drunk
they will have drunk

Conditional

Present

bebería
I should/would drink
you would drink
he/she/it would drink
we should/would drink
you would drink
they would drink

Perfect

habría bebido
I should/would have drunk
you would have drunk
he/she/it would have drunk
we should/would have drunk
you would have drunk
they would have drunk

Subjunctive

Present

beba
I drink
you drink
he/she/it drinks
we drink
you drink
they drink

Present perfect

haya bebido
I have drunk
you have drunk
he/she/it has drunk
we have drunk
you have drunk
they have drunk

Past

bebiera/bebiese
I drank
you drank
he/she/it drank
we drank
you drank
they drank

Past perfect

hubiera/hubiese bebido
I had drunk
you had drunk
he/she/it had drunk
we had drunk
you had drunk
they had drunk

Imperative

let me drink	***no existe (déjame beber)***
drink	***bebe tú***
let him/her/it drink	***beba él/ella/ello***
let us (let's) drink	***bebamos nosotros***
drink	***bebed vosotros***
let them drink	***beban ellos***

Impersonal forms

Infinitive

beber
to drink

Perfect Infinitive

haber bebido
to have drunk

Gerund

bebiendo
drinking

Perfect Gerund

habiendo bebido
having drunk

Participle

bebido
drunk

Perfect Participle

habiendo bebido
having drunk

DRIVE · DROVE · DRIVEN

CONDUCIR

Indicative

Present

conduzco
I drive
you drive
he/she/it drives
we drive
you drive
they drive

Present perfect

he conducido
I have driven
you have driven
he/she/it has driven
we have driven
you have driven
they have driven

Past

conducía/conduje
I drove
you drove
he/she/it drove
we drove
you drove
they drove

Past perfect

había/hube conducido
I had driven
you had driven
he/she/it had driven
we had driven
you had driven
they had driven

Future

conduciré
I shall/will drive
you will drive
he/she/it will drive
we shall/will drive
you will drive
they will drive

Future perfect

habré conducido
I shall/will have driven
you will have driven
he/she/it will have driven
we shall/will have driven
you will have driven
they will have driven

Conditional

Present

conduciría
I should/would drive
you would drive
he/she/it would drive
we should/would drive
you would drive
they would drive

Perfect

habría conducido
I should/would have driven
you would have driven
he/she/it would have driven
we should/would have driven
you would have driven
they would have driven

Subjunctive

Present

conduzca
I drive
you drive
he/she/it drives
we drive
you drive
they drive

Present perfect

haya conducido
I have driven
you have driven
he/she/it has driven
we have driven
you have driven
they have driven

Past

condujera/condujese
I drove
you drove
he/she/it drove
we drove
you drove
they drove

Past perfect

hubiera/hubiese conducido
I had driven
you had driven
he/she/it had driven
we had driven
you had driven
they had driven

Imperative

let me drive	***no existe (déjame conducir)***
drive	***conduce tú***
let him/her/it drive	***conduzca él/ella/ello***
let us (let's) drive	***conduzcamos nosotros***
drive	***conducid vosotros***
let them drive	***conduzcan ellos***

Impersonal forms

Infinitive

conducir
to drive

Perfect Infinitive

haber conducido
to have driven

Gerund

conduciendo
driving

Perfect Gerund

habiendo conducido
having driven

Participle

conducido
driven

Perfect Participle

habiendo conducido
having driven

DWELL · DWELT · DWELT

MORAR, VIVIR, HABITAR.

Indicative

Present

moro
I dwell
you dwell
he/she/it dwells
we dwell
you dwell
they dwell

Present perfect

he morado
I have dwelt
you have dwelt
he/she/it has dwelt
we have dwelt
you have dwelt
they have dwelt

Past

moraba/moré
I dwelt
you dwelt
he/she/it dwelt
we dwelt
you dwelt
they dwelt

Past perfect

había/hube morado
I had dwelt
you had dwelt
he/she/it had dwelt
we had dwelt
you had dwelt
they had dwelt

Future

moraré
I shall/will dwell
you will dwell
he/she/it will dwell
we shall/will dwell
you will dwell
they will dwell

Future perfect

habré morado
I shall/will have dwelt
you will have dwelt
he/she/it will have dwelt
we shall/will have dwelt
you will have dwelt
they will have dwelt

Conditional

Present

moraría
I should/would dwell
you would dwell
he/she/it would dwell
we should/would dwell
you would dwell
they would dwell

Perfect

habría morado
I should/would have dwelt
you would have dwelt
he/she/it would have dwelt
we should/would have dwelt
you would have dwelt
they would have dwelt

Subjunctive

Present

more
I dwell
you dwell
he/she/it dwells
we dwell
you dwell
they dwell

Present perfect

haya morado
I have dwelt
you have dwelt
he/she/it has dwelt
we have dwelt
you have dwelt
they have dwelt

Past

morara o morase
I dwelt
you dwelt
he/she/it dwelt
we dwelt
you dwelt
they dwelt

Past perfect

hubiera o hubiese morado
I had dwelt
you had dwelt
he/she/it had dwelt
we had dwelt
you had dwelt
they had dwelt

Imperative

let me dwell	***no existe (déjame morar)***
dwell	***mora tú***
let him/her/it dwell	***more él/ella/ello***
let us (let's) dwell	***moremos nosotros***
dwell	***morad vosotros***
let them dwell	***moren ellos***

Impersonal forms

Infinitive

morar
to dwell

Perfect Infinitive

haber morado
to have dwelt

Gerund

morando
dwelling

Perfect Gerund

habiendo morado
having dwelt

Participle

morado
dwelt

Perfect Participle

habiendo morado
having dwelt

EAT · ATE · EATEN

COMER

Indicative

Present

como
I eat
you eat
he/she/it eats
we eat
you eat
they eat

Present perfect

he comido
I have eaten
you have eaten
he/she/it has eaten
we have eaten
you have eaten
they have eaten

Past

comía/comí
I ate
you ate
he/she/it ate
we ate
you ate
they ate

Past perfect

había/hube comido
I had eaten
you had eaten
he/she/it had eaten
we had eaten
you had eaten
they had eaten

Future

comeré
I shall/will eat
you will eat
he/she/it will eat
we shall/will eat
you will eat
they will eat

Future perfect

habré comido
I shall/will have eaten
you will have eaten
he/she/it will have eaten
we shall/will have eaten
you will have eaten
they will have eaten

Conditional

Present

comería
I should/would eat
you would eat
he/she/it would eat
we should/would eat
you would eat
they would eat

Perfect

habría comido
I should/would have eaten
you would have eaten
he/she/it would have eaten
we should/would have eaten
you would have eaten
they would have eaten

Subjunctive

Present

coma
I eat
you eat
he/she/it eats
we eat
you eat
they eat

Present perfect

haya comido
I have eaten
you have eaten
he/she/it has eaten
we have eaten
you have eaten
they have eaten

Past

comiera/comiese
I ate
you ate
he/she/it ate
we ate
you ate
they ate

Past perfect

hubiera/hubiese comido
I had eaten
you had eaten
he/she/it had eaten
we had eaten
you had eaten
they had eaten

Imperative

let me eat	***no existe (déjame comer)***
eat	***come tú***
let him/her/it eat	***coma él/ella/ello***
let us (let's) eat	***comamos nosotros***
eat	***comed vosotros***
let them eat	***coman ellos***

Impersonal forms

Infinitive

comer
to eat

Gerund

comiendo
eating

Participle

comido
eaten

Perfect Infinitive

haber comido
to have eaten

Perfect Gerund

habiendo comido
having eaten

Perfect Participle

habiendo comido
having eaten

FALL · FELL · FALLEN

CAER

Indicative

Present

caigo
I fall
you fall
he/she/it falls
we fall
you fall
they fall

Present perfect

he caído
I have fallen
you have fallen
he/she/it has fallen
we have fallen
you have fallen
they have fallen

Past

caía/caí
I fell
you fell
he/she/it fell
we fell
you fell
they fell

Past perfect

había/hube caído
I had fallen
you had fallen
he/she/it had fallen
we had fallen
you had fallen
they had fallen

Future

caeré
I shall/will fall
you will fall
he/she/it will fall
we shall/will fall
you will fall
they will fall

Future perfect

habré caído
I shall/will have fallen
you will have fallen
he/she/it will have fallen
we shall/will have fallen
you will have fallen
they will have fallen

Conditional

Present

caería
I should/would fall
you would fall
he/she/it would fall
we should/would fall
you would fall
they would fall

Perfect

habría caído
I should/would have fallen
you would have fallen
he/she/it would have fallen
we should/would have fallen
you would have fallen
they would have fallen

Subjunctive

Present

caiga
I fall
you fall
he/she/it falls
we fall
you fall
they fall

Present perfect

haya caído
I have fallen
you have fallen
he/she/it has fallen
we have fallen
you have fallen
they have fallen

Past

cayera/cayese
I fell
you fell
he/she/it fell
we fell
you fell
they fell

Past perfect

hubiera/hubiese caído
I had fallen
you had fallen
he/she/it had fallen
we had fallen
you had fallen
they had fallen

Imperative

let me fall	***no existe (déjame caer)***
fall	***cae tú***
let him/her/it fall	***caiga él/ella/ello***
let us (let's) fall	***caigamos nosotros***
fall	***caed vosotros***
let them fall	***caigan ellos***

Impersonal forms

Infinitive

caer
to fall

Perfect Infinitive

to have caído
haber fallen

Gerund

cayendo
falling

Perfect Gerund

having caído
habiendo fallen

Participle

caído
fallen

Perfect Participle

having caído
habiendo fallen

FEED · FED · FED

ALIMENTAR, DAR DE COMER

Indicative

Present

alimento
I feed
you feed
he/she/it feeds
we feed
you feed
they feed

Present perfect

he alimentado
I have fed
you have fed
he/she/it has fed
we have fed
you have fed
they have fed

Past

alimentába/alimenté
I fed
you fed
he/she/it fed
we fed
you fed
they fed

Past perfect

había/hube alimentado
I had fed
you had fed
he/she/it had fed
we had fed
you had fed
they had fed

Future

alimentaré
I shall/will feed
you will feed
he/she/it will feed
we shall/will feed
you will feed
they will feed

Future perfect

habré alimentado
I shall/will have fed
you will have fed
he/she/it will have fed
we shall/will have fed
you will have fed
they will have fed

Conditional

Present

alimentaría
I should/would feed
you would feed
he/she/it would feed
we should/would feed
you would feed
they would feed

Perfect

habría alimentado
I should/would have fed
you would have fed
he/she/it would have fed
we should/would have fed
you would have fed
they would have fed

Subjunctive

Present

alimente
I feed
you feed
he/she/it feeds
we feed
you feed
they feed

Present perfect

haya alimentado
I have fed
you have fed
he/she/it has fed
we have fed
you have fed
they have fed

Past

alimentara o alimentase
I fed
you fed
he/she/it fed
we fed
you fed
they fed

Past perfect

hubiera o hubiese alimentado
I had fed
you had fed
he/she/it had fed
we had fed
you had fed
they had fed

Imperative

let me feed	***no existe (déjame alimentar)***
feed	***alimenta tú***
let him/her/it feed	***alimente él/ella/ello***
let us (let's) feed	***alimentemos nosotros***
feed	***alimentad vosotros***
let them feed	***alimenten ellos***

Impersonal forms

Infinitive

alimentar
to feed

Perfect Infinitive

haber alimentado
to have fed

Gerund

alimentando
feeding

Perfect Gerund

habiendo alimentado
having fed

Participle

alimentado
fed

Perfect Participle

habiendo alimentado
having fed

FEEL · FELT · FELT

SENTIR, PALPAR

Indicative

Present

siento
I feel
you feel
he/she/it feels
we feel
you feel
they feel

Present perfect

he sentido
I have felt
you have felt
he/she/it has felt
we have felt
you have felt
they have felt

Past

sentía/sentí
I felt
you felt
he/she/it felt
we felt
you felt
they felt

Past perfect

había/hube sentido
I had felt
you had felt
he/she/it had felt
we had felt
you had felt
they had felt

Future

sentiré
I shall/will feel
you will feel
he/she/it will feel
we shall/will feel
you will feel
they will feel

Future perfect

habré sentido
I shall/will have felt
you will have felt
he/she/it will have felt
we shall/will have felt
you will have felt
they will have felt

Conditional

Present

sentiría
I should/would feel
you would feel
he/she/it would feel
we should/would feel
you would feel
they would feel

Perfect

habría sentido
I should/would have felt
you would have felt
he/she/it would have felt
we should/would have felt
you would have felt
they would have felt

Subjunctive

Present

sienta
I feel
you feel
he/she/it feels
we feel
you feel
they feel

Present perfect

haya sentido
I have felt
you have felt
he/she/it has felt
we have felt
you have felt
they have felt

Past

sintiera o sintiese
I felt
you felt
he/she/it felt
we felt
you felt
they felt

Past perfect

hubiera o hubiese sentido
I had felt
you had felt
he/she/it had felt
we had felt
you had felt
they had felt

Imperative

let me feel	***no existe (déjame sentir)***
feel	***siente tú***
let him/her/it feel	***sienta él/ella/ello***
let us (let's) feel	***sintamos nosotros***
feel	***sentid vosotros***
let them feel	***sientan ellos***

Impersonal forms

Infinitive

sentir
to feel

Perfect Infinitive

haber sentido
to have felt

Gerund

sintiendo
feeling

Perfect Gerund

habiendo sentido
having felt

Participle

sentido
felt

Perfect Participle

habiendo sentido
having felt

FIND · FOUND · FOUND

ENCONTRAR, HALLAR

Indicative

Present

encuentro
I find
you find
he/she/it finds
we find
you find
they find

Present perfect

he encontrado
I have found
you have found
he/she/it has found
we have found
you have found
they have found

Past

encontraba/encontré
I found
you found
he/she/it found
we found
you found
they found

Past perfect

había/hube encontrado
I had found
you had found
he/she/it had found
we had found
you had found
they had found

Future

encontraré
I shall/will find
you will find
he/she/it will find
we shall/will find
you will find
they will find

Future perfect

habré encontrado
I shall/will have found
you will have found
he/she/it will have found
we shall/will have found
you will have found
they will have found

Conditional

Present

encontraría
I should/would find
you would find
he/she/it would find
we should/would find
you would find
they would find

Perfect

habría encontrado
I should/would have found
you would have found
he/she/it would have found
we should/would have found
you would have found
they would have found

Subjunctive

Present

encuentre
I find
you find
he/she/it finds
we find
you find
they find

Present perfect

haya encontrado
I have found
you have found
he/she/it has found
we have found
you have found
they have found

Past

encontrara/encontrase
I found
you found
he/she/it found
we found
you found
they found

Past perfect

hubiera/hubiese encontrado
I had found
you had found
he/she/it had found
we had found
you had found
they had found

Imperative

let me find	***no existe (déjame encontrar)***
find	***encuentra tú***
let him/her/it find	***encuentre él/ella/ello***
let us (let's) find	***encontremos nosotros***
find	***encontrad vosotros***
let them find	***encuentren ellos***

Impersonal forms

Infinitive

encontrar
to find

Perfect Infinitive

haber encontrado
to have found

Gerund

encontrando
finding

Perfect Gerund

habiendo encontrado
having found

Participle

encontrado
found

Perfect Participle

habiendo encontrado
having found

FIGHT · FOUGHT · FOUGHT

LUCHAR, COMBATIR

Indicative

Present

lucho
I fight
you fight
he/she/it fights
we fight
you fight
they fight

Present perfect

he luchado
I have fought
you have fought
he/she/it has fought
we have fought
you have fought
they have fought

Past

luchaba/luché
I fought
you fought
he/she/it fought
we fought
you fought
they fought

Past perfect

había/hube luchado
I had fought
you had fought
he/she/it had fought
we had fought
you had fought
they had fought

Future

lucharé
I shall/will fight
you will fight
he/she/it will fight
we shall/will fight
they will fight

Future perfect

habré luchado
I shall/will have fought
you will have fought
he/she/it will have fought
we shall/will have fought
you will have fought
they will have fought

Conditional

Present

lucharía
I should/would fight
you would fight
he/she/it would fight
we should/would fight
you would fight
they would fight

Perfect

habría luchado
I should/would have fought
you would have fought
he/she/it would have fought
we should/would have fought
you would have fought
they would have fought

Subjunctive

Present

luche
I fight
you fight
he/she/it fights
we fight
you fight
they fight

Present perfect

haya luchado
I have fought
you have fought
he/she/it has fought
we have fought
you have fought
they have fought

Past

luchara/luchase
I fought
you fought
he/she/it fought
we fought
you fought
they fought

Past perfect

hubiera/hubiese luchado
I had fought
you had fought
he/she/it had fought
we had fought
you had fought
they had fought

Imperative

let me fight	***no existe (déjame luchar)***
fight	***lucha tú***
let him/her/it fight	***luche él/ella/ello***
let us (let's) fight	***luchemos nosotros***
fight	***luchad vosotros***
let them fight	***luchen ellos***

Impersonal forms

Infinitive

luchar
to fight

Perfect Infinitive

haber luchado
to have fought

Gerund

luchando
fighting

Perfect Gerund

habiendo luchado
having fought

Participle

luchado
fought

Perfect Participle

habiendo luchado
having fought

FLEE · FLED · FLED

HUIR, ESCAPAR

Indicative

Present

huyo
I flee
you flee
he/she/it flees
we flee
you flee
they flee

Present perfect

he huido
I have fled
you have fled
he/she/it has fled
we have fled
you have fled
they have fled

Past

huía/huí
I fled
you fled
he/she/it fled
we fled
you fled
they fled

Past perfect

había/hube huido
I had fled
you had fled
he/she/it had fled
we had fled
you had fled
they had fled

Future

huiré
I shall/will flee
you will flee
he/she/it will flee
we shall/will flee
you will flee
they will flee

Future perfect

habré huido
I shall/will have fled
you will have fled
he/she/it will have fled
we shall/will have fled
you will have fled
they will have fled

Conditional

Present

huiría
I should/would flee
you would flee
he/she/it would flee
we should/would flee
you would flee
they would flee

Perfect

habría huido
I should/would have fled
you would have fled
he/she/it would have fled
we should/would have fled
you would have fled
they would have fled

Subjunctive

Present

huya
I flee
you flee
he/she/it flees
we flee
you flee
they flee

Present perfect

haya huido
I have fled
you have fled
he/she/it had fled
we have fled
you have fled
they have fled

Past

huyera o huyese
I fled
you fled
he/she/it fled
we fled
you fled
they fled

Past perfect

hubiera o hubiese huido
I had fled
you had fled
he/she/it had fled
we had fled
you had fled
they had fled

Imperative

let me flee	***no existe (déjame huir)***
flee	***huye tú***
let him/he/it flee	***huya él/ella/ello***
let us (let's) flee	***huyamos nosotros***
flee	***huid vosotros***
let them flee	***huyan ellos***

Impersonal forms

Infinitive

huir
to flee

Perfect Infinitive

haber huido
to have fled

Gerund

huyendo
fleeing

Perfect Gerund

habiendo huido
having fled

Participle

huido
fled

Perfect Participle

habiendo huido
having fled

FLING · FLUNG · FLUNG

TIRAR, ARROJAR, ECHAR, LANZAR, AVENTAR.

Indicative

Present

tiro
I fling
you fling
he/she/it flings
we fling
you fling
they fling

Present perfect

he tirado
I have flung
you have flung
he/she/it has flung
we have flung
you have flung
they have flung

Past

tiraba/tiré
I flung
you flung
he/she/it flung
we flung
you flung
they flung

Past perfect

había/hube tirado
I had flung
you had flung
he/she/it had flung
we had flung
you had flung
they had flung

Future

tiraré
I shall/will fling
you will fling
he/she/it will fling
we shall/will fling
you will fling
they will fling

Future perfect

habré tirado
I shall/will have flung
you will have flung
he/she/it will have flung
we shall/will have flung
you will have flung
they will have flung

Conditional

Present

tiraría
I should/would fling
you would fling
he/she/it would fling
we should/would fling
you would fling
they would fling

Perfect

habría tirado
I should/would have flung
you would have flung
he/she/it would have flung
we should/would have flung
you would have flung
they would have flung

Subjunctive

Present

tire
I fling
you fling
he/she/it flings
we fling
you fling
they fling

Present perfect

haya tirado
I have flung
you have flung
he/she/it has flung
we have flung
you have flung
they have flung

Past

tirara o tirase
I flung
you flung
he/she/it flung
we flung
you flung
they flung

Past perfect

hubiera/hubiese tirado
I had flung
you had flung
he/she/it had flung
we had flung
you had flung
they had flung

Imperative

let me fling	***no existe (déjame tirar)***
fling	***tira tú***
let him/her/it fling	***tire él/ella/ello***
let us (let's) fling	***tiremos nosotros***
fling	***tirad vosotros***
let them fling	***tiren ellos***

Impersonal forms

Infinitive

tirar
to fling

Perfect Infinitive

haber tirado
to have flung

Gerund

tirando
flinging

Perfect Gerund

habiendo tirado
having flung

Participle

tirado
flung

Perfect Participle

habiendo tirado
having flung

FLY · FLEW · FLOWN

VOLAR

Indicative

Present

vuelo
I fly
you fly
he/she/it flies
we fly
you fly
they fly

Present perfect

he volado
I have flown
you have flown
he/she/it has flown
we have flown
you have flown
they have flown

Past

volaba/volé
I flew
you flew
he/she/it flew
we flew
you flew
they flew

Past perfect

había/hube volado
I had flown
you had flown
he/she/it had flown
we had flown
you had flown
they had flown

Future

volaré
I shall/will fly
you will fly
he/she/it will fly
we shall/will fly
you will fly
they will fly

Future perfect

habré volado
I shall/will have flown
you will have flown
he/she/it will have flown
we shall/will have flown
you will have flown
they will have flown

Conditional

Present

volaría
I should/would fly
you would fly
he/she/it would fly
we should/would fly
you would fly
they would fly

Perfect

habría volado
I should/would have flown
you would have flown
he/she/it would have flown
we should/would have flown
you would have flown
they would have flown

Subjunctive

Present

vuele
I fly
you fly
he/she/it flies
we fly
you fly
they fly

Present perfect

haya volado
I have flown
you have flown
he/she/it has flown
we have flown
you have flown
they have flown

Past

volara o volase
I flew
you flew
he/she/it flew
we flew
you flew
they flew

Past perfect

hubiera/hubiese volado
I had flown
you had flown
he/she/it had flown
we had flown
you had flown
they had flown

Imperative

let me fly	***no existe (déjame volar)***
fly	***vuela tú***
let him/her/it fly	***vuele él/ella/ello***
let us (let's) fly	***volemos nosotros***
fly	***volad vosotros***
let them fly	***vuelen ellos***

Impersonal forms

Infinitive

volar
to fly

Perfect Infinitive

haber volado
to have flown

Gerund

volando
flying

Perfect Gerund

habiendo volado
having flown

Participle

volado
flown

Perfect Participle

habiendo volado
having flown

FORBID · FORBADE · FORBIDDEN

PROHIBIR

Indicative

Present

prohibo
I forbid
you forbid
he/she/it forbids
we forbid
you forbid
they forbid

Present perfect

he prohibido
I have forbidden
you have forbidden
he/she/it has forbidden
we have forbidden
you have forbidden
they have forbidden

Past

prohibía/prohibí
I forbade
you forbade
he/she/it forbade
we forbade
you forbade
they forbade

Past perfect

había/hube prohibido
I had forbidden
you had forbidden
he/she/it had forbidden
we had forbidden
you had forbidden
they had forbidden

Future

prohibiré
I shall/will forbid
you will forbid
he/she/it will forbid
we shall/will forbid
you will forbid
they will forbid

Future perfect

habré prohibido
I shall/will have forbidden
you will have forbidden
he/she/it will have forbidden
we shall/will have forbidden
you will have forbidden
they will have forbidden

Conditional

Present

prohibiría
I should/would forbid
you would forbid
he/she/it would forbid
we should/would forbid
you would forbid
they would forbid

Perfect

habría prohibido
I should/would have forbidden
you would have forbidden
he/she/it would have forbidden
we should/would have forbidden
you would have forbidden
they would have forbidden

Subjunctive

Present

prohiba
I forbid
you forbid
he/she/it forbids
we forbid
you forbid
they forbid

Present perfect

they forbade
haya prohibido
I have forbidden
you have forbidden
he/she/it has forbidden
we have forbidden
you have forbidden

Past

prohibiera o
prohibiese
I forbade
you forbade
he/she/it forbade
we forbade
you forbade

Past perfect

they have forbidden
hubiera o hubiese
prohibido
I had forbidden
you had forbidden
he/she/it had forbidden
we had forbidden

Imperative

you had forbidden
they had forbidden
let me forbid
forbid
let him/her/it forbid
let us (let's) forbid

forbid
let them forbid
no existe (déjame prohibir)
prohibe tú
prohiba él/ella/ello
prohibamos nosotros

Impersonal forms

prohibid vosotros
prohiban ellos

prohibido
forbidden

Infinitive

prohibir
to forbid

Perfect Infinitive

haber prohibido
to have forbidden

Gerund

prohibiendo
forbidding

Perfect Gerund

habiendo prohibido
having forbidden

Participle

Perfect Participle

FORGET · FORGOT · FORGOTTEN

OLVIDAR

Indicative

Present

olvido
I forget
you forget
he/she/it forgets
we forget
you forget
they forget

Present perfect

he olvidado
I have forgotten
you have forgotten
he/she/it has forgotten
we have forgotten
you have forgotten
they have forgotten

Past

olvidaba/olvidé
I forgot
you forgot
he/she/it forgot
we forgot
you forgot
they forgot

Past perfect

había/hube olvidado
I had forgotten
you had forgotten
he/she/it had forgotten
we had forgotten
you had forgotten
they had forgotten

Future

olvidaré
I shall/will forget
you will forget
he/she/it will forget
we shall/will forget
you will forget
they will forget

Future perfect

habré olvidado
I shall/will have forgotten
you will have forgotten
he/she/it will have forgotten
we shall/will have forgotten
you will have forgotten
they will have forgotten

Conditional

Present

olvidaría
I should/would forget
you would forget
he/she/it would forget
we should/would forget
you would forget
they would forget

Perfect

habría olvidado
I should/would have forgotten
you would have forgotten
he/she/it would have forgotten
we should/would have forgotten
you would have forgotten
they would have forgotten

Subjunctive

Present

olvide
I forget
you forget
he/she/it forgets
we forget
you forget
they forget

Present perfect

haya olvidado
I have forgotten
you have forgotten
he/she/it has forgotten
we have forgotten
you have forgotten
they have forgotten

Past

olvidara/olvidase
I forgot
you forgot
he/she/it forgot
we forgot
you forgot
they forgot

Past perfect

hubiera/hubiese olvidado
I had forgotten
you had forgotten
he/she/it had forgotten
we had forgotten
you had forgotten
they had forgotten

Imperative

let me forget	***no existe (déjame olvidar)***
forget	***olvida tú***
let him/her/it forget	***olvide él/ella/ello***
let us (let's) forget	***olvidemos nosotros***
forget	***olvidad vosotros***
let them forget	***olviden ellos***

Impersonal forms

Infinitive

olvidar
to forget

Perfect Infinitive

haber olvidado
to have forgotten

Gerund

olvidando
forgetting

Perfect Gerund

habiendo olvidado
having forgotten

Participle

olvidado
forgotten

Perfect Participle

habiendo olvidado
having forgotten

FORSAKE · FORSOOK · FORSAKEN

ABANDONAR, RENUNCIAR

Indicative

Present

abandono
I forsake
you forsake
he/she/it forsakes
we forsake
you forsake
they forsake

Present perfect

he abandonado
I have forsaken
you have forsaken
he/she/it has forsaken
we have forsaken
you have forsaken
they have forsaken

Past

abandonaba/ abandoné
I forsook
you forsook
he/she/it forsook
we forsook
you forsook
they forsook

Past perfect

había/hube abandonado
I had forsaken
you had forsaken
he/she/it had forsaken
we had forsaken
you had forsaken
they had forsaken

Future

abandonaré
I shall/will forsake
you will forsake
he/she/it will forsake
we shall/will forsake
you will forsake
they will forsake

Future perfect

habré abandonado
I shall /will have forsaken
you will have forsaken
he/she/it will have forsaken
we shall/will have forsaken
you will have forsaken
they will have forsaken

Conditional

Present

abandonaría
I should/would forsake
you would forsake
he/she/it would forsake
we should/would forsake
you would forsake
they would forsake

Perfect

habría abandonado
I should/would have forsaken
you would have forsaken
he/she/it would have forsaken
we should/would have forsaken
you would have forsaken
they would have forsaken

Subjunctive

Present

abandone
I forsake
you forsake
he/she/it forsakes
we forsake
you forsake
they forsake

Present perfect

haya abandonado
I have forsaken
you have forsaken
he/she/it has forsaken
we have forsaken
you have forsaken
they have forsaken

Past

abandonara o abandonase
I forsook
you forsook
he/she/it forsook
we forsook
you forsook
they forsook

Past perfect

hubiera o hubiese abandonado
I had forsaken
you had forsaken
he/she/it had forsaken
we had forsaken
you had forsaken
they had forsaken

Imperative

let me forsake	***no existe (déjame abandonar)***
forsake	***abandona tú***
let him/her/it forsake	***abandone él/ella/ello***
let us (let's) forsake	***abandonemos nosotros***
forsake	***abandonad vosotros***
let them forsake	***abandonen ellos***

Impersonal forms

Infinitive

abandonar
to forsake

Perfect Infinitive

haber abandonado
to have forsaken

Gerund

abandonando
forsaking

Perfect Gerund

habiendo abandonado
having forsaken

Participle

abandonado
forsaken

Perfect Participle

habiendo abandonado

FREEZE · FROZE · FROZEN

HELAR, CONGELAR

Indicative

Present

congelo
I freeze
you freeze
he/she/it freezes
we freeze
you freeze
they freeze

Present perfect

he congelado
I have frozen
you have frozen
he/she/it has frozen
we have frozen
you have frozen
they have frozen

Past

congelaba/congelé
I froze
you froze
he/she/it froze
we froze
you froze
they froze

Past perfect

había/hube congelado
I had frozen
you had frozen
he/she/it had frozen
we had frozen
you had frozen
they had forzen

Future

congelaré
I shall/will freeze
you will freeze
he/she/it will freeze
we shall/will freeze
you will freeze
they will freeze

Future perfect

habré congelado
I shall/will have frozen
you will have frozen
he/she/it will have frozen
we shall/will have frozen
you will have frozen
they will have frozen

Conditional

Present

congelaría
I should/would freeze
you would freeze
he/she/it would freeze
we should/would freeze
you would freeze
they would freeze

Perfect

habría congelado
I should/would have frozen
you would have frozen
he/she/it would have frozen
we should/would have frozen
you would have frozen
they would have frozen

Subjunctive

Present

congele
I freeze
you freeze
he/she/it freezes
we freeze
you freeze
they freeze

Present perfect

they froze
haya congelado
I have frozen
you have frozen
he/she/it has frozen
we have frozen
you have frozen

Past

congelara o congelase
I froze
you froze
he/she/it froze
we froze
you froze

Past perfect

they have frozen
hubiera o hubiese congelado
I had frozen
you had frozen
he/she/it had frozen
we had frozen

Imperative

you had frozen
they had frozen
let me freeze
freeze
let him/her/it freeze
let us (let's) freeze

freeze
let them freeze
no existe (déjame congelar)
congela tú
congele él/ella/ello
congelemos nosotros

Impersonal forms

congelad vosotros
congelen ellos

congelado
frozen

Infinitive

congelar
to freeze

Perfect Infinitive

haber congelado
to have frozen

Gerund

congelando
freezing

Perfect Gerund

habiendo congelado
having frozen

Participle

Perfect Participle

GILD · GILDED · GILDED/GILT

DORAR

Indicative

Present	Present perfect
doro	***he dorado***
I gild	I have gilt/gilded
you gild	you have gilt/gilded
he/she/it gilds	he/she/it has gilt/gilded
we gild	we have gilt/gilded
you gild	you have gilt/gilded
they gild	they have gilt/gilded

Past	Past perfect
doraba/doré	***había/hube dorado***
I gilded	I had gilt/gilded
you gilded	you had gilt/gilded
he/she/it gilded	he/she/it had gilt/gilded
we gilded	we had gilt/gilded
you gilded	you had gilt/gilded
they gilded	they had gilt/gilded

Future	Future perfect
doraré	***habré dorado***
I shall/will gild	I shall/will have gilt/gilded
you will gild	you will have gilt/gilded
he/she/it will gild	he/she/it will have gilt/gilded
we shall/will gild	we shall/will have gilt/gilded
you will gild	you will have gilt/gilded
they will gild	they will have gilt/gilded

Conditional

Present	Perfect
doraría	***habría dorado***
I should/would gild	I should/would have gilt/gilded
you would gild	you would have gilt/gilded
he/she/it would gild	he/she/it would have gilt/gilded
we should/would gild	we should/would have gilt/gilded
you would gild	you would have gilt/gilded
they would gild	they would have gilt/gilded

Subjunctive

Present	Present perfect
dore	***haya dorado***
I gild	I have gilt/gilded
you gild	you have gilt/gilded
he/she/it gilds	he/she/it has gilt/gilded
we gild	we have gilt/gilded
you gild	you have gilt/gilded
they gild	they have gilt/gilded

Past	Past perfect
dorara o dorase	***hubiera o hubiese dorado***
I gilded	I had gilt/gilded
you gilded	you had gilt/gilded
he/she/it gilded	he/she/it had gilt/gilded
we gilded	we had gilt/gilded
you gilded	you had gilt/gilded
they gilded	they had gilt/gilded

Imperative

let me gild	***no existe (déjame dorar)***
gild	***dora tú***
let him/her/it gild	***dore él***
let us (let's) gild	***doremos nosotros***
gild	***dorad vosotros***
let them gild	***doren ellos***

Impersonal forms

Infinitive	Perfect Infinitive
dorar	***haber dorado***
to gild	to have gilt/gilded

Gerund	Perfect Gerund
dorando	***habiendo dorado***
gilding	having gilt/gilded

Participle	Perfect Participle
dorado	***habiendo dorado***
gilt/gilded	having gilt/gilded

GIRD · GIRDED/GIRT · GIRDED/GIRT

CEÑIR

Indicative

Present

ciño
I gird
you gird
he/she/it girds
we gird
you gird
they gird

Present perfect

he ceñido
I have girt/girded
you have girt/girded
he/she/it has girt/girded
we have girt/girded
you have girt/girded
they have girt/girded

Past

ceñía/ceñí
I girt/girded
you girt/girded
he/she/it girt/girded
we girt/girded
you girt/girded
they girt/girded

Past perfect

había/hube ceñido
I had girt/girded
you had girt/girded
he/she/it had girt/girded
we had girt/girded
you had girt/girded
they had girt/girded

Future

ceñiré
I shall/will gird
you will gird
he/she/it will gird
we shall/will gird
you will gird
they will gird

Future perfect

habré ceñido
I shall/will have girt/girded
you will have girt/girded
he/she/it will have girt/girded
we shall/will have girt/girded
you will have girt/girded
they will have girlt/girded

Conditional

Present

ceñiría
I should/would gird
you would gird
he/she/it would gird
we should/would gird
you would gird
they would gird

Perfect

habría ceñido
I should/would have girt/girded
you would have girt/girded
he/she/it would have girt/girded
we should/would have girt/girded
you would have girt/girded
they would have girt/girded

Subjunctive

Present

ciña
I gird
you gird
he/she/it girds
we gird
you gird
they gird

Present perfect

haya ceñido
I have girt/girded
you have girt/girded
he/she/it has girt/girded
we have girt/girded
you have girt/girded
they have girt/girded

Past

ciñera o ciñese
I girt/girded
you girt/girded
he/she/it girt/girded
we girt/girded
you girt/girded
they girt/girded

Past perfect

hubiera o hubiese ceñido
I had girt/girded
you had girt/girded
he/she/it had girt/girded
we had girt/girded
you had girt/girded
they had girt/girded

Imperative

let me girt	***no existe (déjame ceñir)***
girt	***ciñe tú***
let him/her/it girt	***ciña él/ella/ello***
let us (let's) girt	***ciñamos nosotros***
girt	***ceñid vosotros***
let them girt	***ciñan ellos***

Impersonal forms

Infinitive

ceñir
to gird

Perfect Infinitive

haber ceñido
to have girt/girded

Gerund

ciñiendo
girding

Perfect Gerund

habiendo ceñido
having girt/girded

Participle

ceñido
girt/girded

Perfect Participle

habiendo ceñido
having girt/girded

GO · WENT · GONE
IR

Indicative

Present

voy
I go
you go
he/she/it goes
we go
you go
they go

Present perfect

he ido
I have gone
you have gone
he/she/it has gone
we have gone
you have gone
they have gone

Past

iba/fu
I went
you went
he/she/it went
we went
you went
they went

Past perfect

había/hube ido
I had gone
you had gone
he/she/it had gone
we had gone
you had gone
they had gone

Future

iré
I shall/will go
you will go
he/she/it will go
we shall/will go
you will go
they will go

Future perfect

habré ido
I shall/will have gone
you will have gone
he/she/it will have gone
we shall/will have gone
you will have gone
they will have gone

Conditional

Present

iría
I should/would go
you would go
he/she/it would go
we should/would go
you would go
they would go

Perfect

habría ido
I should/would have gone
you would have gone
he/she/it would have gone
we should/would have gone
you would have gone
they would have gone

Subjunctive

Present

vaya
I go
you go
he/she/it goes
we go
you go
they go

Present perfect

haya ido
I have gone
you have gone
he/she/it has gone
we have gone
you have gone
they have gone

Past

fuera/fuese
I went
you went
he/she/it went
we went
you went
they went

Past perfect

hubiera/hubiese ido
I had gone
you had gone
he/she/it had gone
we had gone
you had gone
they had gone

Imperative

let me go	***no existe (déjame ir)***
go	***ve tú***
let him/her/it go	***vaya él/ella/ello***
let us (let's) go	***vayamos nosotros***
go	***id vosotros***
let them go	***vayan ellos***

Impersonal forms

Infinitive

ir
to go

Perfect Infinitive

haber ido
to have gone

Gerund

yendo
going

Perfect Gerund

habiendo ido
having gone

Participle

ido
gone

Perfect Participle

habiendo ido
having gone

GRIND · GROUND · GROUND

MOLER

Indicative

Present

muelo
I grind
you grind
he/she/it grinds
we grind
you grind
they grind

Present perfect

he molido
I have ground
you have ground
he/she/it has ground
we have ground
you have ground
they have ground

Past

molía/molí
I ground
you ground
he/she/it ground
we ground
you ground
they ground

Past perfect

había/hube molido
I had ground
you had ground
he/she/it had ground
we had ground
you had ground
they had ground

Future

moleré
I shall/will grind
you will grind
he/she/it will grind
we shall/will grind
you will grind
they will grind

Future perfect

habré molido
I shall/will have ground
you will have ground
he/she/it will have ground
we shall/will have ground
you will have ground
they will have ground

Conditional

Present

molería
I should/would grind
you would grind
he/she/it would grind
we should/would grind
you would grind
they would grind

Perfect

habría molido
I should/would have ground
you would have ground
he/she/it would have ground
we should/would have ground
you would have ground
they would have ground

Subjunctive

Present

muela
I grind
you grind
he/she/it grinds
we grind
you grind
they grind

Present perfect

haya molido
I have ground
you have ground
he/she/it has ground
we have ground
you have ground
they have ground

Past

moliera o moliese
I ground
you ground
he/she/it ground
we ground
you ground
they ground

Past perfect

hubiera o hubiese molido
I had ground
you had ground
he/she/it had ground
we had ground
you had ground
they had ground

Imperative

let me grind	***no existe (déjame moler)***
grind	***muele tú***
let him/her/it grind	***muela él/ella/ello***
let us (let's) grind	***molamos nosotros***
grind	***moled vosotros***
let them grind	***muelan ellos***

Impersonal forms

Infinitive

moler
to grind

Perfect Infinitive

haber molido
to have ground

Gerund

moliendo
grinding

Perfect Gerund

habiendo molido
having ground

Participle

molido
ground

Perfect Participle

habiendo molido
having ground

GROW · GREW · GROWN

CRECER, CULTIVAR

Indicative

Present	Present perfect
crezco	***he crecido***
I grow	I have grown
you grow	you have grown
he/she/it grows	he/she/it has grown
we grow	we have grown
you grow	you have grown
they grow	they have grown

Past	Past perfect
crecía/crecí	***había/hube crecido***
I grew	I had grown
you grew	you had grown
he/she/it grew	he/she/it had grown
we grew	we had grown
you grew	you had grown
they grew	they had grown

Future	Future perfect
creceré	***habré crecido***
I shall/will grow	I shall/will have grown
you will grow	you will have grown
he/she/it will grow	he/she/it will have grown
we shall/will grow	we shall/will have grown
you will grow	you will have grown
they will grow	they will have grown

Conditional

Present	Perfect
crecería	***habría crecido***
I should/would grow	I should/would have grown
you would grow	you would have grown
he/she/it would grow	he/she/it would have grown
we should/would grow	we should/would have grown
you would grow	you would have grown
they would grow	they would have grown

Subjunctive

Present	Present perfect
crezca	***haya crecido***
I grow	I have grown
you grow	you have grown
he/she/it grows	he/she/it has grown
we grow	we have grown
you grow	you have grown
they grow	they have grown

Past	Past perfect
creciera o creciese	***hubiera o hubiese crecido***
I grew	I had grown
you grew	you had grown
he/she/it grew	he/she/it had grown
we grew	we had grown
you grew	you had grown
they grew	they had grown

Imperative

let me grow	***no existe (déjame crecer)***
grow	***crece tú***
let him/her/it grow	***crezca él/ella/ello***
let us (let's) grow	***crezcamos nosotros***
grow	***creced vosotros***
let them grow	***crezcan ellos***

Impersonal forms

Infinitive	Perfect Infinitive
crecer	***haber crecido***
to grow	to have grown

Gerund	Perfect Gerund
creciendo	***habiendo crecido***
growing	having grown

Participle	Perfect Participle
crecido	***habiendo crecido***
grown	having grown

HANG · HUNG/HANGED · HUNG/HANGED

COLGAR, AHORCAR

Indicative

Present

cuelgo
I hang
you hang
he/she/it hangs
we hang
you hang
they hang

Present perfect

he colgado
I have hung/hanged
you have hung/hanged
he/she/it has hung/hanged
we have hung/hanged
you have hung/hanged
they have hung/hanged

Past

colgaba/colgué
I hung/hanged
you hung/hanged
he/she/it hung/hanged
we hung/hanged
you hung/hanged
they hung/hanged

Past perfect

había/hube colgado
I had hung/hanged
you had hung/hanged
he/she/it had hung/hanged
we had hung/hanged
you had hung/hanged
they had hung/hanged

Future

colgaré
I shall/will hang
you will hang
he/she/it will hang
we shall/will hang
you will hang
they will hang

Future perfect

habré colgado
I shall/will have hung/hanged
you will have hung/hanged
he/she/it will have hung/hanged
we shall/will have hung/hanged
you will have hung/hanged
they will have hung/hanged

Present

colgaría
I should/would hang
you would hang
he/she/it would
hang
we should/would
hang
you would hang
they would hang

Perfect

habría colgado
I should/would have hung/hanged
you would have hung/hanged
he/she/it would have hung/
hanged
we should/would have hung/
hanged
you would have hung/hanged
they would have hung/hanged

Subjunctive

Present

cuelgue
I hang
you hang
he/she/it hangs
we hang
you hang
they hang

Present perfect

haya colgado
I have hung/hanged
you have hung/hanged
he/she/it has hung/hanged
we have hung/hanged
you have hung/hanged
they have hung/hanged

Past

colgara o colgase
I hung/hanged
you hung/hanged
he/she/it hung/hanged
we hung/hanged
you hung/hanged
they hung/hanged

Past perfect

hubiera o hubiese colgado
I had hung/hanged
you had hung/hanged
he/she/it had hung/hanged
we had hung/hanged
you had hung/hanged
they had hung/hanged

Imperative

let me hang	***no existe (déjame colgar)***
hang	***cuelga tú***
let him/her/it hang	***cuelgue él/ella/ello***
let us (let's) hang	***colguemos nosotros***
hang	***colgad vosotros***
let them hang	***cuelguen ellos***

Impersonal forms

Infinitive

colgar
to hang

Perfect Infinitive

haber colgado
to have hung/hanged

Gerund

colgando
hanging

Perfect Gerund

habiendo colgado
having hung/hanged

Participle

colgado
hung/hanged

Perfect Participle

habiendo colgado
having hung/hanged

HEAR · HEARD · HEARD

OÍR

Indicative

Present

oigo
I hear
you hear
he/she/it hears
we hear
you hear
they hear

Present perfect

he oído
I have heard
you have heard
he/she/it has heard
we have heard
you have heard
they have heard

Past

oía/oí
I heard
you heard
he/she/it heard
we heard
you heard
they heard

Past perfect

había/hube oído
I had heard
you had heard
he/she/it had heard
we had heard
you had heard
they had heard

Future

oiré
I shall/will hear
you will hear
he/she/it will hear
we shall/will hear
you will hear
they will hear

Future perfect

habré oído
I shall/will have heard
you will have heard
he/she/it will have heard
we shall/will have heard
you will have heard
they will have heard

Conditional

Present

oiría
I should/would hear
you would hear
he/she/it would hear
we should/would hear
you would hear
they would hear

Perfect

habría oído
I should/would have heard
you would have heard
he/she/it would have heard
we should/would have heard
you would have heard
they would have heard

Subjunctive

Present

oiga
I hear
you hear
he/she/it hears
we hear
you hear
they hear

Present perfect

haya oído
I have heard
you have heard
he/she/it has heard
we have heard
you have heard
they have heard

Past

oyera/oyese
I heard
you heard
he/she/it heard
we heard
you heard
they heard

Past perfect

hubiera/hubiese oído
I had heard
you had heard
he/she/it had heard
we had heard
you had heard
they had heard

Imperative

let me hear	***no existe (déjame oír)***
hear	***oye tú***
let him/her/it hear	***oiga él/ella/ello***
let us (let's) hear	***oigamos nosotros***
hear	***oíd vosotros***
let them hear	***oigan ellos***

Impersonal forms

Infinitive

oír
to hear

Perfect Infinitive

haber oído
to have heard

Gerund

oyendo
hearing

Perfect Gerund

habiendo oído
having heard

Participle

oído
heard

Perfect Participle

habiendo oído
having heard

HEW · HEWED · HEWED/HEWN

EXTRAER, LABRAR, TALLAR

Indicative

Present

extraigo
I hew
you hew
he/she/it hews
we hew
you hew
they hew

Present perfect

he extraído
I have hewed/hewn
you have hewed/hewn
he/she/it has hewed/hewn
we have hewed/hewn
you have hewed/hewn
they have hewed/hewn

Past

extraía/extraje
I hewed
you hewed
he/she/it hewed
we hewed
you hewed
they hewed

Past perfect

había/hube extraído
I had hewed/hewn
you had hewed/hewn
he/she/it had hewed/hewn
we had hewed/hewn
you had hewed/hewn
they had hewed/hewn

Future

extraeré
I shall/will hew
you will hew
he/she/it will hew
we shall/will hew
you will hew
they will hew

Future perfect

habré extraído
I shall/will have hewed/hewn
you will have hewed/hewn
he/she/it will have hewed/hewn
we shall/will have hewed/hewn
you will have hewed/hewn
they will have hewed/hewn

Present

extraería
I should/would hew
you would hew
he/she/it would hew
we should/would hew
you would hew
they would hew

Perfect

habría extraído
I should/would have hewed/hewn
you would have hewed/hewn
he/she/it would have hewed/hewn
we should/would have hewed/hewn
you would have hewed/hewn
they would have hewed/hewn

Subjunctive

Present

extraiga
I hew
you hew
he/she/it hews
we hew
you hew
they hew

Present perfect

haya extraído
I have hewed/hewn
you have hewed/hewn
he/she/it has hewed/hewn
we have hewed/hewn
you have hewed/hewn
they have hewed/hewn

Past

extrajera o extrajese
I hewed
you hewed
he/she/it hewed
we hewed
you hewed
they hewed

Past perfect

hubiera o hubiese extraído
I had hewed/hewn
you had hewed/hewn
he/she/it had hewed/hewn
we had hewed/hewn
you had hewed/hewn
they had hewed/hewn

Imperative

let me hew	***no existe (déjame extraer)***
hew	***extrae tú***
let him/her hew	***extraiga él/ella/ello***
let us (let's) hew	***extraigamos nosotros***
hew	***extraed vosotros***
let them hew	***extraigan ellos***

Impersonal forms

Infinitive

extraer
to hew

Perfect Infinitive

haber extraído
to have hewn/hewed

Gerund

extrayendo
hewing

Perfect Gerund

habiendo extraído
having hewn/hewed

Participle

extraído
hewn

Perfect Participle

habiendo extraído
having hewn/hewed

HIDE · HID · HIDDEN

ESCONDER, OCULTAR

Indicative

Present

escondo
I hide
you hide
he/she/it hides
we hide
you hide
they hide

Present perfect

he escondido
I have hidden
you have hidden
he/she/it has hidden
we have hidden
you have hidden
they have hidden

Past

escondía/escondí
I hid
you hid
he/she/it hid
we hid
you hid
they hid

Past perfect

había/hube escondido
I had hidden
you had hidden
he/she/it had hidden
we had hidden
you had hidden
they had hidden

Future

esconderé
I shall/will hide
you will hide
he/she/it will hide
we shall/will hide
you will hide
they will hide

Future perfect

habré escondido
I shall/will have hidden
you will have hidden
he/she/it will have hidden
we shall/will have hidden
you will have hidden
they will have hidden

Conditional

Present

escondería
I should/would hide
you would hide
he/she/it would hide
we should/would hide
you would hide
they would hide

Perfect

habría escondido
I should/would have hidden
you would have hidden
he/she/it would have hidden
we should/would have hidden
you would have hidden
they would have hidden

Subjunctive

Present

esconda
I hide
you hide
he/she/it hides
we hide
you hide
they hide

Present perfect

haya escondido
I had hidden
you had hidden
he/she/it had hidden
we had hidden
you had hidden
they had hidden

Past

escondiera o escondiese
I hid
you hid
he/she/it hid
we hid
you hid
they hid

Past perfect

hubiera o hubiese escondido
I had hidden
you had hidden
he/she/it had hidden
we had hidden
you had hidden
they had hidden

Imperative

let me hide	***no existe (déjame esconder)***
hide	***esconde tú***
let him/her/it hide	***esconda él/ella/ello***
let us (let's) hide	***escondamos nosotros***
hide	***esconded vosotros***
let them hide	***escondan ellos***

Impersonal forms

Infinitive

esconder
to hide

Perfect Infinitive

haber escondido
to have hidden

Gerund

escondiendo
hiding

Perfect Gerund

habiendo escondido
having hidden

Participle

escondido
hidden

Perfect Participle

habiendo escondido
having hidden

HIT · HIT · HIT

GOLPEAR, ACERTAR

Indicative

Present	Present perfect
golpeo	***he golpeado***
I hit	I have hit
you hit	you have hit
he/she/it hits	he/she/it has hit
we hit	we have hit
you hit	you have hit
they hit	they have hit

Past	Past perfect
golpeaba/golpeé	***había/hube golpeado***
I hit	I had hit
you hit	you had hit
he/she/it hit	he/she/it had hit
we hit	we had hit
you hit	you had hit
they hit	they had hit

Future	Future perfect
golpearé	***habré golpeado***
I shall/will hit	I shall/will have hit
you will hit	you will have hit
he/she/it will hit	he/she/it will have hit
we shall/will hit	we shall/will have hit
you will hit	you will have hit
they will hit	they will have hit

Conditional

Present	Perfect
golpearía	***habría golpeado***
I should/would hit	I should/would have hit
you would hit	you would have hit
he/she/it would hit	he/she/it would have hit
we should/would hit	we should/would have hit
you would hit	you would have hit
they would hit	they would have hit

Subjunctive

Present	Present perfect
golpee	***haya golpeado***
I hit	I have hit
you hit	you have hit
he/she/it hits	he/she/it has hit
we hit	we have hit
you hit	you have hit
they hit	they have hit

Past	Past perfect
golpeara o golpease	***hubiera o hubiese golpeado***
I hit	I had hit
you hit	you had hit
he/she/it hit	he/she/it had hit
we hit	we had hit
you hit	you had hit
they hit	they had hit

Imperative

let me hit	***no existe (déjame golpear)***
hit	***golpea tú***
let him/her/it hit	***golpee él/ella/ello***
let us (let's) hit	***golpeemos nosotros***
hit	***golpead vosotros***
let them hit	***golpeen ellos***

Impersonal forms

Infinitive	Perfect Infinitive
golpear	***haber golpeado***
to hit	to have hit
Gerund	**Perfect Gerund**
golpeando	***habiendo golpeado***
hitting	having hit
Participle	**Perfect Participle**
golpeado	***habiendo tolerado***
hit	having hit

HOLD · HELD · HELD

SOSTENER, AGUANTAR, MANTENER

Indicative

Present

sostengo
I hold
you hold
he/she/it holds
we hold
you hold
they hold

Present perfect

he sostenido
I have hold
you have hold
he/she/it has hold
we have hold
you have hold
they have hold

Past

sostenía/sostuve
I held
you held
he/she/it held
we held
you held
they held

Past perfect

había/hube sostenido
I had held
you had held
he/she/it had held
we had held
you had held
they had held

Future

sostendré
I shall/will hold
you will hold
he/she/it will hold
we shall/will hold
you will hold
they will hold

Future perfect

habré sostenido
I shall/will have held
you will have held
he/she/it will have held
we shall/will have held
you will have held
they will have held

Conditional

Present

sostendría
I should/would hold
you would hold
he/she/it would hold
we should/would hold
you would hold
they would hold

Perfect

habría sostenido
I should/would have held
you would have held
he/she/it would have held
we should/would have held
you would have held
they would have held

Subjunctive

Present

sostenga
I hold
you hold
he/she/it holds
we hold
you hold
they hold

Present perfect

they held
haya sostenido
I have held
you have held
he/she/it has held
we have held
you have held

Past

sostuviera o
sostuviese
I held
you held
he/she/it held
we held
you held

Past perfect

they have held
hubiera o hubiese sostenido
I had held
you had held
he had held
we had held
you had held

Imperative

they had held
let me hold
hold
let him/her/it hold
let us (let's) hold
hold

let them hold
no existe (déjame sostener)
sostén tú
sostenga él/ella/ello
sostengamos nosotros
sostened vosotros

Impersonal forms

sostengan ellos

held

Infinitive

sostener
to hold

Perfect Infinitive

haber sostenido
to have held

Gerund

sosteniendo
holding

Perfect Gerund

habiendo sostenido
having held

Participle

sostenido

Perfect Participle

habiendo sostenido

HURT · HURT · HURT

DOLER, HERIR, HACER DAÑO, LASTIMAR

Indicative

Present	Present perfect
hago daño	***he hecho daño***
I hurt	I have hurt
you hurt	you have hurt
he/she/it hurts	he/she/it has hurt
we hurt	we have hurt
you hurt	you have hurt
they hurt	they have hurt

Past	Past perfect
hacía/hice daño	***había/hube hecho daño***
I hurt	I had hurt
you hurt	you had hurt
he/she/it hurt	he/she/it had hurt
we hurt	we had hurt
you hurt	you had hurt
they hurt	they had hurt

Future	Future perfect
haré daño	***habré hecho daño***
I shall/will hurt	I shall/will have hurt
you will hurt	you will have hurt
he/she/it will hurt	he/she/it will have hurt
we shall/will hurt	we shall/will have hurt
you will hurt	you will have hurt
they will hurt	they will have hurt

Conditional

Present	Perfect
haría daño	***habría hecho daño***
I should/would hurt	I should/would have hurt
you would hurt	you would have hurt
he/she/it would hurt	he/she/it would have hurt
we should/would hurt	we should/would have hurt
you would hurt	you would have hurt
they would hurt	they would have hurt

Subjunctive

Present	Present perfect
haga daño	***haya hecho daño***
I hurt	I have hurt
you hurt	you have hurt
he/she/it hurts	he/she/it has hurt
we hurt	we have hurt
you hurt	you have hurt
they hurt	they have hurt

Past	Past perfect
hiciera o hiciese daño	***hubiera o hubiese hecho daño***
I hurt	I had hurt
you hurt	you had hurt
he/she/it hurt	he/she/it had hurt
we hurt	we had hurt
you hurt	you had hurt
they hurt	

Imperative

they had hurt	let them hurt
let me hurt	***no existe (déjame hacer daño)***
hurt	***haz daño***
let him/her/it hurt	***haga daño él/ella/ello***
let us (let's) hurt	***hagamos daño nosotros***
hurt	

Impersonal forms

haced daño vosotros	***hecho daño***
hagan daño ellos	hurt

Infinitive	Perfect infinitive
hacer daño	***haber hecho daño***
to hurt	to have hurt

Gerund	Perfect gerund
haciendo daño	***habiendo hecho daño***
hurting	having hurt

Participle | Perfect participle

KEEP · KEPT · KEPT

GUARDAR, CONSERVAR

Indicative

Present	Present perfect
guardo	***he guardado***
I keep	I have kept
you keep	you have kept
he/she/it keeps	he/she/it has kept
we keep	we have kept
you keep	you have kept
they keep	they have kept

Past	Past perfect
guardaba/guardé	***había /hube guardado***
I kept	I had kept
you kept	you had kept
he/she/it kept	he/she/it had kept
we kept	we had kept
you kept	you had kept
they kept	they had kept

Future	Future perfect
guardaré	***habré guardado***
I shall/will keep	I shall/will have kept
you will keep	you will have kept
he/she/it will keep	he/she/it will have kept
we shall/will keep	we shall/will have kept
you will keep	you will have kept
they will keep	they will have kept

Conditional

Present	Perfect
guardaría	***habría guardado***
I should/would keep	I should/would have kept
you would keep	you would have kept
he/she/it would keep	he/she/it would have kept
we should/would keep	we should/would have kept
you would keep	you would have kept
they would keep	they would have kept

Subjunctive

Present	Present perfect
guarde	***haya guardado***
I keep	I have kept
you keep	you have kept
he/she/it keeps	he/she/it has kept
we keep	we have kept
you keep	you have kept
they keep	they have kept

Past	Past perfect
guardara o guardase	***hubiera o hubiese guardado***
I kept	I had kept
you kept	you had kept
he/she/it kept	he/she/it had kept
we kept	we had kept
you kept	you had kept
they kept	they had kept

Imperative

let me keep	***no existe (déjame guardar)***
keep	***guarda tú***
let him/her/it keep	***guarde él/ella/ello***
let us (let's) keep	***guardemos nosotros***
keep	***guardad vosotros***
let them keep	***guarden ellos***

Impersonal forms

Infinitive	Perfect infinitive
guardar	haber guardado
to keep	to have kept

Gerund	Perfect gerund
guardando	habiendo guardado
keeping	having kept

Participle	Perfect participle
guardado	habiendo guardado
kept	having kept

KNEEL · KNELT · KNELT

ARRODILLAR(SE)

Indicative

Present

me arrodillo
I kneel
you kneel
he/she/it kneels
we kneel
you kneel
they kneel

Present perfect

me he arrodillado
I have knelt
you have knelt
he/she/it has knelt
we have knelt
you have knelt
they have knelt

Past

me arrodillaba/ arrodillé
I knelt
you knelt
he/she/it knelt
we knelt
you knelt
they knelt

Past perfect

me había/hube arrodillado
I had knelt
you had knelt
he/she/it had knelt
we had knelt
you had knelt
they had knelt

Future

me arrodillaré
I shall/will kneel
you will kneel
he/she/it will kneel
we shall/will kneel
you will kneel
they will kneel

Future perfect

me habré arrodillado
I shall/will have knelt
you will have knelt
he/she/it will have knelt
we shall/will have knelt
you will have knelt
they will have knelt

Conditional

Present

me arrodillaría
I should/would kneel
you would kneel
he/she/it would kneel
we should/would kneel
you would kneel
they would kneel

Perfect

me habría arrodillado
I should/would have knelt
you would have knelt
he/she/it would have knelt
we should/would have knelt
you would have knelt
they would have kenlt

Subjunctive

Present

me arrodille
I kneel
you kneel
he/she/it kneels
we kneel
you kneel
they kneel

Present perfect

haya arrodillado
I have knelt
you have knelt
he/she/it has knelt
we have knelt
you have knelt
they have knelt

Past

me arrodillara o arrodillase
I knelt
you knelt
he/she/it knelt
we knelt
you knelt
they knelt

Past perfect

me hubiera o hubiese arrodillado
I had knelt
you had knelt
he/she/it had knelt
we had knelt
you had knelt
they had knelt

Imperative

let me kneel	***no existe (déjame arrodillarme)***
kneel	***arrodíllate tú***
let him/her/it kneel	***arrodíllese él/ella/ello***
let us (let's) kneel	***arrodillémonos nosotros***
kneel	***arrodillaos vosotros***
let them kneel	***arrodíllense ellos***

Impersonal forms

knelt

Infinitive

arrodillar
to kneel

Perfect Infinitive

haber(se) arrodillado
to have knelt

Gerund

arrodillándose
kneeling

Perfect Gerund

habiendo(se) arrodillado
having knelt

Participle

arrodillado

Perfect Participle

habiendo(se) arrodillado

KNIT · KNIT/KNITTED · KNIT/KNITTED

TRICOTAR, TEJER, HACER PUNTO O CALCETA

Indicative

Present

tricoto
I knit
you knit
he/she/it knits
we knit
you knit
they knit

Present perfect

he tricotado
I have knit/knitted
you have knit/knitted
he/she/it has knit/knitted
we have knit/knitted
you have knit/knitted
they have knit/knitted

Past

tricotaba/tricoté
I knit/knitted
you knit/knitted
he/she/it knit/knitted
we knit/knitted
you knit/knitted
they knit/knitted

Past perfect

había/hube tricotado
I had knit/knitted
you had knit/knitted
he/she/it had knit/knitted
we had knit/knitted
you had knit/knitted
they had knit/knitted

Future

tricotaré
I shall/will knit
you will knit
he/she/it will knit
we shall/will knit
you will knit
they will knit

Future perfect

habré tricotado
I shall/will have knit/knitted
you will have knit/knitted
he/she/it will have knit/knitted
we shall/will have knit/knitted
you will have knit/knitted
they will have knit/knitted

Conditional

Present

tricotaría
I should/would knit
you would knit
he/she/it would knit
we should/would knit
you would knit
they would knit

Perfect

habría tricotado
I should/would have knit/knitted
you would have knit/knitted
he/she/it would have knit/knitted
we should/would have knit/knitted
you would have knit/knitted
they would have knit/knitted

Subjunctive

Present

tricote
I knit
you knit
he/she/it knits
we knit
you knit
they knit

Present perfect

haya tricotado
I have knit/knitted
you have knit/knitted
he/she/it has knit/knitted
we have knit/knitted
you have knit/knitted
they have knit/knitted

Past

tricotara o tricotase
I knit/knitted
you knit/knitted
he/she/it knit/knitted
we knit/knitted
you knit/knitted
they knit/knitted

Past perfect

hubiera o hubiese tricotado
I had knit/knitted
you had knit/knitted
he/she/it had knit/knitted
we had knit/knitted
you had knit/knitted
they had knit/knitted

Imperative

let me knit	***no existe (déjame tricotar)***
knit	***tricota tú***
let him/her/it knit	***tricote él/ella/ello***
let us (let's) knit	***tricotemos nosotros***
knit	***tricotad vosotros***
let them knit	***tricoten ellos***

Impersonal forms

Infinitive

tricotar
to knit

Perfect Infinitive

haber tricotado
to have knit/knitted

Gerund

tricotando
knitting

Perfect Gerund

habiendo tricotado
having knit/knitted

Participle

tricotado
knit/knitted

Perfect Participle

habiendo tricotado
having knit/knitted

KNOW · KNEW · KNOWN

SABER, CONOCER

Indicative

Present

sé
I know
you know
he/she/it knows
we know
you know
they know

Present perfect

he sabido
I have known
you have known
he/she/it has known
we have known
you have known
they have known

Past

sabía/supe
I knew
you knew
he/she/it knew
we knew
you knew
they knew

Past perfect

había/hube sabido
I had known
you had known
he/she/it had known
we had known
you had known
they had known

Future

sabré
I shall/will know
you will know
he/she/it will know
we shall/will know
you will know
they will know

Future perfect

habré sabido
I shall/will have known
you will have known
he/she/it will have known
we shall/will have known
you will have known
they will have known

Conditional

Present

sabría
I should/would know
you would know
he/she/it would know
we should/would know
you would know
they would know

Perfect

habría sabido
I should/would have known
you would have known
he/she/it would have known
we should/would have known
you would have known
they would have known

Subjunctive

Present

sepa
I know
you know
he/she/it knows
we know
you know
they know

Present perfect

haya sabido
I have known
you have known
he/she/it has known
we have known
you have known
they have known

Past

supiera o supiese
I knew
you knew
he/she/it knew
we knew
you knew
they knew

Past perfect

hubiera o hubiese sabido
I had known
you had known
he/she/it had known
we had known
you had known
they had known

Imperative

let me know	***no existe (déjame saber)***
know	***sabe tú***
let him/her/it know	***sepa él/ella/ello***
let us (let's) know	***sepamos nosotros***
know	***sabed vosotros***
let them know	***sepan ellos***

Impersonal forms

Infinitive

saber
to know

Perfect Infinitive

haber sabido
to have known

Gerund

sabiendo
knowing

Perfect Gerund

habiendo sabido
having known

Participle

sabido
known

Perfect Participle

habiendo sabido
having known

LAY · LAID · LAID

PONER (HUEVOS, MESA), COLOCAR

Indicative

Present

pongo
I lay
you lay
he/she/it lays
we lay
you lay
they lay

Present perfect

he puesto
I have laid
you have laid
he/she/it has laid
we have laid
you have laid
they have laid

Past

ponía/puse
I laid
you laid
he/she/it laid
we laid
you laid
they laid

Past perfect

había/hube puesto
I had laid
you had laid
he/she/it had laid
we had laid
you had laid
they had laid

Future

pondré
I shall/will lay
you will lay
he/she/it will lay
we shall/will lay
you will lay
they will lay

Future perfect

habré puesto
I shall/will have laid
you will have laid
he/she/it will have laid
we shall/will have laid
you will have laid
they will have laid

Conditional

Present

pondría
I should/would lay
you would lay
he/she/it would lay
we should/would lay
you would lay
they would lay

Perfect

habría puesto
I should/would have laid
you would have laid
he/she/it would have laid
we should/would have laid
you would have laid
they would have laid

Subjunctive

Present

ponga
I lay
you lay
he/she/it lays
we lay
you lay
they lay

Present perfect

haya puesto
I have laid
you have laid
he/she/it has laid
we have laid
you have laid
they have laid

Past

pusiera/pusiese
I laid
you laid
he/she/it laid
we laid
you laid
they laid

Past perfect

hubiera/hubiese puesto
I had laid
you had laid
he/she/it had laid
we had laid
you had laid
they had laid

Imperative

let me lay	***no existe (déjame poner)***
lay	***pon tú***
let him/her/it lay	***ponga él/ella/ello***
let us (let's) lay	***pongamos nosotros***
lay	***poned vosotros***
let them lay	***pongan ellos***

Impersonal forms

Infinitive

poner
to lay

Perfect Infinitive

haber puesto
to have laid

Gerund

poniendo
laying

Perfect Gerund

habiendo puesto
having laid

Participle

puesto
laid

Perfect Participle

habiendo puesto
having laid

LEAD · LED · LED

CONDUCIR, GUIAR, ENCABEZAR, DIRIGIR, MANDAR, ESTAR AL FRENTE

Indicative

Present

encabezo
I lead
you lead
he/she/it leads
we lead
you lead
they lead

Present perfect

he encabezado
I have led
you have led
he/she/it has led
we have led
you have led
they have led

Past

encabezaba/
encabecé
I led
you led
he/she/it led
we led
you led
they led

Past perfect

había/hube
encabezado
I had led
you had led
he/she/it had led
we had led
you had led
they had led

Future

encabezaré
I shall/will lead
you will lead
he/she/it will lead
we shall/will lead
you will lead
they will lead

Future perfect

habré encabezado
I shall/will have led
you will have led
he/she/it will have led
we shall/will have led
you will have led
they will have led

Conditional

Present

encabezaría
I should/would lead
you would lead
he/she/it would lead
we should/would lead
you would lead
they would lead

Perfect

habría encabezado
I should/would have led
you would have led
he/she/it would have led
we should/would have led
you would have led
they would have led

Subjunctive

Present

encabece
I lead
you lead
he/she/it leads
we lead
you lead
they lead

Present perfect

haya encabezado
I have led
you have led
he/she/it has led
we have led
you have led
they have led

Past

encabezara o
encabezase
I led
you led
he/she/it led
we led
you led
they led

Past perfect

hubiera o hubiese
encabezado
I had led
you had led
he/she/it had led
we had led
you had led
they had led

Imperative

let me lead	***no existe (déjame***
lead	***encabezar)***
let him/her/it lead	***encabeza tú***
let us (let's) lead	***encabece él/ella/ello***
lead	***encabecemos nosotros***
let them lead	***encabezad vosotros***

Impersonal forms

encabecen ellos	led

Infinitive

encabezar
to lead

Perfect Infinitive

haber encabezado
to have led

Gerund

encabezando
leading

Perfect Gerund

habiendo encabezado
having led

Participle

encabezado

Perfect Participle

habiendo encabezado

LEAN · LEANED/LEANT · LEANED/LEANT

APOYAR, RECOSTAR

Indicative

Present

apoyo
I lean
you lean
he/she/it leans
we lean
you lean
they lean

Present perfect

he apoyado
I have leaned/leant
you have leaned/leant
he/she/it has leaned/leant
we have leaned/leant
you have leaned/leant
they have leaned/leant

Past

apoyaba/apoyé
I leaned/leant
you leaned/leant
he/she/it leaned/leant
we learned/leant
you learned/leant
they leaned/leant

Past perfect

había/hube apoyado
I had leaned/leant
you had leaned/leant
he/she/it had leaned/leant
we had leaned/leant
you had leaned/leant
they had leaned/leant

Future

apoyaré
I shall/will lean
you will lean
he/she/it will lean
we shall/will lean
you will lean
they will lean

Future perfect

habré apoyado
I shall/will have leaned/leant
you will have leaned/leant
he/she/it will have leaned/leant
we shall/will have leaned/leant
you will have leaned/leant
they will have leaned/leant

Conditional

Present

apoyaría
I should/would lean
you would lean
he/she/it would lean
we should/would lean
you would lean
they would lean

Perfect

habría apoyado
I should/would have leaned/leant
you would have leaned/leant
he/she/it would have leaned/leant
we should/would have leaned/leant
you would have leaned/leant
they would have leaned/leant

Subjunctive

Present

apoye
I lean
you lean
he/she/it leans
we lean
you lean
they lean

Present perfect

haya apoyado
I have leaned/leant
you have leaned/leant
he/she/it has leaned/leant
we have leaned/leant
you have leaned/leant
they have leaned/leant

Past

apoyara o apoyase
I leaned/leant
you leaned/leant
he/she/it leaned/leant
we leaned/leant
you leaned/leant
they leaned/leant

Past perfect

hubiera o hubiese apoyado
I had leaned/leant
you had leaned/leant
he/she/it had leaned/leant
we had leaned/leant
you had leaned/leant
they had leaned/leant

Imperative

let me lean	***no existe (déjame apoyar)***
lean	***apoya tú***
let him/her/it lean	***apoye él/ella/ello***
let us (let's) lean	***apoyemos nosotros***
lead	***apoyad vosotros***
let them lean	***apoyen ellos***

Impersonal forms

Infinitive

apoyar
to lean

Perfect Infinitive

haber apoyado
to have leaned/leant

Gerund

apoyando
leaning

Perfect Gerund

habiendo apoyado
having leaned/leant

Participle

apoyado
leaned/leant

Perfect Participle

habiendo apoyado
having leaned/leant

LEAP · LEAPED/LEPT · LEAPED/LEPT

SALTAR, BRINCAR

Indicative

Present

brinco
I leap
you leap
he/she/it leaps
we leap
you leap
they leap

Present perfect

haya brincado
I have leaped/leapt
you have leaped/leapt
he/she/it has leaped/leapt
we have leaped/leapt
you have leaped/leapt
they have leaped/leapt

Past

brincaba/brinqué
I leaped/leapt
you leaped/leapt
he/she/it leaped/leapt
we leaped/leapt
you leaped/leapt
they leaped/leapt

Past perfect

había/hube brincado
I had leaped/leapt
you had leaped/leapt
he/she/it had leaped/leapt
we had leaped/leapt
you had leaped/leapt
they had leaped/leapt

Future

brincaré
I shall/will leap
you will leap
he/she/it will leap
we shall/will leap
you will leap
they will leap

Future perfect

habré brincado
I shall/will have leaped/leapt
you will have leaped/leapt
he/she/it will have leaped/leapt
we shall/will have leaped/leapt
you will have leaped/leapt
they will have leaped/leapt

Conditional

Present

brincaría
I should/would leap
you would leap
he/she/it would leap
we should/would leap
you would leap
they would leap

Perfect

habría brincado
I should/would have leaped/leapt
you would have leaped/leapt
he/she/it would have leaped/leapt
we should/would have leaped/leapt
you would have leaped/leapt
they would have leaped/leapt

Subjunctive

Present

brinque
I leap
you leap
he/she/it leaps
we leap
you leap
they leap

Present perfect

haya brincado
I have leaped/leapt
you have leaped/leapt
he/she/it has leaped/leapt
we have leaped/leapt
you have leaped/leapt
they have leaped/leapt

Past

brincara o brincase
I leaped/leapt
you leaped/leapt
he/she/it leaped/leapt
we leaped/leapt
you leaped/leapt
they leaped/leapt

Past perfect

hubiera o hubiese brincado
I had leaped/leapt
you had leaped/leapt
he/she/it had leaped/leapt
we had leaped/leapt
you had leaped/leapt
they had leaped/leapt

Imperative

let me leap	***no existe (déjame brincar)***
leap	***brinca tú***
let him/her/it leap	***brinque él/ella/ello***
let us (let's) leap	***brinquemos nosotros***
leap	***brincad vosotros***
let them leap	***brinquen ellos***

Impersonal forms

Infinitive

brincar
to leap

Perfect Infinitive

haber brincado
to have leaped/leaped

Gerund

brincando
leaping

Perfect Gerund

habiendo brincado
having leaped/leapt

Participle

brincado
leaped/leapt

Perfect Participle

habiendo brincado
having leaped/leapt

LEARN · LEARNED/LEARNT · LEARNED/LEARNT

APRENDER

Indicative

Present	Present perfect
aprendo	***he aprendido***
I learn	I have learned/learnt
you learn	you have learned/learnt
he/she/it learns	he/she/it has learned/learnt
we learn	we have learned/learnt
you learn	you have learned/learnt
they learn	they have learned/learnt

Past	Past perfect
aprendía/aprendí	***había/hube aprendido***
I learned/learnt	I had learned/learnt
you learned/learnt	you had learned/learnt
he/she/it learned/learnt	he/she/it had learned/learnt
we learned/learnt	we had leaned/learnt
you learned/learnt	you had learned/learnt
they learned/learnt	they had learned/learnt

Future	Future perfect
aprenderé	***habré aprendido***
I shall/will learn	I shall/will have learned/learnt
you will learned	you will have learnt
he/she/it will learned	he/she/it will have learnt
we shall/will learn	we shall/will have learned/ learnt
you will learn	you will have learned/learnt
they will learn	they will have learned/learnt

Conditional

Present	Perfect
aprendería	***habría aprendido***
I should/would learn	I should/would have learned/learnt
you would learn	you would have learned/learnt
he/she/it would learn	he/she/it would have learned/learnt
we should/would learn	we should/would have learned/ learnt
you would learn	you would have learned/learnt
they would learn	they would have learned/learnt

Subjunctive

Present	Present perfect
aprenda	***haya aprendido***
I learn	I have learned/learnt
you learn	you have learned/learnt
he/she/it learns	he/she/it has learned/learnt
we learn	we have learned/learnt
you learn	you have learned/learnt
they learn	they have learned/learnt

Past	Past perfect
aprendiera o aprendiese	***hubiera o hubiese aprendido***
I learned/learnt	I had learned/learnt
you learned/learnt	you had learned/learnt
he/she/it learned/learnt	he/she/it had learned/learnt
we learned/learnt	we had learned/learnt
you learned/learnt	you had learned/learnt
they learned/learnt	they had learned/learnt

Imperative

let me learn	***no existe (déjame aprender)***
learn	***aprende tú***
let him/her/it learn	***aprenda él/ella/ello***
let us (let's) learn	***aprendamos nosotros***
learn	***aprended vosotros***
let them learn	***aprendan ellos***

Impersonal forms

Infinitive	Perfect Infinitive
aprender	***haber aprendido***
to learn	to have learned/learnt

Gerund	Perfect Gerund
aprendiendo	***habiendo aprendido***
learning	having learned/learnt

Participle	Perfect Participle
aprendido	***habiendo aprendido***
learned/learnt	having learned/learnt

LEAVE · LEFT · LEFT

DEJAR, SALIR, IRSE, ABANDONAR

Indicative

Present

salgo
I leave
you leave
he/she/it leaves
we leave
you leave
they leave

Present perfect

he salido
I have left
you have left
he/she/it has left
we have left
you have left
they have left

Past

salía/salí
I left
you left
he/she/it left
we left
you left
they left

Past perfect

había/hube salido
I had left
you had left
he/she/it had left
we had left
you had left
they had left

Future

saldré
I shall/will leave
you will leave
he/she/it will leave
we shall/will leave
you will leave
they will leave

Future perfect

habré salido
I shall/will have left
you will have left
he/she/it will have left
we shall/will have left
you will have left
they will have left

Conditional

Present

saldría
I should/would leave
you would leave
he/she/it would leave
we should/would leave
you would leave
they would leave

Perfect

habría salido
I should/would have left
you would have left
he/she/it would have left
we should/would have left
you would have left
they would have left

Subjunctive

Present

salga
I leave
you leave
he/she/it leaves
we leave
you leave
they leave

Present perfect

haya salido
I have left
you have left
he/she/it has left
we have left
you have left
they have left

Past

saliera o saliese
I left
you left
he/she/it left
we left
you left
they left

Past perfect

hubiera o hubiese salido
I had left
you had left
he/she/it had left
we had left
you had left
they had left

Imperative

let me leave	***no existe (déjame salir)***
leave	***sal tú***
let him/her/it leave	***salga él/ella/ello***
let us (let's) leave	***salgamos nosotros***
leave	***salid vosotros***
let them leave	***salgan ellos***

Impersonal forms

Infinitive

salir
to leave

Perfect Infinitive

haber salido
to have left

Gerund

saliendo
leaving

Perfect Gerund

habiendo salido
having left

Participle

salido
left

Perfect Participle

habiendo salido
having left

LEND · LENT · LENT

PRESTAR, DEJAR

Indicative

Present

presto
I lend
you lend
he/she/it lends
we lend
you lend
they lend

Present perfect

he prestado
I have lent
you have lent
he/she/it has lent
we have lent
you have lent
they have lent

Past

prestaba/presté
I lent
you lent
he/she/it lent
we lent
you lent
they lent

Past perfect

había/hube prestado
I had lent
you had lent
he/she/it had lent
we had lent
you had lent
they had lent

Future

prestaré
I shall/will lend
you will lend
he/she/it will lend
we shall/will lend
you will lend
they will lend

Future perfect

habré prestado
I shall/will have lent
you will have lent
he/she/it will have lent
we shall/will have lent
you will have lent
they will have lent

Conditional

Present

prestaría
I should/would lend
you would lend
he/she/it would lend
we should/would lend
you would lend
they would lend

Perfect

habría prestado
I should/would have lent
you would have lent
he/she/it would have lent
we should/would have lent
you would have lent
they would have lent

Subjunctive

Present

preste
I lend
you lend
he/she/it lends
we lend
you lend
they lend

Present perfect

haya prestado
I have lent
you have lent
he/she/it has lent
we have lent
you have lent
they have lent

Past

prestara o prestase
I lent
you lent
he/she/it lent
we lent
you lent
they lent

Past perfect

hubiera o hubiese prestado
I had lent
you had lent
he/she/it had lent
we had lent
you had lent
they had lent

Imperative

let me lend	***no existe (déjame prestar)***
lend	***presta tú***
let him/her/it lend	***preste él/ella/ello***
let us (let's) lend	***prestemos nosotros***
lend	***prestad vosotros***
let them lend	***presten ellos***

Impersonal forms

Infinitive

prestar
to lend

Perfect Infinitive

haber prestado
to have lent

Gerund

prestando
lending

Perfect Gerund

habiendo prestado
having lent

Participle

prestado
lent

Perfect Participle

habiendo prestado
having lent

LET · LET · LET

PERMITIR, DEJAR

Indicative

Present

permito
I let
you let
he/she/it lets
we let
you let
they let

Present perfect

he permitido
I have let
you have let
he/she/it has let
we have let
you have let
they have let

Past

permitía/permití
I let
you let
he/she/it let
we let
you let
they let

Past perfect

había/hube permitido
I had let
you had let
he/she/it had let
we had let
you had let
they had let

Future

permitiré
I shall/will let
you will let
he/she/it will let
we shall/will let
you will let
they will let

Future perfect

habré permitido
I shall/will have let
you will have let
he/she/it will have let
we shall/will have let
you will have let
they will have let

Conditional

Present

permitiría
I should/would let
you would let
he/she/it would let
we should/would let
you would let
they would let

Perfect

habría permitido
I should/would have let
you would have let
he/she/it would have let
we should/would have let
you would have let
they would have let

Subjunctive

Present

permita
I let
you let
he/she/it lets
we let
you let
they let

Present perfect

they let
haya permitido
I have let
you have let
he/she/it has let
we have let
you have let

Past

permitiera o permitiese
I let
you let
he/she/it let
we let
you let

Past perfect

they have let
hubiera o hubiese permitido
I had let
you had let
he/she/it had let
we had let
you had let

Imperative

they had let
let me let
let
let him/her/it let
let us (let's) let
let

let them let
no existe (déjame permitir)
permite tú
permita él/ella/ello
permitamos nosotros
permitid vosotros

Impersonal forms

permitan ellos

let

Infinitive

permitir
to let

Perfect Infinitive

haber permitido
to have let

Gerund

permitiendo
letting

Perfect Gerund

habiendo permitido
having let

Participle

permitido

Perfect Participle

habiendo permitido

LIE · LAY · LAIN

ECHARSE, ACOSTARSE, YACER

Indicative

Present	Present perfect
yazgo/yazco	***he yacido***
I lie	I have lain
you lie	you have lain
he/she/it lies	he/she/it has lain
we lie	we have lain
you lie	you have lain
they lie	they have lain

Past	Past perfect
yacía/yací	***había/hube yacido***
I lay	I had lain
you lay	you had lain
he/she/it lay	he/she/it had lain
we lay	we had lain
you lay	you had lain
they lay	they had lain

Future	Future perfect
yaceré	***habré yacido***
I shall/will lie	I shall/will have lain
you will lie	you will have lain
he/she/it will lie	he/she/it will have lain
we shall/will lie	we shall/will have lain
you will lie	you will have lain
they will lie	they will have lain

Conditional

Present	Perfect
yacería	***habría yacido***
I should/would lie	I should/would have lain
you would lie	you would have lain
he/she/it would lie	he/she/it would have lain
we should/would lie	we should/would have lain
you would lie	you would have lain
they would lie	they would have lain

Subjunctive

Present	Present perfect
yazga/yazca	***haya yacido***
I lie	I have lain
you lie	you have lain
he/she/it lies	he/she/it has lain
we lie	we have lain
you lie	you have lain
they lie	they have lain

Past	Past perfect
yaciera/yaciese	***hubiera/hubiese yacido***
I lay	I had lain
you lay	you had lain
he/she/it lay	he/she/it had lain
we lay	we had lain
you lay	you had lain
they lay	they had lain

Imperative

let me lie	***no existe (déjame yacer)***
lie	***yace/yaz tú***
let him/her/it lie	***yazca/yazga él/ella/ello***
let us (let's) lie	***yazcamos/yazgamos nosotros***
lie	***yaced vosotros***
let them lie	***yazcan/yazgan ellos***

Impersonal forms

Infinitive	Perfect Infinitive
yacer	***haber yacido***
to lie	to have lain
Gerund	**Perfect Gerund**
yaciendo	***habiendo yacido***
lying	having lain
Participle	**Perfect Participle**
yacido	***habiendo yacido***
lain	having lain

LIGHT · LIT/LIGHTED · LIT/LIGHTED

ENCENDER, ILUMINAR

Indicative

Present

enciendo
I light
you light
he/she/it lights
we light
you light
they light

Present perfect

he encendido
I have lit/lighted
you have lit/lighted
he/she/it has lit/lighted
we have lit/lighted
you have lit/lighted
they have lit/lighted

Past

encendía/encendí
I lit/lighted
you lit/lighted
he/she/it lit/lighted
we lit/lighted
you lit/lighted
they lit/lighted

Past perfect

había/hube encendido
I had lit/lighted
you had lit/lighted
he/she/it had lit/lighted
we had lit/lighted
you had lit/lighted
they had lit/lighted

Future

encenderé
I shall/will light
you will light
he/she/it will light
we shall/will light
you will light
they will light

Future perfect

habré encendido
I shall/will have lit/lighted
you will have lit/lighted
he/she/it will have lit/lighted
we shall/will have lit/lighted
you will have lit/lighted
they will have lit/lighted

Conditional

Present

encendería
I should/would light
you would light
he/she/it would light
we should/would light
you would light
they would light

Perfect

habría encendido
I should/would have lit/lighted
you would have lit/lighted
he/she/it would have lit/lighted
we should/would have lit/lighted
you would have lit/lighted
they would have lit/lighted

Subjunctive

Present

encienda
I light
you light
he/she/it lights
we light
you light
they light

Present perfect

haya encendido
I have lit/lighted
you have lit/lighted
he/she/it has lit/lighted
we have lit/lighted
you have lit/lighted
they have lit/lighted

Past

encendiera o encendiese
I lit/lighted
you lit/lighted
he/she/it lit/lighted
we lit/lighted
you lit/lighted
they lit/lighted

Past perfect

hubiera o hubiese encendido
I had lit/lighted
you had lit/lighted
he/she/it had lit/lighted
we had lit/lighted
you had lit/lighted
they had lit/lighted

Imperative

let me light	***no existe (déjame encender)***
light	***enciende tú***
let him/her/it light	***encienda él/ella/ello***
let us (let's) light	***encendamos nosotros***
light	***encended vosotros***
let them light	***enciendan ellos***

Impersonal forms

Infinitive

encender
to light

Perfect Infinitive

haber encendido
to have lit/lighted

Gerund

encendiendo
lighting

Perfect Gerund

habiendo encendido
having lit/lighted

Participle

encendido
lit/lighted

Perfect Participle

habiendo encendido
having lit/lighted

LOSE · LOST · LOST

PERDER

Indicative

Present

pierdo
I lose
you lose
he/she/it loses
we lose
you lose
they lose

Present perfect

he perdido
I have lost
you have lost
he/she/it has lost
we have lost
you have lost
they have lost

Past

perdía/perdí
I lost
you lost
he/she/it lost
we lost
you lost
they lost

Past perfect

había/hube perdido
I had lost
you had lost
he/she/it had lost
we had lost
you had lost
they had lost

Future

perderé
I shall/will lose
you will lose
he/she/it will lose
we shall/will lose
you will lose
they will lose

Future perfect

habré perdido
I shall/will have lost
you will have lost
he/she/it will have lost
we shall/will have lost
you will have lost
they will have lost

Conditional

Present

perdería
I should/would lose
you would lose
he/she/it would lose
we should/would lose
you would lose
they would lose

Perfect

habría perdido
I should/would have lost
you would have lost
he/she/it would have lost
we should/would have lost
you would have lost
they would have lost

Subjunctive

Present

pierda
I lose
you lose
he/she/it loses
we lose
you lose
they lose

Present perfect

haya perdido
I have lost
you have lost
he/she/it has lost
we have lost
you have lost
they have lost

Past

perdiera o perdiese
I lost
you lost
he/she/it lost
we lost
you lost
they lost

Past perfect

hubiera o hubiese perdido
I had lost
you had lost
he/she/it had lost
we had lost
you had lost
they had lost

Imperative

let me lose	***no existe (déjame perder)***
lose	***pierde tú***
let him/her/it lose	***pierda él/ella/ello***
let us (let's) lose	***perdamos nosotros***
lose	***perded vosotros***
let them lose	***pierdan ellos***

Impersonal forms

Infinitive

perder
to lose

Perfect Infinitive

haber perdido
to have lost

Gerund

perdiendo
losing

Perfect Gerund

habiendo perdido
having lost

Participle

perdido
lost

Perfect Participle

habiendo perdido
having lost

MAKE · MADE · MADE

HACER, FABRICAR

Indicative

Present

hago
I make
you make
he/she/it makes
we make
you make
they make

Present perfect

he hecho
I have made
you have made
he/she/it has made
we have made
you have made
they have made

Past

hacía/hice
I made
you made
he/she/it made
we made
you made
they made

Past perfect

había/hube hecho
I had made
you had made
he/she/it had made
we had made
you had made
they had made

Future

haré
I shall/will make
you will make
he/she/it will make
we shall/will make
you will make
they will make

Future perfect

habré hecho
I shall/will have made
you will have made
he/she/it will have made
we shall/will have made
you will have made
they will have made

Conditional

Present

haría
I should/would make
you would make
he/she/it would make
we should/would make
you would make
they would make

Perfect

habría hecho
I should/would have made
you would have made
he/she/it would have made
we should/would have made
you would have made
they would have made

Subjunctive

Present

haga
I make
you make
he/she/it makes
we make
you make
they make

Present perfect

haya hecho
I have made
you have made
he/she/it has made
we have made
you have made
they have made

Past

hiciera o hiciese
I made
you made
he/she/it made
we made
you made
they made

Past perfect

hubiera o hubiese hecho
I had made
you had made
he/she/it had made
we had made
you had made
they had made

Imperative

let me make	***no existe (déjame hacer)***
make	***haz tú***
let him/her/it make	***haga él/ella/ello***
let us (let's) make	***hagamos***
make	***haced***
let them make	***hagan ellos***

Impersonal forms

Infinitive

hacer
to make

Perfect Infinitive

haber hecho
to have made

Gerund

haciendo
making

Perfect Gerund

habiendo hecho
having made

Participle

hecho
made

Perfect Participle

habiendo hecho
having made

MEAN · MEANT · MEANT

SIGNIFICAR, QUERER DECIR

Indicative

Present

quiero decir
I mean
you mean
he/she/it means
we mean
you mean
they mean

Present perfect

he querido decir
I have meant
you have meant
he/she/it has meant
we have meant
you have meant
they have meant

Past

quería/quise decir
I meant
you meant
he/she/it meant
we meant
you meant
they meant

Past perfect

había/hube querido decir
I had meant
you had meant
he/she/it had meant
we had meant
you had meant
they had meant

Future

querré decir
I shall/will mean
you will mean
he/she/it will mean
we shall/will mean
you will mean
they will mean

Future perfect

habré querido decir
I shall/will have meant
you will have meant
he/she/it will have meant
we shall/will have meant
you will have meant
they will have meant

Conditional

Present

querría decir
I should/would mean
you would mean
he/she/it would mean
we should/would mean
you would mean
they would mean

Perfect

habría querido decir
I should/would have meant
you would have meant
he/she/it would have meant
we should/would have meant
you would have meant
they would have meant

Subjunctive

Present

quiera decir
I mean
you mean
he/she/it means
we mean
you mean
they mean

Present perfect

haya querido decir
I have meant
you have meant
he/she/it has meant
we have meant
you have meant
they have meant

Past

quisiera o quisiese decir
I meant
you meant
he/she/it meant
we meant
you meant
they meant

Past perfect

hubiera o hubiese querido decir
I had meant
you had meant
he/she/it had meant
we had meant
you had meant
they had meant

Imperative

let me mean	***no existe (déjame querer decir)***
mean	***quiere decir tú***
let him/her/it mean	***quiera decir él/ella/ello***
let us (let's) mean	***queramos decir nosotros***
mean	***quered decir vosotros***
let them mean	***quieran decir ellos***

Impersonal forms

Infinitive

querer decir
to mean

Perfect Infinitive

haber querido decir
to have meant

Gerund

queriendo decir
meaning

Perfect Gerund

habiendo querido decir
having meant

Participle

querido decir
meant

Perfect Participle

habiendo querido decir

MEET · MET · MET

ENCONTRARSE, CONOCER, PRESENTAR, TOPARSE CON

Indicative

Present

me encuentro
I meet
you meet
he/she/it meets
we meet
you meet
they meet

Present perfect

me he encontrado
I have met
you have met
he/she/it has met
we have met
you have met
they have met

Past

me encontraba/ encontré
I met
you met
he/she/it met
we met
you met
they met

Past perfect

me había/hube encontrado
I had met
you had met
he/she/it had met
we had met
you had met
they had met

Future

me encontraré
I shall/will meet
you will meet
he/she/it will meet
we shall/will meet
you will meet
they will meet

Future perfect

me habré encontrado
I shall/will have met
you will have met
he/she/it will have met
we shall/will have met
you will have met
they will have met

Conditional

Present

me encontraría
I should/would meet
you would meet
he/she/it would meet
we should/would meet
you would meet
they would meet

Perfect

me habría encontrado
I should/would have met
you would have met
he/she/it would have met
we should/would have met
you would have met
they would have met

Subjunctive

Present

me encuentre
I meet
you meet
he/she/it meets
we meet
you meet
they meet

Present perfect

me haya encontrado
I have met
you have met
he/she/it has met
we have met
you have met
they have met

Past

me encontrara o encontrase
I met
you met
he/she/it met
we met
you met
they met

Past perfect

me hubiera o hubiese encontrado
I had met
you had met
he/she/it had met
we had met
you had met
they had met

Imperative

let me meet	***no existe (déjame encontrarme)***
meet	***encuéntrate tú***
let him/her/it meet	***encuéntrese él/ella/ello***
let us (let's) meet	***encontrémonos nosotros***
meet	***encontraos vosotros***
let them meet	***encuéntrense ellos***

Impersonal forms

met

Infinitive

encontrarse
to meet

Perfect Infinitive

haber encontrado
to have met

Gerund

encontrándose
meeting

Perfect Gerund

habiendo encontrado
having met

Participle

encontrado

Perfect Participle

habiendo encontrado

MOW · MOWED · MOWN/MOWED

SEGAR, CORTAR EL CÉSPED

Indicative

Present

siego
I mow
you mow
he/she/it mows
we mow
you mow
they mow

Present perfect

he segado
I have mowed/mown
you have mowed/mown
he/she/it has mowed/mown
we have mowed/mown
you have mowed/mown
they have mowed/mown

Past

segaba/segué
I mowed
you mowed
he/she/it mowed
we mowed
you mowed
they mowed

Past perfect

había/hube segado
I had mowed/mown
you had mowed/mown
he/she/it had mowed/mown
we had mowed/mown
you had mowed/mown
they had mowed/mown

Future

segaré
I shall/will mow
you will mow
he/she/it will mow
we shall/will mow
you will mow
they will mow

Future perfect

habré segado
I shall/will have mowed/mown
you will have mowed/mown
he/she/it will have mowed/mown
we shall/will have mowed/mown
you will have mowed/mown
they will have mowed/mown

Conditional

Present

segaría
I should/would mow
you would mow
he/she/it would mow
we should/would mow
you would mow
they would mow

Perfect

habría segado
I should/would have mowed/mown
you would have mowed/mown
he/she/it would have mowed/mown
we should/would have mowed/mown
you would have mowed/mown
they would have mowed/mown

Subjunctive

Present

siegue
I mow
you mow
he/she/it mows
we mow
you mow
they mow

Present perfect

haya segado
I have mowed/mown
you have mowed/mown
he/she/it has mowed/ mown
we have mowed/mown
you have mowed/mown
they have mowed/mown

Past

segara o segase
I mowed
you mowed
he/she/it mowed
we mowed
you mowed
they mowed

Past perfect

hubiera o hubiese segado
I had mowed/mown
you had mowed/mown
he/she/it had mowed/mown
we had mowed/mown
you had mowed/mown
they had mowed/mown

Imperative

let me mow	***no existe (déjame segar)***
mow	***siega tú***
let him/her/it mow	***siegue él/ella/ello***
let us (let's) mow	***seguemos nosotros***
mow	***segad vosotros***
let them mow	***sieguen ellos***

Impersonal forms

Infinitive

segar
to mow

Perfect Infinitive

haber segado
to have mowed

Gerund

segando
mowing

Perfect Gerund

habiendo segado
having mowed/mown

Participle

segado
mowed/mown

Perfect Participle

habiendo segado
having mowed/mown

PAY · PAID · PAID

PAGAR

Indicative

Present

pago
I pay
you pay
he/she/it pays
we pay
you pay
they pay

Present perfect

he pagado
I have paid
you have paid
he/she/it has paid
we have paid
you have paid
they have paid

Past

pagaba/pagué
I paid
you paid
he/she/it paid
we paid
you paid
they paid

Past perfect

había/hube pagado
I had paid
you had paid
he/she/it had paid
we had paid
you had paid
they had paid

Future

pagaré
I shall/will pay
you will pay
he/she/it will pay
we shall/will pay
you will pay
they will pay

Future perfect

habré pagado
I shall/will have paid
you will have paid
he/she/it will have paid
we shall/will have paid
you will have paid
they will have paid

Conditional

Present

pagaría
I should/would pay
you would pay
he/she/it would pay
we should/would pay
you would pay
they would pay

Perfect

habría pagado
I should/would have paid
you would have paid
he/she/it would have paid
we should/would have paid
you would have paid
they would have paid

Subjunctive

Present

pague
I pay
you pay
he/she/it pays
we pay
you pay
they pay

Present perfect

haya pagado
I have paid
you have paid
he/she/it has paid
we have paid
you have paid
they have paid

Past

pagara o pagase
I paid
you paid
he/she/it paid
we paid
you paid
they paid

Past perfect

hubiera o hubiese pagado
I had paid
you had paid
he/she/it had paid
we had paid
you had paid
they had paid

Imperative

let me pay	***no existe (déjame pagar)***
pay	***paga tú***
let him/her/it pay	***pague él/ella/ello***
let us pay (let's) pay	***paguemos nosotros***
pay	***pagad vosotros***
let them pay	***paguen ellos***

Impersonal forms

Infinitive

pagar
to pay

Perfect Infinitive

haber pagado
to have paid

Gerund

pagando
paying

Perfect Gerund

habiendo pagado
having paid

Participle

pagado
paid

Perfect Participle

habiendo pagado
having paid

PUT · PUT · PUT

PONER, COLOCAR

Indicative

Present

pongo
I put
you put
he/she/it puts
we put
you put
they put

Present perfect

he puesto
I have put
you have put
he/she/it has put
we have put
you have put
they have put

Past

ponía/puse
I put
you put
he/she/it put
we put
you put
they put

Past perfect

había/hube puesto
I had put
you had put
he/she/it had put
we had put
you had put
they had put

Future

pondré
I shall/will put
you will put
he/she/it will put
we shall/will put
you will put
they will put

Future perfect

habré puesto
I shall/will have put
you will have put
he/she/it will have put
we shall/will have put
youk will have put
they will have put

Conditional

Present

pondría
I should/would put
you would put
he/she/it would put
we should/would put
you would put
they would put

Perfect

habría puesto
I should/would have put
you would have put
he/she/it would have put
we should/would have put
you would have put
they would have put

Subjunctive

Present

ponga
I put
you put
he/she/it puts
we put
you put
they put

Present perfect

haya puesto
I have put
you have put
he/she/it has put
we have put
you have put
they have put

Past

pusiera o pusiese
I put
you put
he/she/it put
we put
you put
they put

Past perfect

hubiera o hubiese puesto
I had put
you had put
he/she/it had put
we had put
you had put
they had put

Imperative

let me put	***no existe (déjame poner)***
put	***pon tú***
let him/her/it put	***ponga él/ella/ello***
let us (let's) put	***pongamos nosotros***
put	***poned vosotros***
let them put	***pongan ellos***

Impersonal forms

Infinitive

poner
to put

Perfect Infinitive

haber puesto
to have put

Gerund

poniendo
putting

Perfect Gerund

habiendo puesto
having put

Participle

puesto
put

Perfect Participle

habiendo puesto
having put

QUIT · QUIT/QUITTED · QUIT/QUITTED

ABANDONAR, DEJAR, IRSE, RETIRARSE

Indicative

Present

abandono
I quit
you quit
he/she/it quits
we quit
you quit
they quit

Present perfect

he abandonado
I have quit/quitted
you have quit/quitted
he/she/it has quit/quitted
we have quit/quitted
you have quit/quitted
they have quit/quitted

Past

abandonaba/ abandoné
I quit/quitted
you quit/quitted
he/she/it quit/quitted
we quit/quitted
you quit/quitted
they quit/quitted

Past perfect

había/hube abandonado
I had quit/quitted
you had quit/quitted
he/she/it had quit/quitted
we had quit/quitted
you had quit/quitted
they had quit/quitted

Future

abandonaré
I shall/will quit
you will quit
he/she/it will quit
we shall/will quit
you will quit
they will quit

Future perfect

habré abandonado
I shall/will have quit/quitted
you will have quit/quitted
he/she/it will have quit/quitted
we shall/will have quit/quitted
you will have quit/quitted
they will have quit/quitted

Conditional

Present

abandonaría
I should/would quit
you would quit
he/she/it would quit
we should/would quit
you would quit
they would quit

Perfect

habría abandonado
I should/would have quit/quitted
you would have quit/quitted
he/she/it would have quit/quitted
we should/would have quit/quitted
you would have quit/quitted
they would have quit/quitted

Subjunctive

Present

abandone
I quit
you quit
he/she/it quits
we quit
you quit
they quit

Present perfect

haya abandonado
I have quit/quitted
you have quit/quitted
he/she/it has quit/quitted
we have quit/quitted
you have quit/quitted
they have quit/quitted

Past

abandonara o abandonase
I quit/quitted
you quit/quitted
he/she/it quit/quitted
we quit/quitted
you quit/quitted
they quit/quitted

Past perfect

hubiera o hubiese abandonado
I had quit/quitted
you had quit/quitted
he/she/it had quit/quitted
we had quit/quitted
you had quit/quitted
they had quit/quitted

Imperative

let me quit	***no existe (déjame abandonar)***
quit	***abandona tú***
let him/her/it quit	***abandone él/ella/ello***
let us (let's) quit	***abandonemos nosotros***
quit	***abandonad vosotros***
let them quit	***abandonen ellos***

Impersonal forms

Infinitive

abandonar
to quit

Perfect Infinitive

haber abandonado
to have quit/quitted

Gerund

abandonando
quitting

Perfect Gerund

habiendo abandonado
having quit/quitted

Participle

abandonado
quit/quitted

Perfect Participle

habiendo abandonado

READ · READ · READ

LEER

Indicative

Present

leo
I read
you read
he/she/it reads
we read
you read
they read

Present perfect

he leído
I have read
you have read
he/she/it has read
we have read
you have read
they have read

Past

leía/leí
I read
you read
he/she/it read
we read
you read
they read

Past perfect

había/hube leído
I had read
you had read
he/she/it had read
we had read
you had read
they had read

Future

leeré
I shall/will read
you will read
he/she/it will read
we shall/will read
you will read
they will read

Future perfect

habré leído
I shall/will have read
you will have read
he/she/it will have read
we shall/will have read
you will have read
they will have read

Conditional

Present

leería
I should/would read
you would read
he/she/it would read
we should/would read
you would read
they would read

Perfect

habría leído
I should/would have read
you would have read
he/she/it would have read
we should/would have read
you would have read
they would have read

Subjunctive

Present

lea
I read
you read
he/she/it reads
we read
you read
they read

Present perfect

haya leído
I have read
you have read
he/she/it has read
we have read
you have read
they have read

Past

leyera o leyese
I read
you read
he/she/it reads
we read
you read
they read

Past perfect

hubiera o hubiese leído
I had read
you had read
he/she/it had read
we had read
you had read
they had read

Imperative

let me read	***no existe (déjame leer)***
read	***lee tú***
let him/her/it read	***lea él/ella/ello***
let us (let's) read	***leamos nosotros***
read	***leed vosotros***
let them read	***lean ellos***

Impersonal forms

Infinitive

leer
to read

Perfect Infinitive

haber leído
to have read

Gerund

leyendo
reading

Perfect Gerund

habiendo leído
having read

Participle

leído
read

Perfect Participle

habiendo leído
having read

REND · RENT · RENT

RASGAR, DESGARRAR

Indicative

Present

rasgo
I rend
you rend
he/she/it rends
we rend
you rend
they rend

Present perfect

he rasgado
I have rent
you have rent
he/she/it has rent
we have rent
you have rent
they have rent

Past

rasgaba/rasgué
I rent
you rent
he/she/it rent
we rent
you rent
they rent

Past perfect

había/hube rasgado
I had rent
you had rent
he/she/it had rent
we had rent
you had rent
they had rent

Future

rasgaré
I shall/will rend
you will rend
he/she/it will rend
we shall/will rend
you will rend
they will rend

Future perfect

habré rasgado
I shall/will have rent
you will have rent
he/she/it will have rent
we shall/will have rent
you will have rent
they will have rent

Conditional

Present

rasgaría
I should/would rend
you would rend
he/she/it would rend
we should/would rend
you would rend
they would rend

Perfect

habría rasgado
I should/would have rent
you would have rent
he/she/it would have rent
we should/would have rent
you would have rent
they would have rent

Subjunctive

Present

rasgue
I rend
you rend
he/she/it rends
we rend
you rend
they rend

Present perfect

haya rasgado
I have rent
you have rent
he/she/it has rent
we have rent
you have rent
they have rent

Past

rasgara/rasgase
I rent
you rent
he/she/it rent
we rent
you rent
they rent

Past perfect

hubiera o hubiese rasgado
I had rent
you had rent
he/she/it had rent
we had rent
you had rent
they had rent

Imperative

let me rend	***no existe (déjame rasgar)***
rend	***rasga tú***
let him/her/it rend	***rasgue él/ella/ello***
let us (let's) rend	***rasguemos nosotros***
rend	***rasgad vosotros***
let them rend	***rasguen ellos***

Impersonal forms

Infinitive

rasgar
to rend

Perfect Infinitive

haber rasgado
to have rent

Gerund

rasgando
rending

Perfect Gerund

habiendo rasgado
having rent

Participle

rasgado
rent

Perfect Participle

habiendo rasgado
having rent

RID · RID · RID

LIBRAR DE, DESHACERSE, QUITARSE, LIMPIAR, DISIPAR

Indicative

Present

libro de
I rid
you rid
he/she/it rids
we rid
you rid
they rid

Present perfect

he librado de
I have rid
you have rid
he/she/it has rid
we have rid
you have rid
they have rid

Past

libraba/libré de
I rid
you rid
he/she/it rid
we rid
you rid
they rid

Past perfect

había/hube librado de
I had rid
you had rid
he/she/it had rid
we had rid
you had rid
they had rid

Future

libraré de
I shall/will rid
you will rid
he/she/it will rid
we shall/will rid
you will rid
they will rid

Future perfect

habré librado de
I shall/will have rid
you will have rid
he/she/it will have rid
we shall/will have rid
you will have rid
they will have rid

Conditional

Present

libraría de
I should/would rid
you would rid
he/she/it would rid
we should/would rid
you would rid
they would rid

Perfect

habría librado de
I should/would have rid
you would have rid
he/she/it would have rid
we should/would have rid
you would have rid
they would have rid

Subjunctive

Present

libre de
I rid
you rid
he/she/it rids
we rid
you rid
they rid

Present perfect

haya librado de
I have rid
you have rid
he/she/it has rid
we have rid
you have rid
they have rid

Past

librara o librase de
I rid
you rid
he/she/it rid
we rid
you rid
they rid

Past perfect

hubiera o hubiese librado de
I had rid
you had rid
he/she/it had rid
we had rid
you had rid

Imperative

they had rid
let me rid
rid
let him/her/it rid
let us (let's) rid
rid

let them rid
no existe (déjame librarme de)
libra tú de
libre él/ella/ello de
libremos de

Impersonal forms

librad de
libren de

librado de
rid

Infinitive

librar de
to rid

Perfect Infinitive

haber librado de
to have rid

Gerund

librando de
ridding

Perfect Gerund

habiendo librado de
having rid

Participle

Perfect Participle

RIDE · RODE · RIDDEN

CABALGAR, MONTAR

Indicative

Present

cabalgo
I ride
you ride
he/she/it rides
we ride
you ride
they ride

Present perfect

he cabalgado
I have ridden
you have ridden
he/she/it has ridden
we have ridden
you have ridden
they have ridden

Past

cabalgaba/cabalgué
I rode
you rode
he/she/it rode
we rode
you rode
they rode

Past perfect

había/hube cabalgado
I had ridden
you had ridden
he/she/it had ridden
we had ridden
you had ridden
they had ridden

Future

cabalgaré
I shall/will ride
you will ride
he/she/it will ride
we shall/will ride
you will ride
they will ride

Future perfect

habré cabalgado
I shall/will have ridden
you will have ridden
he/she/it will have ridden
we shall/will have ridden
you will have ridden
they will have ridden

Conditional

Present

cabalgaría
I should/would ride
you would ride
he/she/it would ride
we should/would ride
you would ride
they would ride

Perfect

habría cabalgado
I should/would have ridden
you would have ridden
he/she/it would have ridden
we should/would have ridden
you would have ridden
they would have ridden

Subjunctive

Present

cabalgue
I ride
you ride
he/she/it rides
we ride
you ride
they ride

Present perfect

haya cabalgado
I have ridden
you have ridden
he/she/it has ridden
we have ridden
you have ridden
they have ridden

Past

cabalgara o cabalgase
I rode
you rode
he/she/it rode
we rode
you rode
they rode

Past perfect

hubiera o hubiese cabalgado
I had ridden
you had ridden
he/she/it had ridden
we had ridden
you had ridden

Imperative

they had ridden
let me ride
ride
let him/her/it ride
let us ride (let's) ride
ride

let them ride
no existe (déjame cabalgar)
cabalga tú
cabalgue él/ella /ello
cabalguemos nosotros
cabalgad vosotros

Impersonal forms

cabalguen ellos

ridden

Infinitive

cabalgar
to ride

Perfect Infinitive

haber cabalgado
to have ridden

Gerund

cabalgando
riding

Perfect Gerund

habiendo cabalgado
having ridden

Participle

cabalgado

Perfect Participle

habiendo cabalgado

RING · RANG · RUNG

SONAR, REPICAR , TAÑER , TOCAR EL TIMBRE

Indicative

Present

sueno
I ring
you ring
he/she/it rings
we ring
you ring
they ring

Present perfect

he sonado
I have rung
you have rung
he/she/it has rung
we have rung
you have rung
they have rung

Past

sonaba/soné
I rang
you rang
he/she/it rang
we rang
you rang
they rang

Past perfect

había/hube sonado
I had rung
you had rung
he/she/it had rung
we had rung
you had rung
they had rung

Future

sonaré
I shall/will ring
you will ring
he/she/it will ring
we shall/will ring
you will ring
they will ring

Future perfect

habré sonado
I shall/will have rung
you will have rung
he/she/it will have rung
we shall/will have rung
you will have rung
they will have rung

Conditional

Present

sonaría
I should/would ring
you would ring
he/she/it would ring
we should/would ring
you would ring
they would ring

Perfect

habría sonado
I should/would have rung
you would have rung
he/she/it would have rung
we should/would have rung
you would have rung
they would have rung

Subjunctive

Present

suene
I ring
you ring
he/she/it rings
we ring
you ring
they ring

Present perfect

haya sonado
I have rung
you have rung
he/she/it has rung
we have rung
you have rung
they have rung

Past

sonara o sonase
I rang
you rang
he/she/it rang
we rang
you rang
they rang

Past perfect

hubiera o hubiese sonado
I had rung
you had rung
he/she/it had rung
we had rung
you had rung
they had rung

Imperative

let me ring	***no existe (déjame sonar)***
ring	***suena tú***
let him/her/it ring	***suene él/ella/ello***
let us (let's) ring	***sonemos nosotros***
ring	***sonad vosotros***
let them ring	***suenen ellos***

Impersonal forms

Infinitive

sonar
to ring

Perfect Infinitive

haber sonado
to have rung

Gerund

sonando
ringing

Perfect Gerund

habiendo sonado
having rung

Participle

sonado
rung

Perfect Participle

habiendo sonado
having rung

RISE · ROSE · RISEN

ELEVAR, LEVANTAR, SUBIR, SALIR (SOL)

Indicative

Present

elevo
I rise
you rise
he/she/it rises
we rise
you rise
they rise

Present perfect

he elevado
I have risen
you have risen
he/she/it has risen
we have risen
you have risen
they have risen

Past

elevaba/elevé
I rose
you rose
he/she/it rose
we rose
you rose
they rose

Past perfect

había/hube elevado
I had risen
you had risen
he/she/it had risen
we had risen
you had risen
they had risen

Future

elevaré
I shall/will rise
you will rise
he/she/it will rise
we shall/will rise
you will rise
they will rise

Future perfect

habré elevado
I shall/will have risen
you will have risen
he/she/it will have risen
we shall/will have risen
you will have risen
they will have risen

Conditional

Present

elevaría
I should/would rise
you would rise
he/she/it would rise
we should/would rise
you would rise
they would rise

Perfect

habría elevado
I should/would have risen
you would have risen
he/she/it would have risen
we should/would have risen
you would have risen
they would have risen

Subjunctive

Present

eleve
I rise
you rise
he/she/it rises
we rise
you rise
they rise

Present perfect

haya elevado
I have risen
you have risen
he/she/it has risen
we have risen
you have risen
they have risen

Past

elevara/elevase
I rose
you rose
he/she/it rose
we rose
you rose
they rose

Past perfect

hubiera/hubiese elevado
I had risen
you had risen
he/she/it had risen
we had risen
you had risen
they had risen

Imperative

let me rise	***no existe (déjame elevar)***
rise	***eleva tú***
let him/her/it rise	***eleve él/ella/ello***
let us (let's) rise	***elevemos nosotros***
rise	***elevad vosotros***
let them rise	***eleven ellos***

Impersonal forms

Infinitive

elevar
to rise

Perfect Infinitive

haber elevado
to have risen

Gerund

elevando
rising

Perfect Gerund

habiendo elevado
having risen

Participle

elevado
risen

Perfect Participle

habiendo elevado
having risen

RUN · RAN · RUN

CORRER

Indicative

Present

corro
I run
you run
he/she/it runs
we run
you run
they run

Present perfect

he corrido
I have run
you have run
he/she/it has run
we have run
you have run
they have run

Past

corría/corrí
I ran
you ran
he/she/it ran
we ran
you ran
they ran

Past perfect

había/hube corrido
I had run
you had run
he/she/it had run
we had run
you had run
they had run

Future

correré
I shall/will run
you will run
he/she/it will run
we shall/will run
you will run
they will run

Future perfect

habré corrido
I shall/will have run
you will have run
he/she/it will have run
we shall/will have run
you will have run
they will have run

Conditional

Present

correría
I should/would run
you would run
he/she/it would run
we should/would run
you would run
they would run

Perfect

habría corrido
I should/would have run
you would have run
he/she/it would have run
we should/would have run
you would have run
they would have run

Subjunctive

Present

corra
I run
you run
he/she/it runs
we run
you run
they run

Present perfect

haya corrido
I have run
you have run
he/she/it has run
we have run
you have run
they have run

Past

corriera/corriese
I ran
you ran
he/she/it ran
we ran
you ran
they ran

Past perfect

hubiera/hubiese corrido
I had run
you had run
he/she/it had run
we had run
you had run
they had run

Imperative

let me run	***no existe (déjame correr)***
run	***corre tú***
let him/her/it run	***corra él/ella/ello***
let us (let's) run	***corramos nosotros***
run	***corred vosotros***
let them run	***corran ellos***

Impersonal forms

Infinitive

correr
to run

Perfect Infinitive

haber corrido
to have run

Gerund

corriendo
running

Perfect Gerund

habiendo corrido
having run

Participle

corrido
run

Perfect Participle

habiendo corrido
having run

SAW · SAWED · SAWED/SAWN

SERRAR

Indicative

Present	Present perfect
sierro	***he serrado***
I saw	I have sawed/sawn
you saw	you have sawed/sawn
he/she/it saws	he/she/it has sawed/sawn
we saw	we have sawed/sawn
you saw	you have sawed/sawn
they saw	they have sawed/sawn

Past	Past perfect
serraba/serré	***había/hube serrado***
I sawed	I had sawed/sawn
you sawed	you had sawed/sawn
he/she/it sawed	he/she/it had sawed/sawn
we sawed	we had sawed/sawn
you sawed	you had sawed/sawn
they sawed	they had sawed/sawn

Future	Future perfect
serraré	***habré serrado***
I shall/will saw	I shall/will have sawed/sawn
you will saw	you will have sawed/sawn
he/she/it will saw	he/she/it will have sawed/sawn
we shall/will saw	we shall/will have sawed/sawn
you will saw	you will have sawed/sawn
they will saw	they will have sawed/sawn

Conditional

Present	Perfect
serraría	***habría serrado***
I should/would saw	I should/would have sawed/sawn
you would saw	you would have sawed/sawn
he/she/it would saw	he/she/it would have sawed/sawn
we should/would saw	we shouldl/would have sawed/sawn
you would saw	you would have sawed/sawn
they would saw	they would have sawed/sawn

Subjunctive

Present	Present perfect
sierre	***haya serrado***
I saw	I have sawed/sawn
you saw	you have sawed/sawn
he/she/it saws	he/she/it has sawed/sawn
we saw	we have sawed/sawn
you saw	you have sawed/sawn
they saw	they have sawed/sawn

Past	Past perfect
serrara o serrase	***hubiera o hubiese serrado***
I sawed	I had sawed/sawn
you sawed	you had sawed/sawn
he/she/it sawed	he/she/it had sawed/sawn
we sawed	we had sawed/sawn
you sawed	you had sawed/sawn
they sawed	they had sawed/sawn

Imperative

let me saw	***no existe (déjame serrar)***
saw	***sierra tú***
let him/her/it saw	***sierre él/ella/ello***
let us (let's) saw	***serremos nosotros***
saw	***serrad vosotros***
let them saw	***sierren ellos***

Impersonal forms

Infinitive	Perfect Infinitive
serrar	***haber serrado***
to saw	to have sawed/sawn
Gerund	**Perfect Gerund**
serrando	***habiendo serrado***
sawing	having sawed/sawn
Participle	**Perfect Participle**
serrado	***habiendo serrado***
sawed/sawn	having sawed/sawn

SAY · SAID · SAID

DECIR

Indicative

Present

digo
I say
you say
he/she/it says
we say
you say
they say

Present perfect

he dicho
I have said
you have said
he/she/it has said
we have said
you have said
they have said

Past

decía/dije
I said
you said
he/she/it said
we said
you said
they said

Past perfect

había/hube dicho
I had said
you had said
he/she/it had said
we had said
you had said
they had said

Future

diré
I shall/will say
you will say
he/she/it will say
we shall/will say
you will say
they will say

Future perfect

habré dicho
I shall/will have said
you will have said
he/she/it will have said
we shall/will have said
you will have said
they will have said

Conditional

Present

diría
I should/would say
you would say
he/she/it would say
we should/would say
you would say
they would say

Perfect

habría dicho
I should/would have said
you would have said
he/she/it would have said
we should/would have said
you would have said
they would have said

Subjunctive

Present

diga
I say
you say
he/she/it says
we say
you say
they say

Present perfect

haya dicho
I have said
you have said
he/she/it has said
we have said
you have said
they have said

Past

dijera o dijese
I said
you said
he/she/it said
we said
you said
they said

Past perfect

hubiera o hubiese dicho
I had said
you had said
he/she/it had said
we had said
you had said
they had said

Imperative

let me say	***no existe (déjame decir)***
say	***di tú***
let him/her/it say	***diga él/ella/ello***
let us (let's) say	***digamos nosotros***
say	***decid vosotros***
let them say	***digan ellos***

Impersonal forms

Infinitive

decir
to say

Perfect Infinitive

haber dicho
to have said

Gerund

diciendo
saying

Perfect Gerund

habiendo dicho
having said

Participle

dicho
said

Perfect Participle

habiendo dicho
having said

SEE · SAW · SEEN

VER

Indicative

Present

veo
I see
you see
he/she/it sees
we see
you see
they see

Present perfect

he visto
I have seen
you have seen
he/she/it has seen
we have seen
you have seen
they have seen

Past

veía/vi
I saw
you saw
he/she/it saw
we saw
you saw
they saw

Past perfect

había/hube visto
I had seen
you had seen
he/she/it had seen
we had seen
you had seen
they had seen

Future

veré
I shall/will see
you will see
he/she/it will see
we shall/will see
you will see
they will see

Future perfect

habré visto
I shall/will have seen
you will have seen
he/she/it will have seen
we shall/will have seen
you will have seen
they will have seen

Conditional

Present

vería
I should/would see
you would see
he/she/it would see
we should/would see
you would see
they would see

Perfect

habría visto
I should/would have seen
you would have seen
he/she/it would have seen
we should/would have seen
you would have seen
they would have seen

Subjunctive

Present

vea
I see
you see
he/she/it sees
we see
you see
they see

Present perfect

haya visto
I have seen
you have seen
he/she/it has seen
we have seen
you have seen
they have seen

Past

viera/viese
I saw
you saw
he/she/it saw
we saw
you saw
they saw

Past perfect

hubiera/hubiese visto
I had seen
you had seen
he/she/it had seen
we had seen
you had seen
they had seen

Imperative

let me see	***no existe (déjame ver)***
see	***ve tú***
let him/her/it see	***vea él/ella/ello***
let us (let's) see	***veamos nosotros***
see	***ved vosotros***
let them see	***vean ellos***

Impersonal forms

Infinitive

ver
to see

Perfect Infinitive

haber visto
to have seen

Gerund

viendo
seeing

Perfect Gerund

habiendo visto
having seen

Participle

visto
seen

Perfect Participle

habiendo visto
having seen

SEEK · SOUGHT · SOUGHT

BUSCAR, PEDIR AYUDA, IR EN BUSCA DE ALGO, TRATAR DE LOGRAR

Indicative

Present

busco
I seek
you seek
he/she/it seeks
we seek
you seek
they seek

Present perfect

he buscado
I have sought
you have sought
he/she/it has sought
we have sought
you have sought
they have sought

Past

buscaba/busqué
I sought
you sought
he/she/it sought
we sought
you sought
they sought

Past perfect

había/hube buscado
I had sought
you had sought
he/she/it had sought
we had sought
you had sought
they had sought

Future

buscaré
I shall/will seek
you will seek
he/she/it will seek
we shall/will seek
you will seek
they will seek

Future perfect

habré buscado
I shall/will have sought
you will have sought
he/she/it will have sought
we shall/will have sought
you will have sought
they will have sought

Conditional

Present

buscaría
I should/would seek
you would seek
he/she/it would seek
we should/would seek
you would seek
they would seek

Perfect

habría buscado
I should/would have sought
you would have sought
he/she/it would have sought
we should/would have sought
you would have sought
they would have sought

Subjunctive

Present

busque
I seek
you seek
he/she/it seeks
we seek
you seek
they seek

Present perfect

haya buscado
I have sought
you have sought
he/she/it has sought
we have sought
you have sought
they have sought

Past

buscara o buscase
I sought
you sought
he/she/it sought
we sought
you sought
they sought

Past perfect

hubiera o hubiese buscado
I had sought
you had sought
he/she/it had sought
we had sought
you had sought
they had sought

Imperative

let me seek	***no existe (déjame buscar)***
seek	***busca tú***
let him/her/it seek	***busque él/ella/ello***
let us (let's) seek	***busquemos nosotros***
seek	***buscad vosotros***
let them seek	***busquen ellos***

Impersonal forms

Infinitive

buscar
to seek

Perfect Infinitive

haber buscado
to have sought

Gerund

buscando
seeking

Perfect Gerund

habiendo buscado
having sought

Participle

buscado
sought

Perfect particple

habiendo buscado
having sought

SEND · SENT · SENT

ENVIAR, MANDAR

Indicative

Present

envío
I send
you send
he/she/it sends
we send
you send
they send

Present perfect

he enviado
I have sent
you have sent
he/she/it has sent
we have sent
you have sent
they have sent

Past

enviaba/envié
I sent
you sent
he/she/it sent
we sent
you sent
they sent

Past perfect

había/hube enviado
I had sent
you had sent
he/she/it had sent
we had sent
you had sent
they had sent

Future

enviaré
I shall/will send
you will send
he/she/it will send
we shall/will send
you will send
they will send

Future perfect

habré enviado
I shall/will have sent
you will have sent
he/she/it will have sent
we shall/will have sent
you will have sent
they will have sent

Conditional

Present

enviaría
I should/would send
you would send
he/she/it would send
we should/would send
you would send
they would send

Perfect

habría enviado
I should/would have sent
you would have sent
he/she/it would have sent
we should/would have sent
you would have sent
they would have sent

Subjunctive

Present

envíe
I send
you send
he/she/it sends
we send
you send
they send

Present perfect

haya enviado
I have sent
you have sent
he/she/it has sent
we have sent
you have sent
they have sent

Past

enviara o enviase
I sent
you sent
he/she/it sent
we sent
you sent
they sent

Past perfect

hubiera o hubiese enviado
I had sent
you had sent
he/she/it had sent
we had sent
you had sent
they had sent

Imperative

let me send	***no existe (déjame enviar)***
send	***envía tú***
let him/her/it send	***envíe él/ella/ello***
let us (let's) send	***enviemos nosotros***
send	***enviad vosotros***
let them send	***envíen ellos***

Impersonal forms

Infinitive

enviar
to send

Perfect Infinitive

haber enviado
to have sent

Gerund

enviando
sending

Perfect Gerund

habiendo enviado
having sent

Participle

enviado
sent

Perfect Participle

habiendo enviado
having sent

SET · SET · SET

PONER, COLOCAR, PREPARAR, FIJAR, ACORDAR, ESTABLECER, ASIGNAR.

Indicative

Present

coloco
I set
you set
he/she/it sets
we set
you set
they set

Present perfect

he colocado
I have set
you have set
he/she/it has set
we have set
you have set
they have set

Past

colocaba/coloqué
I set
you set
he/she/it set
we set
you set
they set

Past perfect

había/hube colocado
I had set
you had set
he/she/it had set
we had set
you had set
they had set

Future

colocaré
I shall/will set
you will set
he/she/it will set
we shall/will set
you will set
they will set

Future perfect

habré colocado
I shall/will have set
you will have set
he/she/it will have set
we shall/will have set
you will have set
they will have set

Conditional

Present

colocaría
I should/would set
you would set
he/she/it would set
we should/would set
you would set
they would set

Perfect

habría colocado
I should/would have set
you would have set
he/she/it would have set
we should/would have set
you would have set
they would have set

Subjunctive

Present

coloque
I set
you set
he/she/it sets
we set
you set
they set

Present perfect

haya colocado
I have set
you have set
he/she/it has set
we have set
you have set
they have set

Past

colocara o colocase
I set
you set
he/she/it set
we set
you set
they set

Past perfect

hubiera o hubiese colocado
I had set
you had set
he/she/it had set
we had set
you had set
they had set

Imperative

let me set	***no existe (déjame colocar)***
set	***coloca tú***
let him/her/it set	***coloque él/ella/ello***
let us set (let's) set	***coloquemos nosotros***
set	***colocad vosotros***
let them set	***coloquen ellos***

Impersonal forms

Infinitive

colocar
to set

Perfect Infinitive

haber colocado
to have set

Gerund

colocando
setting

Perfect Gerund

habiendo colocado
having set

Participle

colocado
set

Perfect Participle

habiendo colocado
having set

SEW · SEWED · SEWN

COSER

Indicative

Present

coso
I sew
you sew
he/she/it sews
we sew
you sew
they sew

Present perfect

he cosido
I have sewn
you have sewn
he/she/it has sewn
we have sewn
you have sewn
they have sewn

Past

cosía/cosí
I sewed
you sewed
he/she/it sewed
we sewed
you sewed
they sewed

Past perfect

había/hube cosido
I had sewn
you had sewn
he/she/it had sewn
we had sewn
you had sewn
they had sewn

Future

coseré
I shall/will sew
you will sew
he/she/it will sew
we shall/will sew
you will sew
they will sew

Future perfect

habré cosido
I shall/will have sewn
you will have sewn
he/she/it will have sewn
we shall/will have sewn
you will have sewn
they will have sewn

Conditional

Present

cosería
I should/would sew
you would sew
he/she/it would sew
we should/would sew
you would sew
they would sew

Perfect

habría cosido
I should/would have sewn
you would have sewn
he/she/it would have sewn
we should/would have sewn
you would have sewn
they would have sewn

Subjunctive

Present

cosa
I sew
you sew
he/she/it sews
we sew
you sew
they sew

Present perfect

haya cosido
I have sewn
you have sewn
he/she/it has sewn
we have sewn
you have sewn
they have sewn

Past

cosiera o cosiese
I sewed
you sewed
he/she/it sewed
we sewed
you sewed
they sewed

Past perfect

hubiera o hubiese cosido
I had sewn
you had sewn
he/she/it had sewn
we had sewn
you had sewn
they had sewn

Imperative

let me sew	***no existe (déjame coser)***
sew	***cose tú***
let him/her/it sew	***cosa él/ella/ello***
let us (let's) sew	***cosamos nosotros***
sew	***cosed vosotros***
let them sew	***cosan ellos***

Impersonal forms

Infinitive

coser
to sew

Perfect Infinitive

haber cosido
to have sewn

Gerund

cosiendo
sewing

Perfect Gerund

habiendo cosido
having sewn

Participle

cosido
sewn

Perfect Participle

habiendo cosido
having sewn

SHAKE · SHOOK · SHAKEN

AGITAR, REMOVER

Indicative

Present

agito
I shake
you shake
he/she/it shakes
we shake
you shake
they shake

Present perfect

he agitado
I have shaken
you have shaken
he/she/it has shaken
we have shaken
you have shaken
they have shaken

Past

agitaba/agité
I shook
you shook
he/she/it shook
we shook
you shook
they shook

Past perfect

había/hube agitado
I had shaken
you had shaken
he/she/it had shaken
we had shaken
you had shaken
they had shaken

Future

agitaré
I shall/will shake
you will shake
he/she/it will shake
we shall/will shake
you will shake
they will shake

Future perfect

habré agitado
I shall/will have shaken
you will have shaken
he/she/it will have shaken
we shall/will have shaken
you will have shaken
they will have shaken

Conditional

Present

agitaría
I should/would shake
you would shake
he/she/it would shake
we should/would shake
you would shake
they would shake

Perfect

habría agitado
I should/would have shaken
you would have shaken
he/she/it would have shaken
we should/would have shaken
you would have shaken
they would have shaken

Subjunctive

Present

agite
I shake
you shake
he/she/it shakes
we shake
you shake
they shake

Present perfect

haya agitado
I have shaken
you have shaken
he/she/it has shaken
we have shaken
you have shaken
they have shaken

Past

agitara o agitase
I shook
you shook
he/she/it shook
we shook
you shook
they shook

Past perfect

hubiera o hubiese agitado
I had shaken
you had shaken
he/she/it had shaken
we had shaken
you had shaken
they had shaken

Imperative

let me shake	***no existe (déjame agitar)***
shake	***agita tú***
let thim/her/it shake	***agite él/ella/ello***
let us (let's) shake	***agitemos nosotros***
shake	***agitad vosotros***
let them shake	***agiten ellos***

Impersonal forms

Infinitive

agitar
to shake

Perfect Infinitive

haber agitado
to have shaken

Gerund

agitando
shaking

Perfect Gerund

habiendo agitado
having shaken

Participle

agitado
shaken

Perfect Participle

habiendo agitado
having shaken

SHAVE · SHAVED · SHAVED/SHAVEN

AFEITAR

Indicative

Present

afeito
I shave
you shave
he/she/it shaves
we shave
you shave
they shave

Present perfect

he afeitado
I have shaved/shaven
you have shaved/shaven
he/she/it has shaved/shaven
we have shaved/shaven
you have shaved/shaven
they have shaved/shaven

Past

afeitaba/afeité
I shaved
you shaved
he/she/it shaved
we shaved
you shaved
they shaved

Past perfect

había/hube afeitado
I had shaved/shaven
you had shaved/shaven
he/she/it had shaved/shaven
we had shaved/shaven
you had shaved/shaven
they had shaved/shaven

Future

afeitaré
I shall/will shave
you will shave
he/she/it will shave
we shall/will shave
you will shave
they will shave

Future perfect

habré afeitado
I shall/will have shaved/shaven
you will have shaved/shaven
he/she/will have shaved/shaven
we shall/will have shaved / shaven
you will have shaved/shaven
they will have shaved/shaven

Present

afeitaría
I should/would shave
you would shave
he/she/it would shave
we should/would shave
you would shave
they would shave

Perfect

habría afeitado
I should/would have shaved/ shaven
you would have shaved/shaven
he/she/it would have shaved/ shaven
we should/would have shaved/ shaven
you would have shaved/shaven
they would have shaved/shaven

Subjunctive

Present

afeite
I shave
you shave
he/she/it shaves
we shave
you shave
they shave

Present perfect

haya afeitado
I have shaved/shaven
you have shaved/shaven
he/she/it has shaved/shaven
we have shaved/shaven
you have shaved/shaven
they have shaved/shaven

Past

afeitara o afeitase
I shaved
you shaved
he/she/it shaved
we shaved
you shaved
they shaved

Past perfect

hubiera o hubiese afeitado
I had shaved/shaven
you had shaved/shaven
he/she/it had shaved/shaven
we had shaved/shaven
you had shaved/shaven
they had shaved/shaven

Imperative

let me shave	***no existe (déjame afeitar)***
shave	***afeita tú***
let him/her/it shave	***afeite él/ella/ello***
let us shave (let's) shave	***afeitemos nosotros***
shave	***afeitad vosotros***
let them shave	***afeiten ellos***

Impersonal forms

Infinitive

afeitar
to shave

Perfect Infinitive

haber afeitado
to have shaved/shaven

Gerund

afeitando
shaving

Perfect Gerund

habiendo afeitado
having shaved/shaven

Participle

afeitado
shaved/shaven

Perfect Participle

habiendo afeitado
having shaved/shaven

SHEAR · SHEARED · SHORN

ESQUILAR

Indicative

Present

esquilo
I shear
you shear
he/she/it shears
we shear
you shear
they shear

Present perfect

he esquilado
I have shorn
you have shorn
he/she/it has shorn
we have shorn
you have shorn
they have shorn

Past

esquilaba/esquilé
I sheared
you sheared
he/she/it sheared
we sheared
you sheared
they sheared

Past perfect

había/hube esquilado
I had shorn
you had shorn
he/she/it had shorn
we had shorn
you had shorn
they had shorn

Future

esquilaré
I shall/will shear
you will shear
he/she/it will shear
we shall/will shear
you will shear
they will shear

Future perfect

habré esquilado
I shall/will have shorn
you will have shorn
he/she/it will have shorn
we shall/will have shorn
you will have shorn
they will have shorn

Conditional

Present

esquilaría
I should/would shear
you would shear
he/she/it would shear
we should/would shear
you would shear
they would shear

Perfect

habría esquilado
I should/would have shorn
you would have shorn
he/she/it would have shorn
we should/would have shorn
you would have shorn
they would have shorn

Subjunctive

Present

esquile
I shear
you shear
he/she/it shears
we shear
you shear
they shear

Present perfect

haya esquilado
I have shorn
you have shorn
he/she/it has shorn
we have shorn
you have shorn
they have shorn

Past

esquilara o esquilase
I sheared
you sheared
he/she/it sheared
we sheared
you sheared
they sheared

Past perfect

hubiera o hubiese esquilado
I had shorn
you had shorn
he/she/it had shorn
we had shorn
you had shorn
they had shorn

Imperative

let me shear	***no existe (déjame esquilar)***
shear	***esquila tú***
let him/her/it shear	***esquile él/ella/ello***
let us (let's) shear	***esquilemos nosotros***
shear	***esquilad vosotros***
let them shear	***esquilen ellos***

Impersonal forms

Infinitive

esquilar
to shear

Perfect Infinitive

haber esquilado
to have shorn

Gerund

esquilando
shearing

Perfect Gerund

habiendo esquilado
having shorn

Participle

esquilado
shorn

Perfect Participle

habiendo esquilado
having shorn

SHED · SHED · SHED

DERRAMAR · VERTER

Indicative

Present

derramo
I shed
you shed
he/she/it sheds
we shed
you shed
they shed

Present perfect

he derramado
I have shed
you have shed
he/she/it has shed
we have shed
you have shed
they have shed

Past

derramaba/derramé
I shed
you shed
he/she/it shed
we shed
you shed
they shed

Past perfect

había/hube derramado
I had shed
you had shed
he/she/it had shed
we had shed
you had shed
they had shed

Future

derramaré
I shall/will shed
you will shed
he/she/it will shed
we shall/will shed
you will shed
they will shed

Future perfect

habré derramado
I shall/will have shed
you will have shed
he/she/it will have shed
we shall/will have shed
you will have shed
they will have shed

Conditional

Present

derramaría
I should/would shed
you would shed
he/she/it would shed
we should/would shed
you would shed
they would shed

Perfect

habría derramado
I should/would have shed
you would have shed
he/she/it would have shed
we should/would have shed
you would have shed
they would have shed

Subjunctive

Present

derrame
I shed
you shed
he/she/it sheds
we shed
you shed
they shed

Present perfect

they shed
haya derramado
I have shed
you have shed
he/she/it has shed
we have shed
you have shed

Past

derramara o derramase
I shed
you shed
he/she/it shed
we shed
you shed

Past perfect

they have shed
hubiera o hubiese derramado
I had shed
you had shed
he/she/it had shed
we had shed

Imperative

you had shed
they had shed
let me shed
shed
let him/her/it shed
let us (let's) shed

shed
let them shed
no existe (déjame derramar)
derrama tú
derrame él/ella/ello
derramemos nosotros

Impersonal forms

derramad vosotros
derramen ellos

derramado
shed

Infinitive

derramar
to shed

Perfect Infinitive

haber derramado
to have shed

Gerund

derramando
shedding

Perfect Gerund

habiendo derramado
having shed

Participle

Perfect Participle

SHINE · SHONE · SHONE

BRILLAR, RESPLANDECER

Indicative

Present

brillo
I shine
you shine
he/she/it shines
we shine
you shine
they shine

Present perfect

he brillado
I have shone
you have shone
he/she/it has shone
we have shone
you have shone
they have shone

Past

brillaba/brillé
I shone
you shone
he/she/it shone
we shone
you shone
they shone

Past perfect

había/hube brillado
I had shone
you had shone
he/she/it had shone
we had shone
you had shone
they had shone

Future

brillaré
I shall/will shine
you will shine
he/she/it will shine
we shall/will shine
you will shine
they will shine

Future perfect

habré brillado
I shall/will have shone
you will have shone
he/she/it will have shone
we shall/will have shone
you will have shone
they will have shone

Conditional

Present

brillaría
I should/would shine
you would shine
he/she/it would shine
we should/would shine
you would shine
they would shine

Perfect

habría brillado
I should/would have shone
you would have shone
he/she/it would have shone
we should/would have shone
you would have shone
they would have shone

Subjunctive

Present

brille
I shine
you shine
he/she/it shines
we shine
you shine
they shine

Present perfect

haya brillado
I have shone
you have shone
he/she/it has shone
we have shone
you have shone
they have shone

Past

brillara o brillase
I shone
you shone
he/she/it shone
we shone
you shone
they shone

Past perfect

hubiera o hubiese brillado
I had shone
you had shone
he/she/it had shone
we had shone
you had shone
they had shone

Imperative

let me shine	***no existe (déjame brillar)***
shine	***brilla tú***
let him/her/it shine	***brille él/ella/ello***
let us (let's) shine	***brillemos nosotros***
shine	***brillad vosotros***
let them shine	***brillen ellos***

Impersonal forms

Infinitive

brillar
to shine

Perfect Infinitive

haber brillado
to have shone

Gerund

brillando
shining

Perfect Gerund

habiendo brillado
having shone

Participle

brillado
shone

Perfect Participle

habiendo brillado
having shone

SHOE · SHOD · SHOD

HERRAR

Indicative

Present

hierro
I shoe
you shoe
he/she/it shoes
we shoe
you shoe
they shoe

Present perfect

he herrado
I have shod
you have shod
he/she/it has shod
we have shod
you have shod
they have shod

Past

herraba/herré
I shod
you shod
he/she/it shod
we shod
you shod
they shod

Past perfect

había/hube herrado
I had shod
you had shod
he/she/it had shod
we had shod
you had shod
they had shod

Future

herraré
I shall/will shoe
you will shoe
he/she/it will shoe
we shall/will shoe
you will shoe
they will shoe

Future perfect

habré herrado
I shall/will have shod
you will have shod
he/she/it will have shod
we shall/will have shod
you will have shod
they will have shod

Conditional

Present

herraría
I should/would shoe
you would shoe
he/she/it would shoe
we should/would shoe
you would shoe
they would shoe

Perfect

habría herrado
I should/would have shod
you would have shod
he/she/it would have shod
we should/would have shod
you would have shod
they would have shod

Subjunctive

Present

hierre
I shoe
you shoe
he/she/it shoes
we shoe
you shoe
they shoe

Present perfect

haya herrado
I have shod
you have shod
he/she/it has shod
we have shod
you have shod
they have shod

Past

herrara o herrase
I shod
you shod
he/she/it shod
we shod
you shod
they shod

Past perfect

hubiera o hubiese
I had shod
you had shod
he/she/it had shod
we had shod
you had shod
they had shod

Imperative

let me shoe	no existe (déjame herrar)
shoe	hierra tú
let him/her/it shoe	hierre él/ella/ello
let us (let's) shoe	herremos nosotros
shoe	herrad vosotros
let them shoe	hierren ellos

Impersonal forms

Infinitive

herrar
to shoe

Perfect Infinitive

haber herrado
to have shod

Gerund

herrando
shoeing

Perfect Gerund

habiendo herrado
having shod

Participle

herrado
shod

Perfect Participle

habiendo herrado
having shod

SHOOT · SHOT · SHOT
DISPARAR

Indicative

Present	Present perfect
disparo	***he disparado***
I shoot	I have shot
you shoot	you have shot
he/she/it shoots	he/she/it has shot
we shoot	we have shot
you shoot	you have shot
they shoot	they have shot

Past	Past perfect
disparaba/disparé	***había/hube disparado***
I shot	I had shot
you shot	you had shot
he/she/it shot	he/she/it had shot
we shot	we had shot
you shot	you had shot
they shot	they had shot

Future	Future perfect
dispararé	***habré disparado***
I shall/will shoot	I shall/will have shot
you will shoot	you will have shot
he/she/it will shoot	he/she/it will have shot
we shall/will shoot	we shall/will have shot
you will shoot	you will have shot
they will shoot	they will have shot

Conditional

Present	Perfect
dispararía	***habría disparado***
I should/would shoot	I should/would have shot
you would shoot	you would have shot
he/she/it would shoot	he/she/it would have shot
we should/would shoot	we should/would have shot
you would shoot	you would have shot
they would shoot	they would have shot

Subjunctive

Present	Present perfect
dispare	***haya disparado***
I shoot	I have shot
you shoot	you have shot
he/she/it shoots	he/she/it has shot
we shoot	we have shot
you shoot	you have shot
they shoot	they have shot

Past	Past perfect
disparara o disparase	***hubiera o hubiese disparado***
I shot	I had shot
you shot	you had shot
he/she/it shot	he/she/it had shot
we shot	we had shot
you shot	you had shot
they shot	

Imperative

they had shot	let them shoot
let me shoot	***no existe (déjame disparar)***
shoot	***dispara tú***
let him/her/it shoot	***dispare él/ella/ello***
let us (let's) shoot	***disparemos nosotros***
shoot	***disparad vosotros***

Impersonal forms

disparen ellos	shot
Infinitive	**Perfect Infinitive**
disparar	***haber disparado***
to shoot	to have shot
Gerund	**Perfect Gerund**
disparando	***habiendo disparado***
shooting	having shot
Participle	**Perfect Participle**
disparado	***habiendo disparado***

SHOW · SHOWED · SHOWN

MOSTRAR, ENSEÑAR

Indicative

Present

muestro
I show
you show
he/she/it shows
we show
you show
they show

Present perfect

he mostrado
I have shown
you have shown
he/she/it has shown
we have shown
you have shown
they have shown

Past

mostraba/mostré
I showed
you showed
he/she/it showed
we showed
you showed
they showed

Past perfect

había/hube mostrado
I had shown
you had shown
he/she/it had shown
we had shown
you had shown
they had shown

Future

mostraré
I shall/will show
you will show
he/she/it will show
we shall/will show
you will show
they will show

Future perfect

habré mostrado
I shall/will have shown
you will have shown
he/she/it will have shown
we shall/will have shown
you will have shown
they will have shown

Conditional

Present

mostraría
I should/would show
you would show
he/she/it would show
we should/would show
you would show
they would show

Perfect

habría mostrado
I should/would have shown
you would have shown
he/she/it would have shown
we should/would have shown
you would have shown
they would have shown

Subjunctive

Present

muestre
I show
you show
he/she/it shows
we show
you show
they show

Present perfect

haya mostrado
I have shown
you have shown
he/she/it has shown
we have shown
you have shown
they have shown

Past

mostrara o mostrase
I showed
you showed
he/she/it showed
we showed
you showed
they showed

Past perfect

hubiera o hubiese mostrado
I had shown
you had shown
he/she/it had shown
we had shown
you had shown
they had shown

Imperative

let me show	***no existe (déjame mostrar)***
show	***muestra tú***
let him/her/it show	***muestre él/ella/ello***
let us (let's) show	***mostremos nosotros***
show	***mostrad vosotros***
let them show	***muestren ellos***

Impersonal forms

Infinitive

mostrar
to show

Perfect Infinitive

haber mostrado
to have shown

Gerund

mostrando
showing

Perfect Gerund

habiendo mostrado
having shown

Participle

mostrado
shown

Perfect Participle

habiendo mostrado
having shown

SHRINK · SHRANK · SHRUNK

ENCOJER

Indicative

Present

encojo
I shink
you shrink
he/she/it shrinks
we shrink
you shrink
they shrink

Present perfect

he encogido
I have shrunk
you have shrunk
he/she/it has shrunk
we have shrunk
you have shrunk
they have shrunk

Past

encogía/encogí
I shrank
you shrank
he/she/it shrank
we shrank
you shrank
they shrank

Past perfect

había/hube encogido
I had shrunk
you had shurnk
he/she/it had shrunk
we had shrunk
you had shrunk
they had shrunk

Future

encogeré
I shall/will shrink
you will shrink
he/she/it will shrink
we shall/will shrink
you will shrink
they will shrink

Future perfect

habré encogido
I shall/will have shrunk
you will have shrunk
he/she/it will have shrunk
we shall/will have shrunk
you will have shrunk
they will have shrunk

Conditional

Present

encogería
I should/would shrink
you would shrink
he/she/it would shrink
we should/would shrink
you would shrink
they would shrink

Perfect

habría encogido
I should/would have shrunk
you would have shrunk
he/she/it would have shrunk
we should/would have shrunk
you would have shrunk
they would have shrunk

Subjunctive

Present

encoja
I shrink
you shrink
he/she/it shrinks
we shrink
you shrink
they shrink

Present perfect

they shrank
haya encogido
I have shrunk
you have shrunk
he/she/it has shrunk
we have shrunk
you have shrunk

Past

encogiera o
encogiese
I shrank
you shrank
he/she/it shrank
we shrank
you shrank

Past perfect

they have shrunk
hubiera o hubiese encogido
I had shrunk
you had shrunk
he/she/it had shrunk
we had shrunk
you had shrunk

Imperative

they had shrunk
let me shrink
shrink
let him/her/it shrink
let us (let's) shirnk
shrink

let them shrink
no existe (déjame encoger)
encoge tú
encoja él/ella/ello
encojamos nosotros
encoged vosotros

Impersonal forms

encojan ellos

shrunk

Infinitive

encoger
to shrink

Perfect Infinitive

haber encogido
to have shrunk

Gerund

encogiendo
shrinking

Perfect Gerund

habiendo encogido
having shrunk

Participle

encogido

Perfect Participle

habiendo encogido

SHUT · SHUT · SHUT

CERRAR

Indicative

Present

cierro
I shut
you shut
he/she/it shuts
we shut
you shut
they shut

Present perfect

he cerrado
I have shut
you have shut
he/she/it has shut
we have shut
you have shut
they have shut

Past

cerraba/cerré
I shut
you shut
he/she/it shut
we shut
you shut
they shut

Past perfect

había/hube cerrado
I had shut
you had shut
he/she/it had shut
we had shut
you had shut
they had shut

Future

cerraré
I shall/will shut
you will shut
he/she/it will shut
we shall/will shut
you will shut
they will shut

Future perfect

habré cerrado
I shall/will have shut
you will have shut
he/she/it will have shut
we shall/will have shut
you will have shut
they will have shut

Conditional

Present

cerraría
I should/would shut
you would shut
he/she/it would shut
we should/would shut
you would shut
they would shut

Perfect

habría cerrado
I should/would have shut
you would have shut
he/she/it would have shut
we should/would have shut
you would have shut
they would have shut

Subjunctive

Present

cierre
I shut
you shut
he/she/it shuts
we shut
you shut
they shut

Present perfect

haya cerrado
I have shut
you have shut
he/she/it has shut
we have shut
you have shut
they have shut

Past

cerrara o cerrase
I shut
you shut
he/she/it shut
we shut
you shut
they shut

Past perfect

hubiera o hubiese cerrado
I had shut
you had shut
he/she/it had shut
we had shut
you had shut
they had shut

Imperative

let me shut	***no existe (déjame cerrar)***
shut	***cierra tú***
let him/her/it shut	***cierre él/ella/ello***
let us (let's) shut	***cerremos nosotros***
shut	***cerrad vosotros***
let them shut	***cierren ellos***

Impersonal forms

Infinitive

cerrar
to shut

Perfect Infinitive

haber cerrado
to have shut

Gerund

cerrando
shutting

Perfect Gerund

habiendo cerrado
having shut

Participle

cerrado
shut

Perfect Participle

habiendo cerrado
having shut

SING · SANG · SUNG

CANTAR

Indicative

Present

canto
I sing
you sing
he/she/it sings
we sing
you sing
they sing

Present perfect

he cantado
I have sung
you have sung
he/she/it has sung
we have sung
you have sung
they have sung

Past

cantaba/canté
I sang
you sang
he/she/it sang
we sang
you sang
they sang

Past perfect

había/hube cantado
I had sung
you had sung
he/she/it had sung
we had sung
you had sung
they had sung

Future

cantaré
I shall/will sing
you will sing
he/she/it will sing
we shall/will sing
you will sing
they will sing

Future perfect

habré cantado
I shall/will have sung
you will have sung
he/she/it will have sung
we shall/will have sung
you will have sung
they will have sung

Conditional

Present

cantaría
I should/would sing
you would sing
he/she/it would sing
we should/would sing
you would sing
they would sing

Perfect

habría cantado
I should/would have sung
you would have sung
he/she/it would have sung
we should/would have sung
you would have sung
they would have sung

Subjunctive

Present

cante
I sing
you sing
he/she/it sings
we sing
you sing
they sing

Present perfect

haya cantado
I have sung
you have sung
he/she/it has sung
we have sung
you have sung
they have sung

Past

cantara o cantase
I sang
you sang
he/she/it sang
we sang
you sang
they sang

Past perfect

hubiera o hubiese cantado
I had sung
you had sung
he/she/it had sung
we had sung
you had sung
they had sung

Imperative

let me sing	***no existe (déjame cantar)***
sing	***canta tú***
let him/her/it sing	***cante él/ella/ello***
let us (let's) sing	***cantemos nosotros***
sing	***cantad vosotros***
let them sing	***canten ellos***

Impersonal forms

Infinitive

cantar
to sing

Perfect Infinitive

haber cantado
to have sung

Gerund

cantando
singing

Perfect Gerund

habiendo cantado
having sung

Participle

cantado
sung

Perfect Participle

habiendo cantado
having sung

SIT · SAT · SAT

SENTAR(SE)

Indicative

Present

me siento
I sit
you sit
he/she/it sits
we sit
you sit
they sit

Present perfect

me he sentado
I have sat
you have sat
he/she/it has sat
we have sat
you have sat
they have sat

Past

me sentaba/senté
I sat
you sat
he/she/it sat
we sat
you sat
they sat

Past perfect

había/hube sentado
I had sat
you had sat
he/she/it had sat
we had sat
you had sat
they had sat

Future

me sentaré
I shall/will sit
you will sit
he/she/it will sit
we shall/will sit
you will sit
they will sit

Future perfect

me habré sentado
I shall/will have sat
you will have sat
he/she/it will have sat
we shall/will have sat
you will have sat
they will have sat

Conditional

Present

me sentaría
I should/would sit
you would sit
he/she/it would sit
we should/would sit
you would sit
they would sit

Perfect

me habría sentado
I should/would have sat
you would have sat
he/she/it would have sat
we should/would have sat
you would have sat
they would have sat

Subjunctive

Present

me siente
I sit
you sit
he/she/it sits
we sit
you sit
they sit

Present perfect

haya sentado
I have sat
you have sat
he/she/it has sat
we have sat
you have sat
they have sat

Past

me sentara o sentase
I sat
you sat
he/she/it sat
we sat
you sat
they sat

Past perfect

hubiera o hubiese sentado
I had sat
you had sat
he/she/it had sat
we had sat
you had sat
they had sat

Imperative

let me sit	***no existe (déjame sentarme)***
sit	***siéntate tú***
let him/her/it sit	***siéntese él/ella/ello***
let us (let's) sit	***sentémonos nosotros***
sit	***sentaos vosotros***
let them sit	***siéntense ellos***

Impersonal forms

Infinitive

sentar(se)
to sit

Perfect Infinitive

haber sentado
to have sat

Gerund

sentándo(se)
sitting

Perfect Gerund

habiendo sentado
having sat

Participle

sentado
sat

Perfect Participle

habiendo sentado
having sat

SLAY · SLEW · SLAIN

ASESINAR, DAR MUERTE

Indicative

Present

asesino
I slay
you slay
he/she/it slays
we slay
you slay
they slay

Present perfect

he asesinado
I have slain
you have slain
he/she/it has slain
we have slain
you have slain
they have slain

Past

asesinaba/asesiné
I slew
you slew
he/she/it slew
we slew
you slew
they slew

Past perfect

había/hube asesinado
I had slain
you had slain
he/she/it had slain
we had slain
you had slain
they had slain

Future

asesinaré
I shall/will slay
you will slay
he/she/it will slay
we shall/will slay
you will slay
they will slay

Future perfect

habré asesinado
I shall/will have slain
you will have slain
he/she/it will have slain
we shall/will have slain
you will have slain
they will have slain

Conditional

Present

asesinaría
I should/would slay
you would slay
he/she/it would slay
we should/would slay
you would slay
they would slay

Perfect

habría asesinado
I should/would have slain
you would have slain
he/she/it would have slain
we should/would have slain
you would have slain
they would have slain

Subjunctive

Present

asesine
I slay
you slay
he/she/it slays
we slay
you slay
they slay

Present perfect

haya asesinado
I have slain
you have slain
he/she/it has slain
we have slain
you have slain
they have slain

Past

asesinara o asesinase
I slew
you slew
he/she/it slew
we slew
you slew
they slew

Past perfect

hubiera o hubiese asesinado
I had slain
you had slain
he/she/it had slain
we had slain
you had slain

Imperative

they had slain
let me slay
slay
let him/her/it slay
let us (let's) slay
slay

let them slay
no existe (déjame asesinar)
asesina tú
asesine él/ella/ello
asesinemos nosotros
asesinad vosotros

Impersonal forms

asesinen ellos

slain

Infinitive

asesinar
to slay

Perfect Infinitive

haber asesinado
to have slain

Gerund

asesinando
slaying

Perfect Gerund

habiendo asesinado
having slain

Participle

asesinado

Perfect Participle

habiendo asesinado

SLEEP · SLEPT · SLEPT

DORMIR

Indicative

Present

duermo
I sleep
you sleep
he/she/it sleeps
we sleep
you sleep
they sleep

Present perfect

he dormido
I have slept
you have slept
he/she/it has slept
we have slept
you have slept
they have slept

Past

dormía/dormí
I slept
you slept
he/she/it slept
we slept
you slept
they slept

Past perfect

había/hube dormido
I had slept
you had slept
he/she/it had slept
we had slept
you had slept
they had slept

Future

dormiré
I shall/will sleep
you will sleep
he/she/it will sleep
we shall/will sleep
you will sleep
they will sleep

Future perfect

habré dormido
I shall/will have slept
you will have slept
he/she/it will have slept
we shall/will have slept
you will have slept
they will have slept

Conditional

Present

dormiría
I should/would sleep
you would sleep
he/she/it would sleep
we should/would sleep
you would sleep
they would sleep

Perfect

habría dormido
I should/would have slept
you would have slept
he/she/it would have slept
we should/would have slept
you would have slept
they would have slept

Subjunctive

Present

duerma
I sleep
you sleep
he/she/it sleeps
we sleep
you sleep
they sleep

Present perfect

haya dormido
I have slept
you have slept
he/she/it has slept
we have slept
you have slept
they have slept

Past

durmiera o durmiese
I slept
you slept
he/she/it slept
we slept
you slept
they slept

Past perfect

hubiera o hubiese dormido
I had slept
you had slept
he/she/it had slept
we had slept
you had slept
they had slept

Imperative

let me sleep	***no existe (déjame dormir)***
sleep	***duerme tú***
let him/her/it sleep	***duerma él/ella/ello***
let us (let's) sleep	***durmamos***
sleep	***dormid***
let them sleep	***duerman ellos***

Impersonal forms

Infinitive

dormir
to sleep

Perfect Infinitive

haber dormido
to have slept

Gerund

durmiendo
sleeping

Perfect Gerund

habiendo dormido
having slept

Participle

dormido
slept

Perfect Participle

habiendo dormido
having slept

SLIDE · SLID · SLID

DESLIZAR, RESBALAR

Indicative

Present

deslizo
I slide
you slide
he/she/it slides
we slide
you slide
they slide

Present perfect

he deslizado
I have slid
you have slid
he/she/it has slid
we have slid
you have slid
they have slid

Past

deslizaba/deslicé
I slid
you slid
he/she/it slid
we slid
you slid
they slid

Past perfect

había/hube deslizado
I had slid
you had slid
he/she/it had slid
we had slid
you had slid
they had slid

Future

deslizaré
I shall/will slide
you will slide
he/she/it will slide
we shall/will slide
you will slide
they will slide

Future perfect

habré deslizado
I shall/will have slid
you will have slid
he/she/it will have slid
we shall/will have slid
you will have slid
they will have slid

Conditional

Present

deslizaría
I should/would slide
you would slide
he/she/it would slide
we should/would slide
you would slide
they would slide

Perfect

habría deslizado
I should/would have slid
you would have slid
he/she/it would have slid
we should/would have slid
you would have slid
they would have slid

Subjunctive

Present

deslice
I slide
you slide
he/she/it slides
we slide
you slide
they slide

Present perfect

haya deslizado
I have slid
you have slid
he/she/it has slid
we have slid
you have slid
they have slid

Past

deslizara o deslizase
I slid
you slid
he/she/it slid
we slid
you slid
they slid

Past perfect

hubiera o hubiese deslizado
I had slid
you had slid
he/she/it had slid
we had slid
you had slid
they had slid

Imperative

let me slide	***no existe (déjame deslizar)***
slide	***desliza tú***
let him/her/it slide	***deslice él/ella/ello***
let us (let's) slide	***deslicemos nosotros***
slide	***deslizad vosotros***
let them slide	***deslicen ellos***

Impersonal forms

Infinitive

deslizar
to slide

Perfect Infinitive

haber deslizado
to have slid

Gerund

deslizando
sliding

Perfect Gerund

habiendo deslizado
having slid

Participle

deslizado
slid

Perfect Participle

habiendo deslizado
having slid

SLING · SLUNG · SLUNG

TIRAR, LANZAR, ARROJAR, AVENTAR

Indicative

Present

arrojo
I sling
you sling
he/she/it slings
we sling
you sling
they sling

Present perfect

he arrojado
I have slung
you have slung
he/she/it has slung
we have slung
you have slung
they have slung

Past

arrojaba/arrojé
I slung
you slung
he/she/it slung
we slung
you slung
they slung

Past perfect

había/hube arrojado
I had slung
you had slung
he/she/it had slung
we had slung
you had slung
they had slung

Future

arrojaré
I shall/will sling
you will sling
he/she/it will sling
we shall/will sling
you will sling
they will sling

Future perfect

habré arrojado
I shall/will have slung
you will have slung
he/she/it will have slung
we shall/will have slung
you will have slung
they will have slung

Conditional

Present

arrojaría
I should/would sling
you would sling
he/she/it would sling
we should/would sling
you would sling
they would sling

Perfect

habría arrojado
I should/would have slung
you would have slung
he/she/it would have slung
we should/would have slung
you would have slung
they would have slung

Subjunctive

Present

arroje
I sling
you sling
he/she/it slings
we sling
you sling
they sling

Present perfect

haya arrojado
I have slung
you have slung
he/she/it has slung
we have slung
you have slung
they have slung

Past

arrojara o arrojase
I slung
you slung
he/she/it slung
we slung
you slung
they slung

Past perfect

hubiera o hubiese arrrojado
I had slung
you had slung
he/she/it had slung
we had slung
you had slung
they had slung

Imperative

let me sling	***no existe (déjame arrojar)***
sling	***arroja tú***
let him/her/it sling	***arroje él/ella/ello***
let us (let's) sling	***arrojemos nosotros***
sling	***arrojad vosotros***
let them sling	***arrojen ellos***

Impersonal forms

Infinitive

arrojar
to sling

Perfect Infinitive

haber arrojado
to have slung

Gerund

arrojando
slinging

Perfect Gerund

habiendo arrojado
having slung

Participle

arrojado
slung

Perfect Participle

habiendo arrojado
having slung

SLINK · SLUNK · SLUNK

ESCABULLIRSE

Indicative

Present

me escabullo
I slink
you slink
he/she/it slinks
we slink
you slink
they slink

Present perfect

me he escabullido
I have slunk
you have slunk
he/she/it has slunk
we have slunk
you have slunk
they have slunk

Past

me escabullía/ escabullí
I slunk
you slunk
he/she/it slunk
we slunk
you slunk
they slunk

Past perfect

me había/hube escabullido
I had slunk
you had slunk
he/she/it had slunk
we had slunk
you had slunk
they had slunk

Future

me escabulliré
I shall/will slink
you will slink
he/she/it will slink
we shall/will slink
you will slink
they will slink

Future perfect

me habré escabullido
I shall/will have slunk
you will have slunk
he/she/it will have slunk
we shall/will have slunk
you will have slunk
they will have slunk

Conditional

Present

me escabulliría
I should/would slink
you would slink
he/she/it would slink
we should/would slink
you would slink
they would slink

Perfect

me habría escabullido
I should/would have slunk
you would have slunk
he/she/it would have slunk
we should/would have slunk
you would have slunk
they would have slunk

Subjunctive

Present

me escabulla
I slink
you slink
he/she/it slinks
we slink
you slink
they slink

Present perfect

me haya escabullido
I have slunk
you have slunk
he/she/it has slunk
we have slunk
you have slunk
they have slunk

Past

me escabullera o escabullese
I slunk
you slunk
he/she/it slunk
we slunk
you slunk
they slunk

Past perfect

me hubiera o hubiese escabullido
I had slunk
you had slunk
he/she/it had slunk
we had slunk
you had slunk
they had slunk

Imperative

let me slink	***no existe (déjame escabullirme)***
slink	***escabulle(te) tú***
let him/her/it slink	***escabulla él/ella/ello***
let us (let's) slink	***escabullamos nosotros***
slink	***escabullid vosotros***
let them slink	***escabullan ellos***

Impersonal forms

Infinitive

escabullir
to slink

Gerund

escabullendo
slinking

Participle

escabullido
slunk

Perfect Infinitive

haber escabullido
to have slunk

Perfect Gerund

habiendo escabullido
having slunk

Perfect Participle

habiendo escabullido

SLIT · SLIT · SLIT

CORTAR, RAJAR, DEGOLLAR

Indicative

Present

rajo
I slit
you slit
he/she/it slits
we slit
you slit
they slit

Present perfect

he rajado
I have slit
you have slit
he/she/it has slit
we have slit
you have slit
they have slit

Past

rajaba/rajé
I slit
you slit
he/she/it slit
we slit
you slit
they slit

Past perfect

había/hube rajado
I had slit
you had slit
he/she/it had slit
we had slit
you had slit
they had slit

Future

rajaré
I shall/will slit
you will slit
he/she/it will slit
we shall/will slit
you will slit
they will slit

Future perfect

habré rajado
I shall/will have slit
you will have slit
he/she/it will have slit
we shall/will have slit
you will have slit
they will have slit

Conditional

Present

rajaría
I should/would slit
you would slit
he/she/it would slit
we should/would slit
you would slit
they would slit

Perfect

habría rajado
I should/would have slit
you would have slit
he/she/it would have slit
we should/would have slit
you would have slit
they would have slit

Subjunctive

Present

raje
I slit
you slit
he/she/it slits
we slit
you slit
they slit

Present perfect

haya rajado
I have slit
you have slit
he/she/it has slit
we have slit
you have slit
they have slit

Past

rajara o rajase
I slit
you slit
he/she/it slit
we slit
you slit
they slit

Past perfect

hubiera o hubiese rajado
I had slit
you had slit
he/she/it had slit
we had slit
you had slit
they had slit

Imperative

let me slit	***no existe (déjame rajar)***
slit	***raja tú***
let him/her/it slit	***raje él/ella/ello***
let us (let's) slit	***rajemos nosotros***
slit	***rajad vosotros***
let them slit	***rajen ellos***

Impersonal forms

Infinitive

rajar
to slit

Perfect Infinitive

haber rajado
to have slit

Gerund

rajando
slitting

Perfect Gerund

habiendo rajado
having slit

Participle

rajado
slit

Perfect Participle

habiendo rajado
having slit

SMELL · SMELLED/SMELT · SMELLED/SMELT

OLER

Indicative

Present

huelo
I smell
you smell
he/she/it smells
we smell
you smell
they smell

Present perfect

he olido
I have smelled/smelt
you have smelled/smelt
he/she/it has smelled/smelt
we have smelled/smelt
you have smelled/smelt
they have smelled/smelt

Past

olía/olí
I smelled/smelt
you smelled/smelt
he/she/it smelled/smelt
we smelled/smelt
you smelled/smelt
they smelled/smelt

Past perfect

había/hube olido
I had smelled/smelt
you had smelled/smelt
he/she/it had smelled/smelt
we had smelled/smelt
you had smelled/smelt
they had smelled/smelt

Future

oleré
I shall/will smell
you will smell
he/she/it will smell

we shall/will smell
you will smell
they will smell

Future perfect

habré olido
I shall/will have smelled/
smelt
you will have smelled/smelt
he/she/it will have smelled/
smelt
we shall/will have smelled/
smelt

Conditional

Present

olería
I should/would smell
you would smell
he/she/it would smell
we should/would smell
you would smell
they would smell

Perfect

you will have smelled/smelt
they will have smelled/smelt
habría olido
I should/would have smelled/smelt
you would have smelled/smelt
he/she/it would have smelled/smelt
we should/would have smelled/smelt

Subjunctive

Present

you would have
smelled/smelt
they would have
smelled/smelt
huela
I smell
you smell

Present perfect

he/she/it smelled/smelt
we smelled/smelt
you smelled/smelt
they smelled/smelt
haya olido
I have smelled/smelt
you have smelled/smelt

Past

he/she/it smells
we smell
you smell
they smell
oliera u oliese
I smelled/smelt
you smelled/smelt

Past perfect

he/she/it has smelled/smelt
we have smelled/smelt
you have smelled/smelt
they have smelled/smelt
hubiera o hubiese olido
I had smelled/smelt
you had smelled/smelt

Imperative

he/she/it had smelled/
smelt
we had smelled/smelt
you had smelled/smelt
they had smelled/smelt
let me smell

smell
let him/her/it smell
let us (let's) smell
smell
let them smell
no existe (déjame oler)

Impersonal forms

huele tú
huela él/ella/ello
olamos nosotros
oled vosotros
huelan ellos

Infinitive

oler
to smell

Gerund

oliendo
smelling

Participle

olido
smelled/smelt

Perfect Infinitive

haber olido
to have smelled/smelt

Perfect Gerund

SMITE · SMOTE · SMITTEN

GOLPEAR, ATORMENTAR

Indicative

Present

golpeo
I smite
you smite
he/she/it smites
we smite
you smite
they smite

Present perfect

he golpeado
I have smitten
you have smitten
he/she/it has smitten
we have smitten
you have smitten
they have smitten

Past

golpeaba/golpeé
I smote
you smote
he/she/it smote
we smote
you smote
they smote

Past perfect

había/hube golpeado
I had smitten
you had smitten
he/she/it had smitten
we had smitten
you had smitten
they had smitten

Future

golpearé
I shall/will smite
you will smite
he/she/it will smite
we shall/will smite
you will smite
they will smite

Future perfect

habré golpeado
I shall/will have smitten
you will have smitten
he/she/it will have smitten
we shall/will have smitten
you will have smitten
they will have smitten

Conditional

Present

golpearía
I should/would smite
you would smite
he/she/it would smite
we should/would smite
you would smite
they would smite

Perfect

habría golpeado
I should/would have smitten
you would have smitten
he/she/it would have smitten
we should/would have smitten
you would have smitten
they would have smitten

Subjunctive

Present

golpee
I smite
you smite
he/she/it smites
we smite
you smite
they smite

Present perfect

haya golpeado
I have smitten
you have smitten
he/she/it has smitten
we have smitten
you have smitten
they have smitten

Past

golpeara o golpease
I smote
you smote
he/she/it smote
we smote
you smote
they smote

Past perfect

hubiera o hubiese golpeado
I had smitten
you had smitten
he/she/it had smitten
we had smitten
you had smitten
they had smitten

Imperative

let me smite	***no existe (déjame golpear)***
smite	***golpea tú***
let him/her/it smite	***golpee él/ella/ello***
let us (let's) smite	***golpeemos nosotros***
smite	***golpead vosotros***
let them smite	***golpeen ellos***

Impersonal forms

Infinitve

golpear
to smite

Gerund

golpeando
smiting

Participle

golpeado
smitten

Perfect Infinitive

haber golpeado
to have smitten

Perfect Gerund

habiendo golpeado
having smitten

Perfect Participle

habiendo golpeado
having smitten

SOW · SOWED · SOWN

SEMBRAR

Indicative

Present

siembro
I sow
you sow
he/she/it sows
we sow
you sow
they sow

Present perfect

he sembrado
I have sown
you have sown
he/she/it has sown
we have sown
you have sown
they have sown

Past

sembraba/sembré
I sowed
you sowed
he/she/it sowed
we sowed
you sowed
they sowed

Past perfect

había/hube sembrado
I had sown
you had sown
he/she/it had sown
we had sown
you had sown
they had sown

Future

sembraré
I shall/will sow
you will sow
he/she/it will sow
we shall/will sow
you will sow
they will sow

Future perfect

habré sembrado
I shall/will have sown
you will have sown
he/she/it will have sown
we shall/will have sown
you will have sown
they will have sown

Conditional

Present

sembraría
I should/would sow
you would sow
he/she/it would sow
we should/would sow
you would sow
they would sow

Perfect

habría sembrado
I should/would have sown
you would have sown
he/she/it would have sown
we should/would have sown
you would have sown
they would have sown

Subjunctive

Present

siembre
I sow
you sow
he/she/it sows
we sow
you sow
they sow

Present perfect

haya sembrado
I have sown
you have sown
he/she/it has sown
we have sown
you have sown
they have sown

Past

sembrara o sembrase
I sowed
you sowed
he/she/it sowed
we sowed
you sowed
they sowed

Past perfect

hubiera o hubiese sembrado
I had sown
you had sown
he/she/it had sown
we had sown
you had sown
they had sown

Imperative

let me sow — ***no existe (déjame sembrar)***
sow — ***siembra tú***
let him/her/it sow — ***siembre él/ella/ello***
let us (let's) sow — ***sembremos nosotros***
sow — ***sembrad vosotros***
let them sow — ***siembren ellos***

Impersonal forms

Infinitive

sembrar
to sow

Perfect Infinitive

haber sembrado
to have sown

Gerund

sembrando
sowing

Perfect Gerund

habiendo sembrado
having sown

Participle

sembrado
sown

Perfect Participle

habiendo sembrado

SPEAK · SPOKE · SPOKEN

HABLAR

Indicative

Present

hablo
I speak
you speak
he/she/it speaks
we speak
you speak
they speak

Present perfect

he hablado
I have spoken
you have spoken
he/she/it has spoken
we have spoken
you have spoken
they have spoken

Past

hablaba/hablé
I spoke
you spoke
he/she/it spoke
we spoke
you spoke
they spoke

Past perfect

había/hube hablado
I had spoken
you had spoken
he/she/it had spoken
we had spoken
you had spoken
they had spoken

Future

hablaré
I shall/will speak
you will speak
he/she/it will speak
we shall/will speak
you will speak
they will speak

Future perfect

habré hablado
I shall/will have spoken
you will have spoken
he/she/it will have spoken
we shall/will have spoken
you will have spoken
they will have spoken

Conditional

Present

hablaría
I should/would speak
you would speak
he/she/it would speak
we should/would speak
you would speak
they would speak

Perfect

habría hablado
I should/would have spoken
you would have spoken
he/she/it would have spoken
we should/would have spoken
you would have spoken
they would have spoken

Subjunctive

Present

hable
I speak
you speak
he/she/it speaks
we speak
you speak
they speak

Present perfect

haya hablado
I have spoken
you have spoken
he/she/it has spoken
we have spoken
you have spoken
they have spoken

Past

hablara o hablase
I spoke
you spoke
he/she/it spoke
we spoke
you spoke
they spoke

Past perfect

hubiera o hubiese hablado
I had spoken
you had spoken
he/she/it had spoken
we had spoken
you had spoken
they had spoken

Imperative

let me speak	***no existe (déjame hablar)***
speak	***habla tú***
let him/her/it speak	***hable él/ella/ello***
let us (let's) speak	***hablemos nosotros***
speak	***hablad vosotros***
let them speak	***hablen ellos***

Impersonal forms

Infinitive

hablar
to speak

Perfect Infinitive

haber hablado
to have spoken

Gerund

hablando
speaking

Perfect Gerund

habiendo hablado
having spoken

Participle

hablado
spoken

Perfect Participle

habiendo hablado
having spoken

SPEED · SPEEDED/SPED · SPEEDED/SPED

ACELERAR, CONDUCIR RÁPIDO, IR DEPRISA

Indicative

Present

acelero
I speed
you speed
he/she/it speeds
we speed
you speed
they speed

Present perfect

he acelerado
I have speeded/sped
you have speeded/sped
he/she/it has speeded/sped
we have speeded/sped
you have speeded/sped
they have speeded/sped

Past

aceleraba/aceleré
I speeded/sped
you speeded/sped
he/she/it speeded/sped
we speeded/sped
you speeded/sped
they speeded/sped

Past perfect

había/hube acelerado
I had speeded/sped
you had speeded/sped
he/she/it had speeded/sped
we had speeded/sped
you had speeded/sped
they had speeded/sped

Future

aceleraré
I shall/will speed
you will speed
he/she/it will speed
we shall/will speed
you will speed
they will speed

Future perfect

habré acelerado
I shall/will have speeded/
sped
you will have speeded/sped
he/she/it will have speeded/
sped
we shall/will have speeded/
sped
you will have speeded/sped

Conditional

Present

aceleraría
I should/would speed
you would speed
he/she/it would speed
we should/would
speed
you would speed
they would speed

Perfect

they will have speeded/sped
habría acelerado
I should/would have speeded/sped
you would have speeded/sped
he/she/it would have speeded/sped
we should/would have speeded/
sped
you would have speeded/sped

Subjunctive

Present

they would have
speeded/sped
acelere
I speed
you speed
he/she/it speeds
we speed

Present perfect

you speeded/sped
they speeded/sped
haya acelerado
I have speeded/sped
you have speeded/sped
he/she/it has speeded/sped
we have speeded/sped

Past

you speed
they speed
acelerara o acelerase
I speeded/sped
you speeded/sped
he/she/it speeded/sped
we speeded/sped

Past perfect

you have speeded/sped
they have speeded/sped
hubiera o hubiese acelerado
I had speeded/sped
you had speeded/sped
he/she/it had speeded/sped
we had speeded/sped

Imperative

you had speeded/sped
they had speeded/sped
let me speed
speed
let him/her/it speed
let us (let's) speed

speed
let them speed
no existe (déjame acelerar)
acelera tú
acelere él/ella/ello
aceleremos nosotros

Impersonal forms

acelerad vosotros
aceleren ellos

acelerado
speeded/sped

Infinitive

acelerar
to speed

Perfect Infinitive

haber acelerado
to have speeded/sped

Gerund

acelerando
speeding

Perfect Gerund

habiendo acelerado
having speeded/sped

Participle

Perfect Participle

SPELL · SPELLED/SPELT · SPELLED/SPELT

DELETREAR

Indicative

Present

deletreo
I spell
you spell
he/she/it spells
we spell
you spell
they spell

Present perfect

he deletreado
I have spelled/spelt
you have spelled/spelt
he/she/it has spelled/spelt
we have spelled/spelt
you have spelled/spelt
they have spelled/spelt

Past

deletreaba/deletreé
I spelled/spelt
you spelled/spelt
he/she/it spelled/spelt
we spelled/spelt
you spelled/spelt
they spelled/spelt

Past perfect

había/hube deletreado
I had spelled/spelt
you had spelled/spelt
he/she/it had spelled/spelt
we had spelled/spelt
you had spelled/spelt
they had spelled/spelt

Future

deletrearé
I shall/will spell
you will spell
he/she/it wil spell
we shall/will spell
you will spell
they will spell

Future perfect

habré deletreado
I shall/will have spelled/spelt
you will have spelled/spelt
he/she/it will have spelled/spelt
we shall/will have spelled/spelt
you will have spelled/spelt
they will have spelled/spelt

Present

deletrearía
I should/would spell
you would spell
he/she/it would spell
we should/would spell
you would spell
they would spell

Perfect

habría deletreado
I should/would have spelled/spelt
you would have spelled/spelt
he/she/it would have spelled/spelt
we should/would have spelled/spelt
you would have spelled/spelt
they would have spelled/spelt

Subjunctive

Present

deletree
I spell
you spell
he/she/it spells
we spell
you spell
they spell

Present perfect

they spelled/spelt
haya deletreado
I have spelled/spelt
you have spelled/spelt
he/she/it has spelled/spelt
we have spelled/spelt
you have spelled/spelt

Past

deletreara o deletrease
I spelled/spelt
you spelled/spelt
he/she/it spelled/spelt
we spelled/spelt
you spelled/spelt

Past perfect

they have spelled/spelt
hubiera o hubiese deletreado
I had spelled/spelt
you had spelled/spelt
he/she/it had spelled/spelt
we had spelled/spelt
you had spelled/spelt

Imperative

they had spelled/spelt
let me spell
spell
let him/her/it spell
let us (let's) spell
spell

let them spell
no existe (déjame deletrear)
deletrea tú
deletree él/ella/ello
deletreemos nosotros
deletread vosotros

Impersonal forms

deletreen ellos

spelled/spelt

Infinitive

deletrear
to spell

Perfect Infinitive

haber deletreado
to have spelled/spelt

Gerund

deletreando
spelling

Perfect Gerund

habiendo deletreado
having spelled/spelt

Participle

deletreado

Perfect Participle

habiendo deletreado

SPEND · SPENT · SPENT

PASAR, GASTAR

Indicative

Present

gasto
I spend
you spend
he/she/it spends
we spend
you spend
they spend

Present perfect

he gastado
I have spent
you have spent
he/she/it has spent
we have spent
you have spent
they have spent

Past

gastaba/gasté
I spent
you spent
he/she/it spent
we spent
you spent
they spent

Past perfect

había/hube gastado
I had spent
you had spent
he/she/it had spent
we had spent
you had spent
they had spent

Future

gastaré
I shall/will spend
you will spend
he/she/it will spend
we shall/will spend
you will spend
they will spend

Future perfect

habrá gastado
I shall/will have spent
you will have spent
he/she/it will have spent
we shall/will have spent
you will have spent
they will have spent

Conditional

Present

gastaría
I should/would spend
you would spend
he/she/it would spend
we should/would spend
you would spend
they would spend

Perfect

habría gastado
I should/would have spent
you would have spent
he/she/it would have spent
we should/would have spent
you would have spent
they would have spent

Subjunctive

Present

gaste
I spend
you spend
he/she/it spends
we spend
you spend
they spend

Present perfect

haya gastado
I have spent
you have spent
he/she/it has spent
we have spent
you have spent
they have spent

Past

gastara o gastase
I spent
you spent
he/she/it spent
we spent
you spent
they spent

Past perfect

hubiera o hubiese gastado
I had spent
you had spent
he/she/it had spent
we had spent
you had spent
they had spent

Imperative

let me spend	***no existe (déjame gastar)***
spend	***gasta tú***
let him/her/it spend	***gaste él/ella/ello***
let us (let's) spend	***gastemos nosotros***
spend	***gastad vosotros***
let them spend	***gasten ellos***

Impersonal forms

Infinitive

gastar
to spend

Perfect Infinitive

haber gastado
to have spent

Gerund

gastando
spending

Perfect Gerund

habiendo gastado
having spent

Participle

gastado
spent

Perfect Participle

habiendo gastado
having spent

SPILL · SPILLED/SPILT · SPILLED/SPILT

DERRAMAR

Indicative

Present

derramo
I spill
you spill
he/she/it spills
we spill
you spill
they spill

Present perfect

he derramado
I have spilled/spilt
you have spilled/spilt
he/she/it has spilled/spilt
we have spilled/spilt
you have spilled/spilt
they have spilled/spilt

Past

derramaba/derramé
I spilled/spilt
you spilled/spilt
he/she/it spilled/spilt
we spilled/spilt
you spilled/spilt
they spilled/spilt

Past perfect

había/hube derramado
I had spilled/spilt
you had spilled/spilt
he/she/it had spilled/spilt
we had spilled/spilt
you had spilled/spilt
they had spilled/spilt

Future

derramaré
I shall/will spill
you will spill
he/she/it will spill
we shall/will spill
you will spill
they will spill

Future perfect

habré derramado
I shall/will have spilled/spilt
you will have spilled/spilt
he/she/it will have spilled/spilt
we shall/will have spilled/spilt
you will have spilled/spilt
they will have spilled/spilt

Conditional

Present

derramaría
I should/would spill
you would spill
he/she/it would spill
we should/would spill
you would spill
they would spill

Perfect

habría derramado
I should/would have spilled/spilt
you would have spilled/spilt
he/she/it would have spilled/spilt
we should/would have spilled/spilt
you would have spilled/spilt
they would have spilled/spilt

Subjunctive

Present

derrame
I spill
you spill
he/she/it spills
we spill
you spill
they spill

Present perfect

they spilled/spilt
haya derramado
I have spilled/spilt
you have spilled/spilt
he/she/it has spilled/spilt
we have spilled/spilt
you have spilled/spilt

Past

derramara o derramase
I spilled/spilt
you spilled/spilt
he/she/it spilled/spilt
we spilled/spilt
you spilled/spilt

Past perfect

they have spilled/spilt
hubiera o hubiese derramado
I had spilled/spilt
you had spilled/spilt
he/she/it had spilled/spilt
we had spilled/spilt
you had spilled/spilt

Imperative

they had spilled/spilt
let me spill
spill
let him/her/it spill
let us (let's) spill
spill

let them spill
no existe (déjame derramar)
derrama tú
derrame él/ella/ello
derramemos nosotros
derramad vosotros

Impersonal forms

derramen ellos
spilled/spilt

Infinitive

derramar
to spill

Perfect Infinitive

haber derramado
to have spilled/spilt

Gerund

derramando
spilling

Perfect Gerund

habiendo derramado
having spilled/spilt

Participle

derramado

Perfect Participle

habiendo derramado

SPIN · SPAN/SPUN · SPUN

GIRAR, HACER GIRAR, CENTRIFUGAR, HILAR

Indicative

Present

giro
I spin
you spin
he/she/it spins
we spin
you spin
they spin

Present perfect

he girado
I have spun
you have spun
he/she/it has spun
we have spun
you have spun
they have spun

Past

giraba/giré
I span/spun
you span/spun
he/she/it span/spun
we span/spun
you span/spun
they span/spun

Past perfect

había/hube girado
I had spun
you had spun
he/she/it had spun
we had spun
you had spun
they had spun

Future

giraré
I shall/will spin
you will spin
he/she/it will spin
we shall/will spin
you will spin
they will spìn

Future perfect

habré girado
I shall/will have spun
you will have spun
he/she/it will have spun
we shall/will have spun
you will have spun
they will have spun

Conditional

Present

giraría
I should/would spin
you would spin
he/she/it would spin
we should/would spin
you would spin
they would spin

Perfect

habría girado
I should/would have spun
you would have spun
he/she/it would have spun
we should/would have spun
you would have spun
they would have spun

Subjunctive

Present

gire
I spin
you spin
he/she/it spins
we spin
you spin
they spin

Present perfect

haya girado
I have spun
you have spun
he/she/it has spun
we have spun
you have spun
they have spun

Past

girara o girase
I span/spun
you span/spun
he/she/it span/spun
we span/spun
you span/spun
they span/spun

Past perfect

hubiera o hubiese girado
I had spun
you had spun
he/she/it had spun
we had spun
you had spun
they had spun

Imperative

let me spin	***no existe (déjame girar)***
spin	***gira tú***
let him/her/it spin	***gire él/ella/ello***
let us (let's) spin	***giremos nosotros***
spin	***girad vosotros***
let them spin	***giren ellos***

Impersonal forms

Infinitive

girar
to spin

Perfect Infinitive

haber girado
to have spun

Gerund

girando
spinning

Perfect Gerund

habiendo girado
having spun

Participle

girado
spun

Perfect Participle

habiendo girado
having spun

SPIT · SPAT · SPAT

ESCUPIR

Indicative

Present

escupo
I spit
you spit
he/she/it spits
we spit
you spit
they spit

Present perfect

he escupido
I have spat
you have spat
he/she/it has spat
we have spat
you have spat
they have spat

Past

escupía/escupí
I spat
you spat
he/she/it spat
we spat
you spat
they spat

Past perfect

había/hube escupido
I had spat
you had spat
he/she/it had spat
we had spat
you had spat
they had spat

Future

escupiré
I shall/will spit
you will spit
he/she/it will spit
we shall/will spit
you will spit
they will spit

Future perfect

habré escupido
I shall/will have spat
you will have spat
he/she/it will have spat
we shall/will have spat
you will have spat
they will have spat

Conditional

Present

escupiría
I should/would spit
you would pit
he/she/it would spit
we should/would spit
you would spit
they would spit

Perfect

habría escupido
I should/would have spat
you would have spat
he/she/it would have spat
we should/would have spat
you would have spat
they would have spat

Subjunctive

Present

escupa
I spit
you spit
he/she/it spits
we spit
you spit
they spit

Present perfect

haya escupido
I have spat
you have spat
he/she/it has spat
we have spat
you have spat
they have spat

Past

escupiera o escupiese
I spat
you spat
he/she/it spat
we spat
you spat
they spat

Past perfect

hubiera o hubiese escupido
I had spat
you had spat
he/she/it had spat
we had spat
you had spat
they had spat

Imperative

let me spit	***no existe (déjame escupir)***
spit	***escupe tú***
let him/her/it spit	***escupa él/ella/ello***
let us (let's) spit	***escupamos nosotros***
spit	***escupid vosotros***
let them spit	***escupan ellos***

Impersonal forms

Infinitive

escupir
to spit

Perfect Infinitive

haber escupido
to have spat

Gerund

escupiendo
spitting

Perfect Gerund

habiendo escupido
having spat

Participle

escupido
spat

Perfect Participle

habiendo escupido
having spat

SPLIT · SPLIT · SPLIT

PARTIR, REPARTIR, ESCINDIR, DIVIDIR

Indicative

Present

parto
I split
you split
he/she/it splits
we split
you split
they split

Present perfect

he partido
I have split
you have split
he/she/it has split
we have split
you have split
they have split

Past

partía/partí
I split
you split
he/she/it split
we split
you split
they split

Past perfect

había/hube partido
I had split
you had split
he/she/it had split
we had split
you had split
they had split

Future

partiré
I shall/will split
you will split
he/she/it will split
we shall/will split
you will split
they will split

Future perfect

habré partido
I shall/will have split
you will have split
he/she/it will have split
we shall/will have split
you will have split
they will have split

Conditional

Present

partiría
I should/would split
you would split
he/she/it would split
we should/would split
you would split
they would split

Perfect

habría partido
I should/would have split
you would have split
he/she/it would have split
we should/would have split
you would have split
they would have split

Subjunctive

Present

parta
I split
you split
he/she/it splits
we split
you split
they split

Present perfect

haya partido
I have split
you have split
he/she/it has split
we have split
you have split
they have split

Past

partiera o partiese
I split
you split
he/she/it split
we split
you split
they split

Past perfect

hubiera o hubiese partido
I had split
you had split
he/she/it had split
we had split
you had split
they had split

Imperative

let me split	***no existe (déjame partir)***
split	***parte tú***
let him/her/it split	***parta él/ella/ello***
let us (let's) split	***partamos nosotros***
split	***partid vosotros***
let them split	***partan ellos***

Impersonal forms

Infinitive

partir
to split

Perfect Infinitive

haber partido
to have split

Gerund

partiendo
splitting

Perfect Gerund

habiendo partido
having split

Participle

partido
split

Perfect Participle

habiendo partido
having split

SPOIL · SPOILED/SPOILT · SPOILED/SPOILT

ECHAR A PERDER, ESTROPEAR, ARRUINAR, CONSENTIR, MALCRIAR

Indicative

Present

consiento
I spoil
you spoil
he/she/it spoils
we spoil
you spoil
they spoil

Present perfect

he consentido
I have spoiled/spoilt
you have spoiled/spoilt
he/she/it has spoiled/spoilt
we have spoiled/spoilt
you have spoiled/spoilt
they have spoiled/spoilt

Past

consentía/consentí
I spoiled/spoilt
you spoiled/spoilt
he/she/it spoiled/spoilt
we spoiled/spoilt
you spoiled/spoilt
they spoiled/spoilt

Past perfect

había/hube consentido
I had spoiled/spoilt
you had spoiled/spoilt
he/she/it had spoiled/spoilt
we had spoiled/spoilt
you had spoiled/spoilt
they had spoiled/spoilt

Future

consentiré
I shall/will spoil
you will spoil
he/she/ti will spoil
we shall/will spoil
you will spoil
they will spoil

Future perfect

habré consentido
I shall/will have spoiled/spoilt
you will have spoiled/spoilt
he/she/it will have spoiled/spoilt
we shall/will have spoiled/spoilt
you will have spoiled/spoilt
they will have spoiled/spoilt

Present

consentiría
I should/would spoil
you would spoil
he/she/it would spoil
we should/would spoil
you would spoil
they would spoil

Perfect

habría consentido
I should/would have spoiled/spoilt
you would have spoiled/spoilt
he/she/it would have spoiled/spoilt
we should/would have spoiled/spoilt
you would have spoiled/spoilt
they would have spoiled/spoilt

Subjunctive

Present

consienta
I spoil
you spoil
he/she/it spoils
we spoil
you spoil
they spoil

Present perfect

haya consentido
I have spoiled/spoilt
you have spoiled/spoilt
he/she/it has spoiled/spoilt
we have spoiled/spoilt
you have spoiled/spoilt
they have spoiled/spoilt

Past

consintiera o consintiese
I spoiled/spoilt
you spoiled/spoilt
he/she/it spoiled/spoilt
we spoiled/spoilt
you spoiled/spoilt
they spoiled/spoilt

Past perfect

hubiera o hubiese consentido
I had spoiled/spoilt
you had spoiled/spoilt
he/she/it had spoiled/spoilt
we had spoiled/spoilt
you had spoiled/spoilt
they had spoiled/spoilt

Imperative

let me spoil	***no existe (déjame consentir)***
spoil	***consiente tú***
let him/her/it spoil	***consienta él/ella/ello***
let us (let's) spoil	***consintamos nosotros***
spoil	***consentid vosotros***
let them spoil	***consientan ellos***

Impersonal forms

Infinitive

consentir
to spoil

Perfect Infinitive

haber consentido
to have spoiled/spoilt

Gerund

consintiendo
spoiling

Perfect Gerund

habiendo consentido
having spoiled/spoilt

Participle

consentido
spoiled/spoilt

Perfect Participle

habiendo consentido
having spoiled/spoilt

SPREAD · SPREAD · SPREAD

ESPARCIR

Indicative

Present

esparzo
I spread
you spread
he/she/it spreads
we spread
you spread
they spread

Present perfect

he esparcido
I have spread
you have spread
he/she/it has spread
we have spread
you have spread
they have spread

Past

esparcía/esparcí
I spread
you spread
he/she/it spread
we spread
you spread
they spread

Past perfect

había/hube esparcido
I had spread
you had spread
he/she/it had spread
we had spread
you had spread
they had spread

Future

esparciré
I shall/will spread
you will spread
he/she/it will spread
we shall/will spread
you will spread
they will spread

Future perfect

habré esparcido
I shall/will have spread
you will have spread
he/she/it will have spread
we shall/will have spread
you will have spread
they will have spread

Conditional

Present

esparciría
I should/would spread
you would spread
he/she/it would spread
we should/would spread
you would spread
they would spread

Perfect

habría esparcido
I should/would have spread
you would have spread
he/she/it would have spread
we should/would have spread
you would have spread
they would have spread

Subjunctive

Present

esparza
I spread
you spread
he/she/it spreads
we spread
you spread
they spread

Present perfect

they spread
haya esparcido
I have spread
you have spread
he/she/it has spread
we have spread
you have spread

Past

esparciera o
esparciese
I spread
you spread
he/she/it spread
we spread
you spread

Past perfect

they have spread
hubiera o hubiese esparcido
I had spread
you had spread
he/she/it had spread
we had spread
you had spread

Imperative

they had spread
let me spread
spread
let him/her/it spread
let us (let's) spread
spread

let them spread
no existe (déjame esparcir)
esparce tú
esparza él/ella/ello
esparzamos nosotros
esparced vosotros

Impersonal forms

esparzan ellos

spread

Infinitive

esparcir
to spread

Perfect Infinitive

haber esparcido
to have spread

Gerund

esparciendo
spreading

Perfect Gerund

habiendo esparcido
having spread

Participle

esparcido

Perfect Participle

habiendo esparcido

SPRING · SPRANG · SPRUNG

SALTAR, SURGIR, BROTAR, NACER, BRINCAR.

Indicative

Present

salto
I spring
you spring
he/she/it springs
we spring
you spring
they spring

Present perfect

saltado
I have sprung
you have sprung
he/she/it has sprung
we have sprung
you have sprung
they have sprung

Past

saltaba/salté
I sprang
you sprang
he/she/it sprang
we sprang
you sprang
they sprang

Past perfect

había/hube saltado
I had sprung
you had sprung
he/she/it had sprung
we had sprung
you had sprung
they had sprung

Future

saltaré
I shall/will spring
you will spring
he/she/it will spring
we shall/will spring
you will spring
they will spring

Future perfect

habré saltado
I shall/will have sprung
you will have sprung
he/she/it will have sprung
we shall/will have sprung
you will have sprung
they will have sprung

Conditional

Present

saltaría
I should/would spring
you would spring
he/she/it would pring
we should/would spring
you would spring
they would spring

Perfect

habría saltado
I should/would have sprung
you would have sprung
he/she/it would have sprung
we should/would have sprung
you would have sprung
they would have sprung

Subjunctive

Present

salte
I spring
you spring
he/she/it springs
we spring
you spring
they spring

Present perfect

haya saltado
I have sprung
you have sprung
he/she/it has sprung
we have sprung
you have sprung
they have sprung

Past

saltara o saltase
I sprang
you sprang
he/she/it sprang
we sprang
you sprang
they sprang

Past perfect

hubiera o hubiese saltado
I had sprung
you had sprung
he/she/it had sprung
we had sprung
you had sprung
they had sprung

Imperative

let me spring	***no existe (déjame saltar)***
spring	***salta tú***
let him/her/it spring	***salte él/ella/ello***
let us (let's) spring	***saltemos nosotros***
spring	***saltad vosotros***
let them spring	***salten ellos***

Impersonal forms

Infinitive

saltar
to spring

Perfect Infinitive

haber saltado
to have sprung

Gerund

saltando
springing

Perfect Gerund

habiendo saltado
having sprung

Participle

saltado
sprung

Perfect Participle

habiendo saltado
having sprung

STAND · STOOD · STOOD

ESTAR, PONER (DE PIE), RESISTIR, INCORPORARSE.

Indicative

Present

incorporo
I stand
you stand
he/she/it stands
we stand
you stand
they stand

Present perfect

he incorporado
I have stood
you have stood
he/she/it has stood
we have stood
you have stood
they have stood

Past

incorporaba/ incorporé
I stood
you stood
he/she/it stood
we stood
you stood
they stood

Past perfect

había/hube incorporado
I had stood
you had stood
he/she/it had stood
we had stood
you had stood
they had stood

Future

incorporaré
I shall/will stand
you will stand
he/she/it will stand
we shall/will stand
you will stand
they will stand

Future perfect

habré incorporaré
I shall/will have stood
you will have stood
he/she/it will have stood
we shall/will have stood
you will have stood
they will have stood

Conditional

Present

incorporaría
I should/would stand
you would stand
he/she/it would stand
we should/would stand
you would stand
they would stand

Perfect

habría incorporado
I should/would have stood
you would have stood
he/she/it would have stood
we should/would have stood
you would have stood
they would have stood

Subjunctive

Present

incorpore
I stand
you stand
he/she/it stands
we stand
you stand
they stand

Present perfect

haya incorporado
I have stood
you have stood
he/she/it has stood
we have stood
you have stood
they have stood

Past

incorporara / incorporase
I stood
you stood
he/she/it stood
we stood
you stood
they stood

Past perfect

hubiera/hubiese incorporado
I had stood
you had stood
he/she/it had stood
we had stood
you had stood
they had stood

Imperative

let me stand	***no existe (déjame incorporar)***
stand	***incorpora tú***
let him/her/it stand	***incorpore él/ella/ello***
let us (let's) stand	***incorporemos nosotros***
stand	***incorporad vosotros***
let them stand	

Impersonal forms

Infinitive

incorporar
to stand

Perfect Infinitive

haber incorporado
to have stood

Gerund

incorporando
standing

Perfect Gerund

habiendo incorporado
having stood

Participle

incorporado
stood

Perfect Participle

habiendo incorporado
having stood

STEAL · STOLE · STOLEN

ROBAR

Indicative

Present

robo
I steal
you steal
he/she/it steals
we steal
you steal
they steal

Present perfect

he robado
I have stolen
you have stolen
he/she/it has stolen
we have stolen
you have stolen
they have stolen

Past

robaba/robé
I stole
you stole
he/she/it stole
we stole
you stole
they stole

Past perfect

había/hube robado
I had stolen
you had stolen
he/she/it had stolen
we had stolen
you had stolen
they had stolen

Future

robaré
I shall/will steal
you will steal
he/she/it will steal
we shall/will steal
you will steal
they will steal

Future perfect

habré robado
I shall/will have stolen
you will have stolen
he/she/it will have stolen
we shall/will have stolen
you will have stolen
they will have stolen

Conditional

Present

robaría
I should/would steal
you would steal
he/she/it would steal
we should/would steal
you would steal
they would steal

Perfect

habría robado
I should/would have stolen
you would have stolen
he/she/it would have stolen
we should/would have stolen
you would have stolen
they would have stolen

Subjunctive

Present

robe
I steal
you steal
he/she/it steals
we steal
you steal
they steal

Present perfect

haya robado
I have stolen
you have stolen
he/she/it has stolen
we have stolen
you have stolen
they have stolen

Past

robara o robase
I stole
you stole
he/she/it stole
we stole
you stole
they stole

Past perfect

hubiera o hubiese robado
I had stolen
you had stolen
he/she/it had stolen
we had stolen
you had stolen
they had stolen

Imperative

let me steal	***no existe (déjame robar)***
steal	***roba tú***
let him/her/it steal	***robe él/ella/ello***
let us (let's) steal	***robemos nosotros***
steal	***robad vosotros***
let them steal	***roben ellos***

Impersonal forms

Infinitive

robar
to steal

Perfect Infinitive

haber robado
to have stolen

Gerund

robando
stealing

Perfect Gerund

habiendo robado
having stolen

Participle

robado
stolen

Perfect Participle

habiendo robado
having stolen

STICK · STUCK · STUCK

PEGAR, ADHERIR, COLOCAR, ATASCAR(SE), AGUANTAR, SOPORTAR

Indicative

Present

pego
I stick
you stick
he/she/it sticks
we stick
you stick
they stick

Present perfect

he pegado
I have stuck
you have stuck
he/she/it has stuck
we have stuck
you have stuck
they have stuck

Past

pegaba/pegué
I stuck
you stuck
he/she/it stuck
we stuck
you stuck
they stuck

Past perfect

había/hube pegado
I had stuck
you had stuck
he/she/it had stuck
we had stuck
you had stuck
they had stuck

Future

pegaré
I shall/will stick
you will stick
he/she/it will stick
we shall/will stick
you will stick
they will stick

Future perfect

habré pegado
I shall/will have stuck
you will have stuck
he/she/it will have stuck
we shall/will have stuck
you will have stuck
they will have stuck

Conditional

Present

pegaría
I should/would stick
you would stick
he/she/it would stick
we should/would stick
you would stick
they would stick

Perfect

habría pegado
I should/would have stuck
you would have stuck
he/she/it would have stuck
we should/would have stuck
you would have stuck
they would have stuck

Subjunctive

Present

pegue
I stick
you stick
he/she/it sticks
we stick
you stick
they stick

Present perfect

haya pegado
I have stuck
you have stuck
he/she/it has stuck
we have stuck
you have stuck
they have stuck

Past

pegara o pegase
I stuck
you stuck
he/she/it stuck
we stuck
you stuck
they stuck

Past perfect

hubiera o hubiese pegado
I had stuck
you had stuck
he/she/it had stuck
we had stuck
you had stuck
they had stuck

Imperative

let me stick	***no existe (déjame pegar)***
stick	***pega tú***
let him/her/it stick	***pegue él/ella/ello***
let us (let's) stick	***peguemos nosotros***
stick	***pegad vosotros***
let them stick	***peguen ellos***

Impersonal forms

Infinitive

pegar
to stick

Perfect Infinitive

haber pegado
to have stuck

Gerund

pegando
sticking

Perfect Gerund

habiendo pegado
having stuck

Participle

pegado
stuck

Perfect Participle

habiendo pegado
having stuck

STING · STUNG · STUNG

PICAR · MORDER

Indicative

Present

pico
I sting
you sting
he/she/it stings
we sting
you sting
they sting

Present perfect

he picado
I have stung
you have stung
he/she/it has stung
we have stung
you have stung
they have stung

Past

picaba/piqué
I stung
you stung
he/she/it stung
we stung
you stung
they stung

Past perfect

había/hube picado
I had stung
you had stung
he/she/it had stung
we had stung
you had stung
they had stung

Future

picaré
I shall/will sting
you will sting
he/she/it will sting
we shall/will sting
you will sting
they will sting

Future perfect

habré picado
I shall/will have stung
you will have stung
he/she/it will have stung
we shall/will have stung
you will have stung
they will have stung

Conditional

Present

picaría
I should/would sting
you would sting
he/she/it would sting
we should/would sting
you would sting
they would sting

Perfect

habría picado
I should/would have stung
you would have stung
he/she/it would have stung
we should/would have stung
you would have stung
they would have stung

Subjunctive

Present

pique
I sting
you sting
he/she/it stings
we sting
you sting
they sting

Present perfect

haya picado
I have stung
you have stung
he/she/it has stung
we have stung
you have stung
they have stung

Past

picara o picase
I stung
you stung
he/she/it stung
we stung
you stung
they stung

Past perfect

hubiera o hubiese picado
I had stung
you had stung
he/she/it had stung
we had stung
you had stung
they had stung

Imperative

let me sting	***no existe (déjame picar)***
sting	***pica tú***
let him/her/it sting	***pique él/ella/ello***
let us (let's) sting	***piquemos nosotros***
sting	***picad vosotros***
let them sting	***piquen ellos***

Impersonal forms

Infinitive

picar
to sting

Perfect Infinitive

haber picado
to have stung

Gerund

picando
stinging

Perfect Gerund

habiendo picado
having stung

Participle

picado
stung

Perfect Participle

habiendo picado
having stung

STINK · STANK · STUNK

APESTAR

Indicative

Present

apesto
I stink
you stink
he/she/it stinks
we stink
you stink
they stink

Present perfect

he apestado
I have stunk
you have stunk
he/she/it has stunk
we have stunk
you have stunk
they have stunk

Past

apestaba/apesté
I stank
you stank
he/she/it stank
we stank
you stank
they stank

Past perfect

había/hube apestado
I had stunk
you had stunk
he/she/it had stunk
we had stunk
you had stunk
they had stunk

Future

apestaré
I shall/will stink
you will stink
he/she/it will stink
we shall/will stink
you will stink
they will stink

Future perfect

habré apestado
I shall/will have stunk
you will have stunk
he/she/it will have stunk
we shall/will have stunk
you will have stunk
they will have stunk

Conditional

Present

apestaría
I should/would stink
you would stink
he/she/it would stink
we should/would stink
you would stink
they would stink

Perfect

habría apestado
I should/would have stunk
you would have stunk
he/she/it would have stunk
we should/would have stunk
you would have stunk
they would have stunk

Subjunctive

Present

apeste
I stink
you stink
he/she/it stinks
we stink
you stink
they stink

Present perfect

haya apestado
I have stunk
you have stunk
he/she/it has stunk
we have stunk
you have stunk
they have stunk

Past

apestara o apestase
I stank
you stank
he/she/it stank
we stank
you stank
they stank

Past perfect

hubiera o hubiese apestado
I had stunk
you had stunk
he/she/it had stunk
we had stunk
you had stunk
they had stunk

Imperative

let me stink	***no existe (déjame apestar)***
stink	***apesta tú***
let him/her/it stink	***apeste él/ella/ello***
let us (let's) stink	***apestemos nosotros***
stink	***apestad vosotros***
let them stink	***apesten ellos***

Impersonal forms

Infinitive

apestar
to stink

Perfect Infinitive

haber apestado
to have stunk

Gerund

apestando
stinking

Perfect Gerund

habiendo apestado
having stunk

Participle

apestado
stunk

Perfect Participle

habiendo apestado
having stunk

STREW · STREWED · STREWED/STREWN

ESPARCIR, DERRAMAR

Indicative

Present

esparzo
I strew
you strew
he/she/it strews
we strew
you strew
they strew

Present perfect

he esparcido
I have strewed/strewn
you have strewed/strewn
he/she/it has strewed/strewn
we have strewed/strewn
you have strewed/strewn
they have strewed/strewn

Past

esparcía/esparcí
I strewed
you strewed
he/she/it strewed
we strewed
you strewed
they strewed

Past perfect

había/hube esparcido
I had strewed/strewn
you had strewed/strewn
he/she/it had strewed/strewn
we had strewed/strewn
you had strewed/strewn
they had strewed/strewn

Future

esparciré
I shall/will strew
you will strew
he/she/it will strew
we shall/will strew
you will strew
they will strew

Future perfect

habré esparcido
I shall/will have strewed/strewn
you will have strewed/strewn
he/she/it will have strewed/ strewn
we shall/will have strewed/ strewn
you will have strewed/strewn
they will have strewed/strewn

Present

esparciría
I should/would strew
you would strew
he/she/it would strew
we should/would strew
you would strew
they would strew

Perfect

habría esparcido
I should/would have strewed/ strewn
you would have strewed/strewn
he/she/it would have strewed/ strewn
we should/would have strewed/ strewn
you would have strewed/strewn
they would have strewed/strewn

Subjunctive

Present

esparza
I strew
you strew
he/she/it strews
we strew
you strew
they strew

Present perfect

they strewed
haya esparcido
I have strewed/strewn
you have strewed/strewn
he/she/it has strewed/strewn
we have strewed/strewn
you have strewed/strewn

Past

esparciera o esparciese
I strewed
you strewed
he/she/it strewed
we strewed
you strewed

Past perfect

they have strewed/strewn
hubiera o hubiese esparcido
I had strewed/strewn
you had strewed/strewn
he/she/it had strewed/strewn
we had strewed/strewn
you had strewed/strewn

Imperative

they had strewed/ strewn
let me strew
strew
let him/her/it strew
let us (let's) strew

strew
let them strew
no existe (déjame esparcir)
esparce tú
esparza él
esparzamos nosotros

Impersonal forms

esparced vosotros
esparzan ellos

esparcido
strewed/strewn

Infinitive

esparcir
to strew

Perfect Infinitive

haber esparcido
to have strewed/strewn

Gerund

esparciendo
strewing

Perfect Gerund

habiendo esparcido
having strewed/strewn

Participle

Perfect Participle

STRIDE · STRODE · STRIDDEN

DAR ZANCADAS

Indicative

Present

doy zancadas
I stride
you stride
he/she/it strides
we stride
you stride
they stride

Present perfect

he dado zancadas
I have stridden
you have stridden
he/she/it has stridden
we have stridden
you have stridden
they have stridden

Past

daba/di zancadas
I strode
you strode
he/she/it strode
we strode
you strode
they strode

Past perfect

había/hube dado zancadas
I had stridden
you had stridden
he/she/it had stridden
we had stridden
you had stridden
they had stridden

Future

daré zancadas
I shall/will stride
you will stride
he/she/it will stride
we shall/will stride
you will stride
they will stride

Future perfect

había/hube dado zancadas
I shall/will have stridden
you will have stridden
he/she/it will have stridden
we shall/will have stridden
you will have stridden
they will have stridden

Conditional

Present

daría zancadas
I should/would stride
you would stride
he/she/it would stride
we should/would stride
you would stride
they would stride

Perfect

habría dado zancadas
I should/would have stridden
you would have stridden
he/she/it would have stridden
we should/would have stridden
you would have stridden
they would have stridden

Subjunctive

Present

dé zancadas
I stride
you stride
he/she/it strides
we stride
you stride
they stride

Present perfect

haya dado zancadas
I have stridden
you have stridden
he/she/it has stridden
we have stridden
you have stridden
they have stridden

Past

diera o diese zancadas
I strode
you strode
he/she/it strode
we strode
you strode
they strode

Past perfect

hubiera o hubiese dado zancadas
I had stridden
you had stridden
he/she/it had stridden
we had stridden
you had stridden
they had stridden

Imperative

let me stride	***no existe (déjame dar zancadas)***
stride	***da tú zancadas***
let him/her/it stride	***dé zancadas él/ella/ello***
let us (let's) stride	***demos zancadas nosotros***
stride	***dad zancadas vosotros***
let them stride	***den zancadas ellos***

Impersonal forms

Infinitive

dar zancadas
to stride

Perfect Infinitive

haber dado zancadas
to have stridden

Gerund

dando zancadas
striding

Perfect Gerund

habiendo dado zancadas
having stridden

Participle

dado zancadas
stridden

Perfect Participle

habiendo dado zancadas
having stridden

STRIKE · STRUCK · STRUCK

GOLPEAR · HACER HUELGA

Indicative

Present

golpeo
I strike
you strike
he/she/it strikes
we strike
you strike
they strike

Present perfect

he golpeado
I have struck
you have struck
he/she/it has struck
we have struck
you have struck
they have struck

Past

golpeaba/golpeé
I struck
you struck
he/she/it struck
we struck
you struck
they struck

Past perfect

había/hube golpeado
I had struck
you had struck
he/she/it had struck
we had struck
you had struck
they had struck

Future

golpearé
I shall/will strike
you will strike
he/she/it will strike
we shall/will strike
you will strike
they will strike

Future perfect

habré golpeado
I shall/will have struck
you will have struck
he/she/it will have struck
we shall/will have struck
you will have struck
they will have struck

Conditional

Present

golpearía
I should/would strike
you would strike
he/she/it would strike
we should/would strike
you would strike
they would strike

Perfect

habría golpeado
I should/would have struck
you would have struck
he/she/it would have struck
we should/would have struck
you would have struck
they would have struck

Subjunctive

Present

golpee
I strike
you strike
he/she/it strikes
we strike
you strike
they strike

Present perfect

haya golpeado
I have struck
you have struck
he/she/it has struck
we have struck
you have struck
they have struck

Past

golpeara o golpease
I struck
you struck
he/she/it struck
we struck
you struck
they struck

Past perfect

hubiera o hubiese golpeado
I had struck
you had struck
he/she/it had struck
we had struck
you had struck
they had struck

Imperative

let me strike	***no existe (déjame golpear)***
strike	***golpea tú***
let him/her/it strike	***golpee él/ella/ello***
let us (let's) strike	***golpeemos nosotros***
strike	***golpead vosotros***
let them strike	***golpeen ellos***

Impersonal forms

Infinitive

golpear
to strike

Perfect Infinitive

haber golpeado
to have struck

Gerund

golpeando
striking

Perfect Gerund

habiendo golpeado
having struck

Participle

golpeado
struck

Perfect Participle

habiendo golpeado
having struck

STRING · STRUNG · STRUNG

PONER CUERDAS, ENCORDAR, COLGAR, ENSARTAR, ENHEBRAR.

Indicative

Present

pongo cuerda
I string
you string
he/she/it strings
we string
you string
they string

Present perfect

he puesto cuerda
I have strung
you have strung
he/she/it has strung
we have strung
you have strung
they have strung

Past

ponía/puse cuerda
I strung
you strung
he/she/it strung
we strung
you strung
they strung

Past perfect

había/hube puesto cuerda
I had strung
you had strung
he/she/it had strung
we had strung
you had strung
they had strung

Future

pondré cuerda
I shall/will string
you will string
he/she/it will string
we shall/will string
you will string
they will string

Future perfect

habré puesto cuerda
I shall/will have strung
you will have strung
he/she/it will have strung
we shall/will have strung
you will have strung
they will have strung

Conditional

Present

pondría cuerda
I should/would string
you would string
he/she/it would string
we should/would string
you would string
they would string

Perfect

habría puesto cuerda
I should/would have strung
you would have strung
he/she/it would have strung
we should/would have strung
you would have strung
they would have strung

Subjunctive

Present

ponga cuerda
I string
you string
he/she/it strings
we string
you string
they string

Present perfect

haya puesto cuerda
I have strung
you have strung
he/she/it has strung
we have strung
you have strung
they have strung

Past

pusiera o pusiese cuerda
I strung
you strung
he/she/it strung
we strung
you strung
they strung

Past perfect

hubiera o hubiese puesto cuerda
I had strung
you had strung
he/she/it had strung
we had strung
you had strung
they had strung

Imperative

let me string	***no existe (déjame poner cuerda)***
string	***pon cuerda tú***
let him/her/it string	***ponga cuerda él/ella/ello***
let us (let's) string	***pongamos cuerda nosotros***
string	***poned cuerda vosotros***
let them string	***pongan cuerda ellos***

Impersonal forms

Infinitive

poner cuerda
to string

Perfect Infinitive

haber puesto cuerda
to have strung

Gerund

poniendo cuerda
stringing

Perfect Gerund

habiendo puesto cuerda
having strung

Participle

puesto cuerda
strung

Perfect Participle

habiendo puesto cuerda

STRIVE · STROVE · STRIVEN

ESFORZARSE, LUCHAR POR ALGO.

Indicative

Present

me esfuerzo
I strive
you strive
he/she/it strives
we strive
you strive
they strive

Present perfect

me he esforzado
I have striven
you have striven
he/she/it has striven
we have striven
you have striven
they have striven

Past

esforzaba
I strove
you strove
he/she/it strove
we strove
you strove
they strove

Past perfect

me había/hube esforzado
I had striven
you had striven
he/she/it had striven
we had striven
you had striven
they had striven

Future

me esforzaré
I shall/will strive
you will strive
he/she/it will strive
we shall/will strive
you will strive
they will strive

Future perfect

me habré esfozado
I shall/will have striven
you will have striven
he/she/it will have striven
we shall/will have striven
you will have striven
they will have striven

Conditional

Present

me esforzaría
I should/would strive
you would strive
he/she/it would strive
we should/would strive
you would strive
they would strive

Perfect

me habría esforzado
I should/would have striven
you would have striven
he/she/it would have striven
we should/would have striven
you would have striven
they would have striven

Subjunctive

Present

me esfuerce
I strive
you strive
he/she/it strives
we strive
you strive
they strive

Present perfect

me haya esforzado
I have striven
you have striven
he/she/it has striven
we have striven
you have striven
they have striven

Past

me esforzara o esforzase
I strove
you strove
he/she/it strove
we strove
you strove
they strove

Past perfect

me hubiera o hubiese esforzado
I had striven
you had striven
he/she/it had striven
we had striven
you had striven
they had striven

Imperative

let me strive	***no existe (déjame esforzarme)***
strive	***esfuérzate tú***
let him/her/it strive	***esfuércese él/ella/ello***
let us (let's) strive	***esforcémonos nosotros***
strive	***esforzaos vosotros***
let them strive	***esfuercen ellos***

Impersonal forms

striven

Infinitive

esforzarse
to strive

Perfect Infinitive

haberse esforzado
to have striven

Gerund

esforzándose
striving

Perfect Gerund

habiéndose esforzado
having striven

Participle

esforzado

Perfect Participle

habiéndose esforzado

SWEAR · SWORE · SWORN
JURAR

Indicative

Present
juro
I swear
you swear
he/she/it swears
we swear
you swear
they swear

Present perfect
he jurado
I have sworn
you have sworn
he/she/it has sworn
we have sworn
you have sworn
they have sworn

Past
juraba/juré
I swore
you swore
he/she/it swore
we swore
you swore
they swore

Past perfect
había/hube jurado
I had sworn
you had sworn
he/she/it had sworn
we had sworn
you had sworn
they had sworn

Future
juraré
I shall/will swear
you will swear
he/she/it will swear
we shall/will swear
you will swear
they will swear

Future perfect
habré jurado
I shall/will have sworn
you will have sworn
he/she/it will have sworn
we shall/will have sworn
you will have sworn
they will have sworn

Conditional

Present
juraría
I should/would swear
you would swear
he/she/it would swear
we should/would swear
you would swear
they would swear

Perfect
habría jurado
I should/would have sworn
you would have sworn
he/she/it would have sworn
we should/would have sworn
you would have sworn
they would have sworn

Subjunctive

Present
jure
I swear
you swear
he/she/it swears
we swear
you swear
they swear

Present perfect
haya jurado
I have sworn
you have sworn
he/she/it has sworn
we have sworn
you have sworn
they have sworn

Past
jurara o jurase
I swore
you swore
he/she/it swore
we swore
you swore
they swore

Past perfect
hubiera o hubiese jurado
I had sworn
you had sworn
he/she/it had sworn
we had sworn
you had sworn
they had sworn

Imperative

let me swear	***no existe (déjame jurar)***
swear	***jura tú***
let him/her/it swear	***jure él/ella/ello***
let us (let's) swear	***juremos nosotros***
swear	***jurad vosotros***
let them swear	***juren ellos***

Impersonal forms

Infinitive
jurar
to swear

Perfect Infinitive
haber jurado
to have sworn

Gerund
jurando
swearing

Perfect Gerund
habiendo jurado
having sworn

Participle
jurado
sworn

Perfect Participle
habiendo jurado
having sworn

SWEEP · SWEPT · SWEPT

BARRER

Indicative

Present

barro
I sweep
you sweep
he/she/it sweeps
we sweep
you sweep
they sweep

Present perfect

he barrido
I have swept
you have swept
he/she/it has swept
we have swept
you have swept
they have swept

Past

barría/barrí
I swept
you swept
he/she/it swept
we swept
you swept
they swept

Past perfect

había/hube barrido
I had swept
you had swept
he/she/it had swept
we had swept
you had swept
they had swept

Future

barreré
I shall/will sweep
you will sweep
he/she/it will sweep
we shall/will sweep
you will sweep
they will sweep

Future perfect

habré barrido
I shall/will have swept
you will have swept
he/she/it will have swept
we shall/will have swept
you will have swept
they will have swept

Conditional

Present

barrería
I should/would sweep
you would sweep
he/she/it would sweep
we should/would sweep
you would sweep
they would sweep

Perfect

habría barrido
I should/would have swept
you would have swept
he/she/it would have swept
we should/would have swept
you would have swept
they would have swept

Subjunctive

Present

barra
I sweep
you sweep
he/she/it sweeps
we sweep
you sweep
they sweep

Present perfect

haya barrido
I have swept
you have swept
he/she/it has swept
we have swept
you have swept
they have swept

Past

barriera o barriese
I swept
you swept
he/she/it swept
we swept
you swept
they swept

Past perfect

hubiera o hubiese barrido
I had swept
you had swept
he/she/it had swept
we had swept
you had swept
they had swept

Imperative

let me sweep	***no existe (déjame barrer)***
sweep	***barre tú***
let him/her/it sweep	***barra él/ella/ello***
let us (let's) sweep	***barramos nosotros***
sweep	***barred vosotros***
let them sweep	***barran ellos***

Impersonal forms

Infinitive

barrer
to sweep

Perfect Infinitive

haber barrido
to have swept

Gerund

barriendo
sweeping

Perfect Gerund

habiendo barrido
having swept

Participle

barrido
swept

Perfect Participle

habiendo barrido
having swept

SWELL · SWELLED · SWOLLEN

HINCHAR, INFLAMAR

Indicative

Present

inflamo
I swell
you swell
he/she/it swells
we swell
you swell
they swell

Present perfect

he inflamado
I have swollen
you have swollen
he/she/it has swollen
we have swollen
you have swollen
they have swollen

Past

inflamaba/inflamé
I swelled
you swelled
he/she/it swelled
we swelled
you swelled
they swelled

Past perfect

había/hube inflamado
I had swollen
you had swollen
he/she/it had swollen
we had swollen
you had swollen
they had swollen

Future

inflamaré
I shall/will swell
you will swell
he/she/it will swell
we shall/will swell
you will swell
they will swell

Future perfect

habré inflamado
I shall/will have swollen
you will have swollen
he/she/it will have swollen
we shall/will have swollen
you will have swollen
they will have swollen

Conditional

Present

inflamaría
I should/would swell
you would swell
he/she/it would swell
we should/would swell
you would swell
they would swell

Perfect

habría inflado
I should/would have swollen
you would have swollen
he/she/it would have swollen
we should/would have swollen
you would have swollen
they would have swollen

Subjunctive

Present

inflame
I swell
you swell
he/she/it swells
we swell
you swell
they swell

Present perfect

haya inflamado
I have swollen
you have swollen
he/she/it has swollen
we have swollen
you have swollen
they have swollen

Past

inflamara o inflamase
I swelled
you swelled
he/she/it swelled
we swelled
you swelled
they swelled

Past perfect

hubiera o hubiese inflamado
I had swollen
you had swollen
he/she/it had swollen
we had swollen
you had swollen

Imperative

they had swollen
let me swell
swell
let him/her/it swell
let us (let's) swell
swell

let them swell
no existe (déjame inflamar)
inflama tú
inflame él/ella/ello
inflamemos nosotros
inflamad vosotros

Impersonal forms

inflamen ellos

swollen

Infinitive

inflamar
to swell

Perfect Infinitive

haber inflamado
to have swollen

Gerund

inflamando
swelling

Perfect Gerund

habiendo inflamado
having swollen

Participle

inflamado

Perfect Participle

habiendo inflamado

SWIM · SWAM · SWUM

NADAR

Indicative

Present

nado
I swim
you swim
he/she/it swims
we swim
you swim
they swim

Present perfect

he nadado
I have swum
you have swum
he/she/it has swum
we have swum
you have swum
they have swum

Past

nadaba/nadé
I swam
you swam
he/she/it swam
we swam
you swam
they swam

Past perfect

había/hube nadado
I had swum
you had swum
he/she/it had swum
we had swum
you had swum
they had swum

Future

nadaré
I shall/will swim
you will swim
he/she/it will swim
we shall/will swim
you will swim
they will swim

Future perfect

habré nadado
I shall/will have swum
you will have swum
he/she/it will have swum
we shall/will have swum
you will have swum
they will have swum

Conditional

Present

nadaría
I should/would swim
you would swim
he/she/it would swim
we should/would swim
you would swim
they would swim

Perfect

habría nadado
I should/would have swum
you would have swum
he/she/it would have swum
we should/would have swum
you would have swum
they would have swum

Subjunctive

Present

nade
I swim
you swim
he/she/it swims
we swim
you swim
they swim

Present perfect

haya nadado
I have swum
you have swum
he/she/it has swum
we have swum
you have swum
they have swum

Past

nadara o nadase
I swam
you swam
he/she/it swam
we swam
you swam
they swam

Past perfect

hubiera o hubiese nadado
I had swum
you had swum
he/she/it had swum
we had swum
you had swum
they had swum

Imperative

let me swim	***no existe (déjame nadar)***
swim	***nada tú***
let him/her/it swim	***nade él/ella/ello***
let us (let's) swim	***nademos nosotros***
swim	***nadad vosotros***
let them swim	***naden ellos***

Impersonal forms

Infinitive

nadar
to swim

Perfect Infinitive

haber nadado
to have swum

Gerund

nadando
swimming

Perfect Gerund

habiendo nadado
having swum

Participle

nadado
swum

Perfect Participle

habiendo nadado
having swum

SWING · SWUNG · SWUNG

COLUMPIARSE, COLGAR, BALANCEARSE

Indicative

Present

columpio
I swing
you swing
he/she/it swings
we swing
you swing
they swing

Present perfect

they would swing
he columpiado
I have swung
you have swung
he/she/it has swung
we have swung
you have swung

Past

columpiaba/
columpié
I swung
you swung
he/she/it swung
we swung
you swung

Past perfect

they have swung
había/hube columpiado
I had swung
you had swung
he/she/it had swung
we had swung
you had swung

Future

they swung
columpiaré
I shall/will swing
you will swing
he/she/it will swing
we shall/will swing
you will swing

Future perfect

they had swung
habré columpiado
I shall/will have swung
you will have swung
he/she/it will have swung
we shall/will have swung
you will have swung

Conditional

Present

they will swing
columpiaría
I should/would swing
you would swing
he/she/it would swing
we should/would swing
you would swing

Perfect

they will have swung
habría columpiado
I should/would have swung
you would have swung
he/she/it would have swung
we should/would have swung
you would have swung

Subjunctive

Present

they would have swung
columpie
I swing
you swing
he/she/it swings
we swing
you swing

Present perfect

they swung
haya columpiado
I have swung
you have swung
he/she/it has swung
we have swung
you have swung

Past

they swing
columpiara o
columpiase
I swung
you swung
he/she/it swung
we swung
you swung

Past perfect

they have swung
hubiera o hubiese
columpiado
I had swung
you had swung
he/she/it had swung
we had swung
you had swung

Imperative

they had swung
let me swing
swing
let him/her/it swing
let us (let's) swing
swing

let them swing
no existe (déjame
columpiar)
columpia tú
columpie él/ella/ello
columpiemos nosotros

Impersonal forms

columpiad vosotros
columpien ellos

columpiado
swung

Infinitive

columpiar
to swing

Perfect Infinitive

haber columpiado
to have swung

Gerund

columpiando
swinging

Perfect Gerund

habiendo columpiado
having swung

Participle

Perfect Participle

TAKE · TOOK · TAKEN

COGER, TOMAR

Indicative

Present

cojo
I take
you take
he/she/it takes
we take
you take
they take

Present perfect

he cogido
I have taken
you have taken
he/she/it has taken
we have taken
you have taken
they have taken

Past

cogía/cogí
I took
you took
he/she/it took
we took
you took
they took

Past perfect

había/hube cogido
I had taken
you had taken
he/she/it had taken
we had taken
you had taken
they had taken

Future

cogeré
I shall/will take
you will take
he/she/it will take
we shall/will take
you will take
they will take

Future perfect

habré cogido
I shall/will have taken
you will have taken
he/she/it will have taken
we shall/will have taken
you will have taken
they will have taken

Conditional

Present

cogería
I should/would take
you would take
he/she/it would take
we should/would take
you would take
they would take

Perfect

habría cogido
I should/would have taken
you would have taken
he/she/it would have taken
we should/would have taken
you would have taken
they would have taken

Subjunctive

Present

coja
I take
you take
he/she/it takes
we take
you take
they take

Present perfect

haya cogido
I have taken
you have taken
he/she/it has taken
we have taken
you have taken
they have taken

Past

cogiera/cogiese
I took
you took
he/she/it took
we took
you took
they took

Past perfect

hubiera/hubiese cogido
I had taken
you had taken
he/she/it had taken
we had taken
you had taken
they had taken

Imperative

let me take	***no existe (déjame coger)***
take	***coge tú***
let him/her/it take	***coja él/ella/ello***
let us (let's) take	***cojamos nosotros***
take	***coged vosotros***
let them take	***cojan ellos***

Impersonal forms

Infinitive

coger
to take

Perfect Infinitive

haber cogido
to have taken

Gerund

cogiendo
taking

Perfect Gerund

habiendo cogido
having taken

Participle

cogido
taken

Perfect Participle

habiendo cogido
having taken

TEACH · TAUGHT · TAUGHT

ENSEÑAR

Indicative

Present

enseño
I teach
you teach
he/she/it teaches
we teach
you teach
they teach

Present perfect

he enseñado
I have taught
you have taught
he/she/it has taught
we have taught
you have taught
they have taught

Past

enseñaba/enseñé
I taught
you taught
he/she/it taught
we taught
you taught
they taught

Past perfect

había/hube enseñado
I had taught
you had taught
he/she/it had taught
we had taught
you had taught
they had taught

Future

enseñaré
I shall/will teach
you will teach
he/she/it will teach
we shall/will teach
you will teach
they will teach

Future perfect

habré enseñado
I shall/will have taught
you will have taught
he/she/it will have taught
we shall/will have taught
you will have taught
they will have taught

Conditional

Present

enseñaría
I should/would teach
you would teach
he/she/it would teach
we should/would teach
you would teach
they would teach

Perfect

habría enseñado
I should/would have taught
you would have taught
he/she/it would have taught
we should/would have taught
you would have taught
they would have taught

Subjunctive

Present

enseñe
I teach
you teach
he/she/it teaches
we teach
you teach
they teach

Present perfect

haya enseñado
I have taught
you have taught
he/she/it has taught
we have taught
you have taught
they have taught

Past

enseñara o enseñase
I taught
you taught
he/she/it taught
we taught
you taught
they taught

Past perfect

hubiera o hubiese enseñado
I had taught
you had taught
he/she/it had taught
we had taught
you had taught
they had taught

Imperative

let me teach	***no existe (déjame enseñar)***
teach	***enseña tú***
let him/her/it teach	***enseñe él/ella/ello***
let us (let's) teach	***enseñemos nosotros***
teach	***enseñad vosotros***
let them teach	***enseñen ellos***

Impersonal forms

Infinitive

enseñar
to teach

Perfect Infinitive

haber enseñado
to have taught

Gerund

enseñando
teaching

Perfect Gerund

habiendo enseñado
having taught

Participle

enseñado
taught

Perfect Participle

habiendo enseñado
having taught

TEAR · TORE · TORN

DESGARRAR, ARRANCAR, RASGAR

Indicative

Present

desgarro
I tear
you tear
he/she/it tears
we tear
you tear
they tear

Present perfect

he arrancado
I have torn
you have torn
he/she/it has torn
we have torn
you have torn
they have torn

Past

arrancaba/arranqué
I tore
you tore
he/she/it tore
we tore
you tore
they tore

Past perfect

había/hube arrancado
I had torn
you had torn
he/she/it had torn
we had torn
you had torn
they had torn

Future

arrancaré
I shall/will tear
you will tear
he/she/it will tear
we shall/will tear
you will tear
they will tear

Future perfect

habré arrancado
I shall/will have torn
you will have torn
he/she/it will have torn
we shall/will have torn
you will have torn
they will have torn

Conditional

Present

arrancaría
I should/would tear
you would tear
he/she/it would tear
we should/would tear
you would tear
they would tear

Perfect

habría arrancado
I should/would have torn
you would have torn
he/she/it would have torn
we should/would have torn
you would have torn
they would have torn

Subjunctive

Present

desgarre
I tear
you tear
he/she/it tears
we tear
you tear
they tear

Present perfect

haya arrancado
I have torn
you have torn
he/she/it has torn
we have torn
you have torn
they have torn

Past

arrancara o arrancase
I tore
you tore
he/she/it tore
we tore
you tore
they tore

Past perfect

hubiera o hubiese arrancado
I had torn
you had torn
he/she/it had torn
we had torn
you had torn

Imperative

let me tear	***no existe (déjame desgarrar)***
tear	***desgarra tú***
let him/her/it tear	***desgarre él/ella/ello***
let us (let's) tear	***desgarremos nosotros***
tear	***desgarrad vosotros***
let them tear	***desgarren ellos***

Impersonal forms

Infinitive

desgarrar
to tear

Perfect Infinitive

haber desgarrado
to have torn

Gerund

desgarrando
tearing

Perfect Gerund

habiendo desgarrado
having torn

Participle

desgarrado
torn

Perfect Participle

habiendo desgarrado
having torn

TELL · TOLD · TOLD

DECIR, CONTAR

Indicative

Present

digo
I tell
you tell
he/she/it tells
we tell
you tell
they tell

Present perfect

he dicho
I have told
you have told
he/she/it has told
we have told
you have told
they have told

Past

decía/dije
I told
you told
he/she/it told
we told
you told
they told

Past perfect

había/hube dicho
I had told
you had told
he/she/it had told
we had told
you had told
they had told

Future

diré
I shall/will tell
you will tell
he/she/it will tell
we shall/will tell
you will tell
they will tell

Future perfect

habré dicho
I shall/will have told
you will have told
he/she/it will have told
we shall/will have told
you will have told
they will have told

Conditional

Present

diría
I should/would tell
you would tell
he/she/it would tell
we should/would tell
you would tell
they would tell

Perfect

habría dicho
I should/would have told
you would have told
he/she/it would have told
we should/would have told
you would have told
they would have told

Subjunctive

Present

diga
I tell
you tell
he/she/it tells
we tell
you tell
they tell

Present perfect

haya dicho
I have told
you have told
he/she/it has told
we have told
you have told
they have told

Past

dijera/dijese
I told
you told
he/she/it told
we told
you told
they told

Past perfect

hubiera/hubiese dicho
I had told
you had told
he/she/it had told
we had told
you had told
they had told

Imperative

let me tell	***no existe (déjame decir)***
tell	***di tú***
let him/her/it tell	***diga él/ella/ello***
let us (let's) tell	***digamos nosotros***
tell	***decid vosotros***
let them tell	***digan ellos***

Impersonal forms

Infinitive

decir
to tell

Perfect Infinitive

haber dicho
to have told

Gerund

diciendo
telling

Perfect Gerund

habiendo dicho
having told

Participle

dicho
told

Perfect Participle

habiendo dicho
having told

THINK · THOUGHT · THOUGHT

PENSAR, CREER

Indicative

Present

creo
I think
you think
he/she/it thinks
we think
you think
they think

Present perfect

he creído
I have thought
you have thought
he/she/it has thought
we have thought
you have thought
they have thought

Past

creía/creí
I thought
you thought
he/she/it thought
we thought
you thought
they thought

Past perfect

había/hube creído
I had thought
you had thought
he/she/it had thought
we had thought
you had thought
they had thought

Future

creeré
I shall/will think
you will think
he/she/it will think
we shall/will think
you will think
they will think

Future perfect

habré creído
I shall/will have thought
you will have thought
he/she/it will have thought
we shall/will have thought
you will have thought
they will have thought

Conditional

Present

creería
I should/would think
you would think
he/she/it would think
we should/would think
you would think
they would think

Perfect

habría creído
I should/would have thought
you would have thought
he/she/it would have thought
we should/would have thought
you would have thought
they would have thought

Subjunctive

Present

crea
I think
you think
he/she/it thinks
we think
you think
they think

Present perfect

haya creído
I have thought
you have thought
he/she/it has thought
we have thought
you have thought
they have thought

Past

creyera o creyese
I thought
you thought
he/she/it thought
we thought
you thought
they thought

Past perfect

hubiera o hubiese creído
I had thought
you had thought
he/she/it had thought
we had thought
you had thought
they had thought

Imperative

let me think	***no existe (déjame pensar)***
think	***piensa***
let him/her/it think	***let him/her/it think***
let us (let's) think	***let us (let's) think***
think	***think***
let them think	***let them think***

Impersonal forms

Infinitive

creer
to think

Perfect Infinitive

haber creído
to have thought

Gerund

creído
thinking

Perfect Gerund

habiendo creído
having thought

Participle

creído
thought

Perfect Participle

habiendo creído
having thought

THRIVE · THROVE/THRIVED · THRIVEN

PROSPERAR

Indicative

Present

prospero
I thrive
you thrive
he/she/it thrives
we thrive
you thrive
they thrive

Present perfect

they would thrive
he prosperado
I have thrived/thriven
you have thrived/thriven
he/she/it has thrived/thriven
we have thrived/thriven
you have thrived/thriven

Past

prosperaba/
prosperé
I thrived/throve
you thrived/throve
he/she/it thrived/throve
we thrived/throve
you thrived/throve

Past perfect

they have thrived/thriven
había/hube prosperado
I had thrived/thriven
you had thrived/thriven
he/she/it had thrived/thriven
we had thrived/thriven
you had thrived/thriven

Future

they thrived/throve
prosperaré
I shall/will thrive
you will thrive
he/she/it will thrive

we shall/will thrive
you will thrive

Future perfect

they had thrived/thriven
habré properado
I shall/will have thrived/
thriven
you will have thrived/thriven
he/she/it will have thrived/
thriven
we shall/will have thrived/thriven

Present

they will thrive
prosperaría
I should/would thrive

you would thrive
he/she/it would
thrive
we should/would
thrive
you would thrive

Perfect

you will have thrived/thriven
they will have thrived/thriven
habría prosperado
I should/would have thrived/
thriven
you would have thrived/thriven
he/she/it would have thrived/
thriven
we should/would have thrived/
thriven

Subjunctive

Present

you would have
thrived/thriven
they would have
thrived/thriven
prospere
I thive
you thrive

Present perfect

he/she/it thrived/throve
we thrived/throve
you thrived/throve
they thrived/throve
haya prosperado
I have thrived/thriven
you have thrived/thriven

Past

he/she/it thrives
we thrive
you thrive
they thrive
prosperara o
prosperase
I thrived/throve
you thrived/throve

Past perfect

he/she/it has thrived/thriven
we have thrived/thriven
you have thrived/thriven
they have thrived/thriven
hubiera o hubiese
prosperado
I had thrived/thriven
you had thrived/thriven

Imperative

he/she/it had thrived/
thriven
we had thrived/thriven
you had thrived/thriven
they had thrived/thriven
let me thrive

thrive
let him/her/it thrive
let us (let's) thrive
thrive
let them thrive
no existe (déjame prosperar)

Impersonal forms

prospera tú
prospere él/ella/ello
prosperemos
nosotros
prosperad vosotros
prosperen ellos

Infinitive

prosperar
to thrive

Gerund

prosperando
thriving

Participle

prosperado
thrived/thriven

Perfect Infinitive

haber prosperado
to have thrived/thriven

THROW · THREW · THROWN

ARROJAR · TIRAR

Indicative

Present

arrojo
I throw
you throw
he/she/it throws
we throw
you throw
they throw

Present perfect

he arrojado
I have thrown
you have thrown
he/she/it has thrown
we have thrown
you have thrown
they have thrown

Past

arrojaba/arrojé
I threw
you threw
he/she/it threw
we threw
you threw
they threw

Past perfect

había/hube arrojado
I had thrown
you had thrown
he/she/it had thrown
we had thrown
you had thrown
they had thrown

Future

arrojaré
I shall/will throw
you will throw
he/she/it will throw
we shall/will throw
you will throw
they will throw

Future perfect

habré arrojado
I shall/will have thrown
you will have thrown
he/she/it will have thrown
we shall/will have thrown
you will have thrown
they will have thrown

Conditional

Present

arrojaría
I should/would throw
you would throw
he/she/it would throw
we should/would throw
you would throw
they would throw

Perfect

habría arrojado
I should/would have thrown
you would have thrown
he/she/it would have thrown
we should/would have thrown
you would have thrown
they would have thrown

Subjunctive

Present

arroje
I throw
you throw
he/she/it throws
we throw
you throw
they throw

Present perfect

haya arrojado
I have thrown
you have thrown
he/she/it has thrown
we have thrown
you have thrown
they have thrown

Past

arrojara o arrojase
I threw
you threw
he/she/it threw
we threw
you threw
they threw

Past perfect

hubiera o hubiese arrojado
I had thrown
you had thrown
he/she/it had thrown
we had thrown
you had thrown
they had thrown

Imperative

let me throw	***no existe (déjame arrojar)***
throw	***arroja tú***
let him/her/it throw	***arroje él/ella/ello***
let us (let's) throw	***arrojemos nosotros***
throw	***arrojad vosotros***
let them throw	***arrojen ellos***

Impersonal forms

Infinitive

arrojar
to throw

Perfect Infinitive

haber arrojado
to have thrown

Gerund

arrojando
throwing

Perfect Gerund

habiendo arrojado
having thrown

Participle

arrojado
thrown

Perfect Participle

habiendo arrojado
having thrown

THRUST · THRUST · THRUST

CLAVAR · INSERTAR · EMPUJAR

Indicative

Present

clavo
I thrust
you thrust
he/she/it thrusts
we thrust
you thrust
they thrust

Present perfect

he clavado
I have thrust
you have thrust
he/she/it has thrust
we have thrust
you have thrust
they have thrust

Past

clavaba/clavé
I thrust
you thrust
he/she/it thrust
we thrust
you thrust
they thrust

Past perfect

había/hube clavado.
I had thrust
you had thrust
he/she/it had thrust
we had thrust
you had thrust
they had thrust

Future

clavaré
I shall/will thrust
you will thrust
he/she/it will thrust
we shall/will thrust
you will thrust
they will thrust

Future perfect

habré clavado
I shall/will have thrust
you will have thrust
he/she/it will have thrust
we shall/will have thrust
you will have thrust
they will have thrust

Conditional

Present

clavaría
I should/would thrust
you would thrust
he/she/it would thrust
we should/would thrust
you would thrust
they would thrust

Perfect

habría clavado
I should/would have thrust
you would have thrust
he/she/it would have thrust
we should/would have thrust
you would have thrust
they would have thrust

Subjunctive

Present

clave
I thrust
you thrust
he/she/it thrusts
we thrust
you thrust
they thrust

Present perfect

haya clavado
I have thrust
you have thrust
he/she/it has thrust
we have thrust
you have thrust
they have thrust

Past

clavara o clavase
I thrust
you thrust
he/she/it thrust
we thrust
you thrust
they thrust

Past perfect

hubiera o hubiese clavado
I had thrust
you had thrust
he/she/it had thrust
we had thrust
you had thrust
they had thrust

Imperative

let me thrust	***no existe (déjame clavar)***
thrust	***clava tú***
let him/her/it thrust	***clave él/ella/ello***
let us (let's) thrust	***clavemos nosotros***
thrust	***clavad vosotros***
let them thrust	***claven ellos***

Impersonal forms

Infinitive

clavar
to thrust

Perfect Infinitive

haber clavado
to have thrust

Gerund

clavando
thrusting

Perfect Gerund

habiendo clavado
having thrust

Participle

clavado
thrust

Perfect Participle

habiendo clavado
having thrust

TREAD · TROD · TRODDEN
PISAR · APISONAR

Indicative

Present

piso
I tread
you tread
he/she/it treads
we tread
you tread
they tread

Present perfect

he pisado
I have trodden
you have trodden
he/she/it has trodden
we have trodden
you have trodden
they have trodden

Past

pisaba/pisé
I trod
you trod
he/she/it trod
we trod
you trod
they trod

Past perfect

había/hube pisado
I had trodden
you had trodden
he/she/it had trodden
we had trodden
you had trodden
they had trodden

Future

pisaré
I shall/will tread
you will tread
he/she/it will tread
we shall/will tread
you will tread
they will tread

Future perfect

habré pisado
I shall/will have trodden
you will have trodden
he/she/it will have trodden
we shall/will have trodden
you will have trodden
they will have trodden

Conditional

Present

pisaría
I should/would tread
you would tread
he/she/it woudl tread
we should/would tread
you would tread
they would tread

Perfect

habría pisado
I should/would have trodden
you would have trodden
he/she/it would have trodden
we should/would have trodden
you would have trodden
they would have trodden

Subjunctive

Present

pise
I tread
you tread
he/she/it treads
we tread
you tread
they tread

Present perfect

haya pisado
I have trodden
you have trodden
he/she/it has trodden
we have trodden
you have trodden
they have trodden

Past

pisara o pisase
I trod
you trod
he/she/it trod
we trod
you trod
they trod

Past perfect

hubiera o hubiese pisado
I had trodden
you had trodden
he/she/it had trodden
we had trodden
you had trodden
they had trodden

Imperative

let me tread	***no existe (déjame pisar)***
tread	***pisa tú***
let him/her/it tread	***pise él/ella/ello***
let us (let's) tread	***pisemos nosotros***
tread	***pisad vosotros***
let them tread	***pisen ellos***

Impersonal forms

Infinitive

pisar
to tread

Perfect infintive

haber pisado
to have trodden

Gerund

pisando
treading

Perfect Gerund

habiendo pisado
having trodden

Participle

pisado
trodden

Perfect Participle

habiendo pisado
having trodden

WAKE · WOKE · WOKEN

DESPERTAR

Indicative

Present

despierto
I wake
you wake
he/she/it wakes
we wake
you wake
they wake

Present perfect

he despertado
I have woken
you have woken
he/she/it has woken
we have woken
you have woken
they have woken

Past

despertaba/desperté
I woke
you woke
he/she/it woke
we woke
you woke
they woke

Past perfect

había/hube despertado
I had woken
you had woken
he/she/it had woken
we had woken
you had woken
they had woken

Future

despertaré
I shall/will wake
you will wake
he/she/it will wake
we shall/will wake
you will wake
they will wake

Future perfect

habré despertado
I shall/will have woken
you will have woken
he/she/it will have woken
we shall/will have woken
you will have woken
they will have woken

Conditional

Present

despertaría
I should/would wake
you would wake
he/she/it would wake
we should/would wake
you would wake
they would wake

Perfect

habría despertado
I should/would have woken
you would have woken
he/she/it would have woken
we should/would have woken
you would have woken
they would have woken

Subjunctive

Present

despierte
I wake
you wake
he/she/it wakes
we wake
you wake
they wake

Present perfect

haya despertado
I have woken
you have woken
he/she/it has woken
we have woken
you have woken
they have woken

Past

despertara o despertas
I woke
you woke
he/she/it woke
we woke
you woke
they woke

Past perfect

hubiera o hubiese despertado
I had woken
you had woken
he/she/it had woken
we had woken
you had woken

Imperative

they had woken
let me wake
wake
let him/her/it wake
let us (let's) wake
wake

let them wake
no existe (déjame despertar)
despierta tú
despierte él/ella/ello
despertemos nosotros
despertad vosotros

Impersonal forms

despierten ellos

woken

Infinitive

despertar
to wake

Perfect Infinitive

haber despertado
to have woken

Gerund

despertando
waking

Perfect Gerund

habiendo despertado
having woken

Participle

despertado

Perfect Participle

habiendo despertado

WEAR · WORE · WORN

LLEVAR PUESTO

Indicative

Present

llevo puesto
I wear
you wear
he/she/it wears
we wear
you wear
they wear

Present perfect

he llevado puesto
I have worn
you have worn
he/she/it has worn
we have worn
you have worn
they have worn

Past

llevaba/llevé puesto
I wore
you wore
he/she/it wore
we wore
you wore
they wore

Past perfect

había/hube llevado puesto
I had worn
you had worn
he/she/it had worn
we had worn
you had worn
they had worn

Future

llevaré puesto
I shall/will wear
you will wear
he/she/it will wear
we shall/will wear
you will wear
they will wear

Future perfect

habré llevado puesto
I shall/will have worn
you will have worn
he/she/it will have worn
we shall/will have worn
you will have worn
they will have worn

Conditional

Present

llevaría puesto
I should/would wear
you would wear
he/she/it would wear
we should/would wear
you would wear
they would wear

Perfect

habría llevado puesto
I should/would have worn
you would have worn
he/she/it would have worn
we should/would have worn
you would have worn
they would have worn

Subjunctive

Present

lleve puesto
I wear
you wear
he/she/it wears
we wear
you wear
they wear

Present perfect

haya llevado puesto
I have worn
you have worn
he/she/it has worn
we have worn
you have worn
they have worn

Past

llevara/llevase puesto
I wore
you wore
he/she/it wore
we wore
you wore
they wore

Past perfect

hubiera/hubiese llevado puesto
I had worn
you had worn
he/she/it had worn
we had worn
you had worn
they had worn

Imperative

let me wear	***no existe (déjame llevar puesto)***
wear	***lleva puesto tú***
let him/her/it wear	***lleve puesto él/ella/ello***
let us (let's) wear	***llevemos puesto nosotros***
wear	***llevad puesto vosotros***
let them wear	

Impersonal forms

Infinitive

llevar puesto
to wear

Perfect Infinitive

haber llevado puesto
to have worn

Gerund

llevando puesto
wearing

Perfect Gerund

habiendo llevado puesto
having worn

Participle

llevado puesto
worn

Perfect Participle

habiendo llevado puesto
having worn

WEAVE · WOVE · WOVEN

TEJER, HILAR

Indicative

Present

tejo
I weave
you weave
he/she/it weaves
we weave
you weave
they weave

Present perfect

he tejido
I have woven
you have woven
he/she/it has woven
we have woven
you have woven
they have woven

Past

tejía/tejí
I wove
you wove
he/she/it wove
we wove
you wove
theey wove

Past perfect

había/hube tejido
I had woven
you had woven
he/she/it had woven
we had woven
you had woven
they had woven

Future

tejeré
I shall/will weave
you will weave
he/she/it will weave
we shall/will weave
you will weave
they will weave

Future perfect

habré tejido
I shall/wil have woven
you will have woven
he/she/it will have woven
we shall/will have woven
you will have woven
they will have woven

Present

tejería
I should/would weave
you would weave
he/she/it would weave
we should/would weave
you would weave
they would weave

Perfect

habría tejido
I should/would have woven
you would have woven
he/she/it would have woven
we should/would have woven
you would have woven
they would have woven

Subjunctive

Present

teja
I weave
you weave
he/she/it weaves
we weave
you weave
they weave

Present perfect

haya tejido
I have woven
you have woven
he/she/it has woven
we have woven
you have woven
they have woven

Past

tejiera o tejiese
I wove
you wove
he/she/it wove
we wove
you wove
they wove

Past perfect

hubiera o hubiese tejido
I had woven
you had woven
he/she/it had woven
we had woven
you had woven
they had woven

Imperative

let me weave	***no existe (déjame tejer)***
weave	***teje tú***
let him/her/it weave	***teja él/ella/ello***
let us (let's) weave	***tejamos nosotros***
weave	***tejed vosotros***
let them weave	***tejan ellos***

Impersonal forms

Infinitive

tejer
to weave

Perfect Infinitive

haber tejido
to have woven

Gerund

tejiendo
weaving

Perfect Gerund

habiendo tejido
having woven

Participle

tejido
woven

Perfect Participle

habiendo tejido
having woven

WEEP · WEPT · WEPT

SOLLOZAR

Indicative

Present

sollozo
I weep
you weep
he/she/it weeps
we weep
you weep
they weep

Present perfect

he sollozado
I have wept
you have wept
he/she/it has wept
we have wept
you have wept
they have wept

Past

sollozaba/sollocé
I wept
you wept
he/she/it wept
we wept
you wept
they wept

Past perfect

había/hube sollozado
I had wept
you had wept
he/she/it had wept
we had wept
you had wept
they had wept

Future

sollozaré
I shall/will weep
you will weep
he/she/it will weep
we shall/will weep
you will weep
they will weep

Future perfect

habré sollozado
I shall/will have wept
you will have wept
he/she/it will have wept
we shall/will have wept
you will have wept
they will have wept

Conditional

Present

sollozaría
I should/would weep
you would weep
he/she/it would weep
we should/would weep
you would weep
they would weep

Perfect

habría sollozado
I should/would have wept
you would have wept
he/she/it would have wept
we should/would have wept
you would have wept
they would have wept

Subjunctive

Present

solloce
I weep
you weep
he/she/it weeps
we weep
you weep
they weep

Present perfect

haya sollozado
I have wept
you have wept
he/she/it has wept
we have wept
you have wept
they have wept

Past

sollozara o sollozase
I wept
you wept
he/she/it wept
we wept
you wept
they wept

Past perfect

hubiera o hubiese sollozado
I had wept
you had wept
he/she/it had wept
we had wept
you had wept
they had wept

Imperative

let me weep	***no existe (déjame sollozar)***
weep	***solloza tú***
let him/her/it weep	***solloce él/ella/ello***
let us (let's) weep	***sollocemos nosotros***
weep	***sollozad vosotros***
let them weep	***sollocen ellos***

Impersonal forms

Infinitive

sollozar
to weep

Perfect Infinitive

haber sollozado
to have wept

Gerund

sollozando
weeping

Perfect Gerund

habiendo sollozado
having wept

Participle

sollozado
wept

Perfect Participle

habiendo sollozado
having swept

WIN · WON · WON

GANAR

Indicative

Present

gano
I win
you win
he/she/it wins
we win
you win
they win

Present perfect

he ganado
I have won
you have won
he/she/it has won
we have won
you have won
they have won

Past

ganaba/gané
I won
you won
he/she/it won
we won
you won
they won

Past perfect

había/hube ganado
I had won
you had won
he/had won
we had won
you had won
they had won

Future

ganaré
I shall/will win
you will win
he/she/it will win
we shall/will win
you will win
they will win

Future perfect

habré ganado
I shall/will have won
you will have won
he/she/it will have won
we shall/will have won
you will have won
they will have won

Conditional

Present

ganaría
I should/would win
you would win
he/she/it would win
we should/would win
you would win
they would win

Perfect

habría ganado
I should/would have won
you would have won
he/she/it would have won
we should/would have won
you would have won
they would have won

Subjunctive

Present

gane
I win
you win
he/she/it wins
we win
you win
they win

Present perfect

haya ganado
I have won
you have won
he/she/it has won
we have won
you have won
they have won

Past

ganara o ganase
I won
you won
he/she/it won
we won
you won
they won

Past perfect

hubiera o hubiese ganado
I had won
you had won
he had won
we had won
you had won
they had won

Imperative

let me win	***no existe (déjame ganar)***
win	***gana tú***
let him/her/it win	***gane él/ella/ello***
let us (let's) win	***ganemos nosotros***
win	***ganad vosotros***
let them win	***ganen ellos***

Impersonal forms

Infinitive

ganar
to win

Perfect Infinitive

haber ganado
to have won

Gerund

ganando
winning

Perfect Gerund

habiendo ganado
having won

Participle

ganado
won

Perfect Participle

habiendo ganado
having won

WIND · WOUND · WOUND

ENROSCAR · ENROLLAR · DEVANAR · OVILLAR

Indicative

Present

enrollo
I wind
you wind
he/she/it winds
we wind
you wind
they wind

Present perfect

he enrollado
I have wound
you have wound
he/she/it has wound
we have wound
you have wound
they have wound

Past

enrollaba/enrollé
I wound
you wound
he/she/it wound
we wound
you wound
they wound

Past perfect

había/hube enrollado
I had wound
you had wound
he/she/it had wound
we had wound
you had wound
they had wound

Future

enrollaré
I shall/will wind
you will wind
he/she/it will wind
we shall/will wind
you will wind
they will wind

Future perfect

habré enrollado
I shall/will have wound
you will have wound
he/she/it will have wound
we shall/will have wound
you will have wound
they will have wound

Conditional

Present

enrollaría
I should/would wind
you would wind
he/she/it would wind
we should/would wind
you would wind
they would wind

Perfect

habría enrollado
I should/would have wound
you would have wound
he/she/it would have wound
we should/would have wound
you would have wound
they would have wound

Subjunctive

Present

enrolle
I wind
you wind
he/she/it winds
we wind
you wind
they wind

Present perfect

haya enrollado
I have wound
you have wound
he/she/it has wound
we have wound
you have wound
they have wound

Past

enrollara o enrollase
I wound
you wound
he/she/it wound
we wound
you wound
they wound

Past perfect

hubiera o hubiese enrollado
I had wound
you had wound
he/she/it had wound
we had wound
you had wound
they had wound

Imperative

let me wind	***no existe (déjame enrollar)***
wind	***enrolla tú***
let him/her/it wind	***enrolle él/ella/ello***
let us (let's) wind	***enrollemos nosotros***
wind	***enrollad vosotros***
let them wind	***enrollen ellos***

Impersonal forms

Infinitive

enrollar
to wind

Perfect Infinitive

haber enrollado
to have wound

Gerund

enrollando
winding

Perfect Gerund

habiendo enrollado
having wound

Participle

enrollado
wound

Perfect Participle

habiendo enrollado
having wound

WRING · WRUNG · WRUNG

RETORCER · ESTRUJAR

Indicative

Present

retuerzo
I wring
you wring
he/she/it wrings
we wring
you wring
they wring

Present perfect

he retorcido
I have wrung
you have wrung
he/she/it has wrung
we have wrung
you have wrung
they have wrung

Past

retorcía/retorcí
I wrung
you wrung
he/she/it wrung
we wrung
you wrung
they wrung

Past perfect

había/hube retorcido
I had wrung
you had wrung
he/she/it had wrung
we had wrung
you had wrung
they had wrung

Future

retorceré
I shall/will wring
you will wring
he/she/it will wring
we shall/will wring
you will wring
they will wring

Future perfect

habré retorcido
I shall/will have wrung
you will have wrung
he/she/it will have wrung
we shall/will have wrung
you will have wrung
they will have wrung

Conditional

Present

retorcería
I should/would wring
you would wring
he/she/it would wring
we should/would wring
you would wring
they would wring

Perfect

habría retorcido
I should/would have wrung
you would have wrung
he/she/it would have wrung
we should/would have wrung
you would have wrung
they would have wrung

Subjunctive

Present

retuerza
I wring
you wring
he/she/it wrings
we wring
you wring
they wring

Present perfect

haya retorcido
I have wrung
you have wrung
he/she/it has wrung
we have wrung
you have wrung
they have wrung

Past

retorciera o retorciese
I wrung
you wrung
he/she/it wrung
we wrung
you wrung
they wrung

Past perfect

hubiera o hubiese retorcido
I had wrung
you had wrung
he/she/it had wrung
we had wrung
you had wrung
they had wrung

Imperative

let me wring	***no existe (déjame retorcer)***
wring	***retuerce tú***
let him/her/it wring	***retuerza él/ella/ello***
let us (let's) wring	***retorzamos nosotros***
wring	***retorced vosotros***
let them wring	***retuerzan ellos***

Impersonal forms

Infinitive

retorcer
to wring

Perfect Infinitive

haber retorcido
to have wrung

Gerund

retorciendo
wringing

Perfect Gerund

habiendo retorcido
having wrung

Participle

retorcido
wrung

Perfect Participle

habiendo retorcido
having wrung

WRITE · WROTE · WRITTEN

ESCRIBIR

Indicative

Present

escribo
I write
you write
he/she/it writes
we write
you write
they write

Present perfect

he escrito
I have written
you have written
he/she/it has written
we have written
you have written
they have written

Past

escribía/escribí
I wrote
you wrote
he/she/it wrote
we wrote
you wrote
they wrote

Past perfect

había/hube escrito
I had written
you had written
he/she/it had written
we had written
you had written
they had written

Future

escribiré
I shall/will write
you will write
he/she/it will write
we shall/will write
you will write
they will write

Future perfect

habré escrito
I shall/will have written
you will have written
he/she/it will have written
we shall/will have written
you will have written
they will have written

Conditional

Present

escribiría
I should/would write
you would write
he/she/it would write
we should/would write
you would write
they would write

Perfect

habría escrito
I should/would have written
you would have written
he/she/it would have written
we should/would have written
you would have written
they would have written

Subjunctive

Present

escriba
I write
you write
he/she/it writes
we write
you write
they write

Present perfect

haya escrito
I have written
you have written
he/she/it has written
we have written
you have written
they have written

Past

escribiera/escribiese
I wrote
you wrote
he/she/it wrote
we wrote
you wrote
they wrote

Past perfect

hubiera/hubiese escrito
I had written
you had written
he/she/it had written
we had written
you had written
they had written

Imperative

let me write	***no existe (déjame escribir)***
write	***escribe tú***
let him/her/it write	***escriba él/ella/ello***
let us (let's) write	***escribamos nosotros***
write	***escribid vosotros***
let them write	***escriban ellos***

Impersonal forms

Infinitive

escribir
to write

Perfect Infinitive

haber escrito
to have written

Gerund

escribiendo
writing

Perfect Gerund

habiendo escrito
having written

Participle

escrito
written

Perfect Participle

habiendo escrito
having written

AUXILIARY OR MODALS

BE · WAS · BEEN

SER, ESTAR.

Indicative

Present

soy/estoy
I am
you are
he/she/it is
we are
you are
they are

Present perfect

he sido/estado
I have been
you have been
he/she/it has been
we have been
you have been
they have been

Past

era/estaba/fui/estuve
I was
you were
he/she/it was
we were
you were
they were

Past perfect

había/hube sido/estado
I had been
you had been
he/she/it had been
we had been
you had been
they had been

Future

seré/estaré
I shall/will be
you will be
he/she/it will be
we shall/will be
you will be
they will be

Future perfect

habré sido/estado
I shall/will have been
you will have been
he/she/it will have been
we shall/will have been
you will have been
they will have been

Conditional

Present

seria/estaría
I should/would be
you would be
he/she/it would be
we should/would be
you would be
they would be

Perfect

habría sido/estado
I should/would have been
you would have been
he/she/it would have been
we should/would have been
you would have been
they would have been

Subjunctive

Present

sea/esté
I am
you are
he/she/it is
we are
you are
they are

Present perfect

haya sido/estado
I have been
you have been
he/she/it has been
we have been
you have been
they have been

Past

fuera/estuviera/fuese/ estuviese
I were
you were
he/she/it were
we were
you were
they were

Past perfect

hubiera/hubiese sido/estado
I had been
you had been
he/she/it had been
we had been
you had been
they had been

Imperative

let me be	***no existe (déjame ser/estar)***
be	***sé/está tú***
let him/her/it be	***sea/esté él/ella/ello***
let us (let's) be	***seamos/estemos nosotros***
be	***sed/estad vosotros***
let them be	***sean/estén ellos***

Impersonal forms

Infinitive

ser/estar
to be

Perfect Infinitive

haber sido/estado
to have been

Gerund

siendo/estando
being

Perfect Gerund

habiendo sido/estado
having been

Participle

sido/estado
been

Perfect Participle

habiendo sido/estado
having been

CAN/BE ABLE TO

PODER

Indicative

Present

puedo
I can / I am able to
you can / you are able to
he can / he is able to
we can / we are able to
you can / you are able to
they can / they are able to

Present Perfect

he podido
I have been able to
you have been able to
he has been able to
we have been able to
you have been able to
they have been able to

Past

podía/pude
I could/I was able to
you could/you were able to
he could/he was able to
we could/ we were able to
you could/you were able to
they could/they were able to

Past perfect

había/hube podido
I had been able to
you had been able to
he had been able to
we had been able to
you had been able to
they had been able to

Future

podré
I shall/will be able to
you will be able to
he will be able to
we shall/will be able to
you will be able
they will be able to

Future perfect

habré podido
I shall/will have been able to
you will have been able to
he will have been able to
we shall/will have been able to
you will have been able to
they will have been able to

Present

podría
I could/would be able to
you could/would be able to
he could/would be able to
we could/would be able to
you could/would be able to
they could/would be able to

Perfect

habría podido
I should/would have been able to
you would have been able to
he would have been able to
we should/would have been able to
you would have been able to
they would have been able to

Subjunctive

Present

pueda
I can / I am able to
you can / you are able to
he can / he is able to
we can / we are able to
you can / you are able to
they can / they are able to

Present Perfect

haya podido
I have been able to
you have been able to
he has been able to
we have been able to
you have been able to
they have been able to

Past

pudiera/pudiese
I could / I was able to
you could / you were able to
he could / he was able to
we could / we were able to
you could / you were able to
they could / they were able to

Past perfect

hubiera/hubiese podido
I had been able to
you had been able to
he had been able to
we had been able to
you had been able to
they had been able to

Imperative

NO HAY

Impersonal forms

Infinitive

poder
to be able

Perfect Infinitive

haber podido
to have been able

Gerund

pudiendo
being able

Perfect Gerund

habiendo podido
having been able

Participle

podido
been able

Perfect Participle

habiendo podido
having been able

AUXILIARY OR MODALS

HAVE · HAD · HAD

TENER, TOMAR

Indicative

Present

tengo
I have
you have
he/she/it has
we have
you have
they have

Present perfect

he tenido
I have had
You have had
he/she/it has had
we have had
you have had
they have had

Past

tenía/tuve
I had
you had
he/she/it had
we had
you had
they had

Past perfect

había/hube tenido
I had had
you had had
he/she/it had had
we had had
you had had
they had had

Future

tendré
I shall/will have
you will have
he/she/it will have
we shall/will have
you will have
they will have

Future perfect

habré tenido
I shall/will have had
you will have had
he/she/it will have had
we shall/will have had
you will have had
they will have had

Conditional

Present

tendría
I should/would have
you would have
he/she/it would have
we should/would have
you would have
they would have

Perfect

habría tenido
I should/would have had
you would have had
he/she/it would have had
we should/would have had
you would have had
they would have had

Subjunctive

Present

tenga
I have
you have
he/she/it has
we have
you have
they have

Present perfect

haya tenido
I have had
you have had
he/she/it has had
we have had
you have had
they have had

Past

tuviera/tuviese
I had
you had
he/she/it had
we had
you had
they had

Past perfect

hubiera/hubiese tenido
I had had
you had had
he/she/it had had
we had had
you had had
they had had

Imperative

let me have	***no existe (déjame tener)***
have	***ten tú***
let him/her/it have	***tenga él/ella/ello***
let us (let's) have	***tengamos nosotros***
have	***tened vosotros***
let them have	***tengan ellos***

Impersonal forms

Infinitive

tener
to have

Perfect Infinitive

haber tenido
to have had

Gerund

teniendo
having

Perfect Gerund

habiendo tenido
having had

Participle

tenido
had

Perfect Participle

habiendo tenido
having had

MAY · MIGHT

PODER

Indicative

Present

puedo

I may
you may
he may
we may
you may
they may

Present perfect

Past

podía/pude

I might
you might
he might
we might
you might
they might

Past perfect

Future

Future perfect

Conditional

Present

podría

I might
you might
he might
we might
you might
they might

Perfect

Subjunctive

Present

Present perfect

Past

Past perfect

Imperative

Impersonal forms

MUST

DEBO, TENGO QUE.

Indicative

Present

debo
I must / I have to
you must / you have to
he/she/it must / he/she/it has to
we must / we have to
you must / you have to
they must /they have to

Present Perfect

he debido
I have had to
you have had to
he/she/it has had to
we have had to
you have had to
they have had to

Past

debía/debí
I had to
you had to
he/she/it had to
we had to
you had to
they had to

Past perfect

había/hube debido
I had had to
you had had to
he/she/it had had to
we had had to
you had had to
they had had to

Future

deberé
I shall/will have to
you will have to
he/she/it will have to
we shall/will have to
you will have to
they will have to

Future perfect

habré debido
I shall/will have had to
you will have had to
he/she/it will have had to
we shall/will have had to
you will have had to
they will have had to

Conditional

Present

debería
I should/would have to
you would have to
he/she/it would have to
we should/would have to
you would have to
they would have to

Perfect

habría debido
I should/would have had to
you would have had to
he/she/it would have had to
we should/would have had to
you would have had to
they would have had to

Subjunctive

Present

deba
I must / I have to
you must / you have to
he/she/it must / he/she/it has to
we must / we have to
you must / you have to
they must /they have to

Present perfect

haya debido
I have had to
you have had to
he/she/it has had to
we have had to
you have had to
they have had to

Past

debiera/debieses
I had to
you had to
he/she/it had to
we had to
you had to
they had to

Past perfect

hubiera/hubiese debido
I had had to
you had had to
he/she/it had had to
we had had to
you had had to
they had had to

Imperative

NO HAY

Impersonal forms

Infinitive

deber
to have to

Perfect Infinitive

haber debido
to have had

Gerund

debiendo
having to

Perfect Gerund

habiendo debido
having had

Participle

debido
had to

Perfect Participle

habiendo debido
having had

OUGHT TO

DEBERÍA

Indicative

Present

Present perfect

Past

Past perfect

Future

Future perfect

Subjunctive

Present

Present perfect

Past

Past perfect

Imperative

Impersonal forms

Infinitive

Perfect Infinitive

Gerund

Perfect Gerund

Participle

Perfect Participle

Present

debería

I ought to
you ought to
he/she/it ought to
we ought to
you ought to
they ought to

Perfect

debería haber/tener

I ought to have
you ought to have
he/she/it ought to have
we ought to have
you ought to have
they ought to have

SHOULD

DEBERÍA

Indicative

Present

Present perfect

Past

Past perfect

Future

Future perfect

Subjunctive

Present

Present perfect

Past

Past perfect

Imperative

Impersonal forms

Infinitive

Perfect Infinitive

Gerund

Perfect Gerund

Participle

Perfect Participle

Present	Perfect
debería	***debería haber/tener***
I should	I should have
you should	you should have
he/she/it should	he/she/it should have
we should	we should have
you should	you should have
they should	they should have

THERE TO BE

HABER (IMPERSONAL)

Indicative

Present

hay
there is
there are

Present perfect

hay
there has been
there have been

Past

había
there was
there were

Past perfect

había habido
there had been

Future

habrá
there will be

Future perfect

there will have been

Conditional

Present

habría
there would be

Perfect

habría
there would have been

Subjunctive

Present

haya
there is
there are

Present perfect

haya habido
there has been
there have been

Past

hubiera/hubiese
there was
there were

Past perfect

hubiera/hubiese habido
there had been

Imperative

haya
let there be

Impersonal forms

Infinitive

haber
there to be

Perfect Infinitive

Gerund

habiendo
there being

Perfect Gerund

habiendo habido
there having been

Participle

Perfect Participle

habiendo habido
there having been

OTHER TITLES

Complementary books:

Elementary Tests · 3 levels
Advanced Tests · 2 levels
Structured Tests · 3 levels
Bilingual Phrases · 5 levels
Bilingual Translations · 5 levels
Fill in the gaps · 3 levels
Guide to Prepositions (English to Spanish)
Guide to Prepositions - **exercises**
Guide to Phrasal Verbs
Phrasal Verbs - **exercises**
English Verbs one by one
My English telltale
Conversation in Action - Let's Talk (for teachers)
English irregular verbs

Grammars:

English Grammar · 3 levels

Pastimes:

Didactical crosswords

Reading:

Reading books
Reading books with tape
Bilingual reading books
Graded reading - French

Textbooks:

Stanley
Stanley, book of exercises
Stanley, Teacher's book
On Second Thoughts (children)
In the Third Place (children)

Others:

Traveller's guide
- English - French - Italian - German - Portuguese

Business:

Bilingual Business Letters
· English - Spanish · Italian - Spanish · French - Spanish
· Business idioms

EDITORIAL STANLEY

Apdo. 207 - 20302 IRUN - SPAIN
Telf. (943) 64 04 12 - Fax. (943) 64 38 63
e-mail: rrossetg.stanley@nexo.es